Karl Heyer (1888–1964), lawyer a
foremost pupils of Rudolf Steine:
1888, he held doctorates in History and Jurisprudence. In 1911 he heard a lecture by Rudolf Steiner and began an intensive study of history. He wrote the nine-volume work *Beiträge zur Geschichte des Abendlandes* ('Contributions to the History of the West'), which includes the present book on Kaspar Hauser.

KASPAR HAUSER

and the Destiny of Middle Europe in the Nineteenth Century

Karl Heyer

Translated by Terry M. Boardman

TEMPLE LODGE

Temple Lodge Publishing Ltd.
Hillside House, The Square
Forest Row, RH18 5ES

www.templelodge.com

First published in English by Temple Lodge Publishing, 2024

Originally printed privately in German in Kressbronn/Lake Constance in 1958. Most recently republished by Perseus Verlag, Basel, in 1999

A CIP catalogue record for this book is available from the British Library

ISBN 978 1 915776 21 1

Cover by Morgan Creative
Typeset by Symbiosys Technologies, Visakhapatnam, India
Printed by 4Edge Ltd., Essex

Dedicated with gratitude to Margarete, my wife and companion

Contents

Karl Heyer and his Kaspar Hauser Work

Foreword to the 4th Edition

'You can see what kind of person you are by your inner attitude towards the phenomenon of Kaspar Hauser.'

Karl Heyer's book about Kaspar Hauser was the first comprehensive work on this multifaceted and mysterious subject that was based on perspectives drawn from spiritual science. In the book, Heyer did not intend to add to the already existing factual material on the subject but rather, limited himself to 'allowing illuminating light from Anthroposophy to fall upon these facts (...)'. This was his inaugural deed for all the anthroposophically oriented literature which followed the publication of this book. And until now (1999) none of those subsequent works has surpassed Heyer's brilliant book in this respect.

In his autobiography* Karl Heyer relates how he received the first indirect stimulus for this work in a decisive conversation with Rudolf Steiner on 29 September 1912—through the fact that this conversation took place exactly a hundred years after the birth of the Crown Prince of Baden, as Heyer realised only later.

The concrete, direct stimulus that led him to embark on the work came forty years later, through something Heyer heard at the beginning of the 1950s:

> At an anthroposophical meeting in Stuttgart I learned of a very important remark Rudolf Steiner had made about Kaspar Hauser, which had been unknown to me until that time.† It struck me like a lightning bolt, which I had also experienced decades earlier when I had been greatly moved by the novel by [Jakob] Wassermann, although I had not felt that the Kaspar Hauser affair itself could be illumined anthroposophically, despite Rudolf Steiner's words in a public lecture in Nuremberg on 17 June 1908. Now that illumination appeared possible, and I began through extensive correspondence to

---

**Aus meinem Leben*, Perseus Verlag Basel 1990, p. 130f.

†The source who communicated the remark has remained unknown.

> gather all the traceable comments by Dr Steiner about Kaspar Hauser and to test their authenticity. I travelled to various places and studied the external literature on Kaspar Hauser, looking at the facts gathered through this research together with the indications received from Rudolf Steiner. (On my search, I met or heard from many people in the Anthroposophical Society who had long had a deep interest in Kaspar Hauser and who probably somehow had a karmic connection with the affair.) The result of all this was volume IX of my series of books titled *Beiträge zur Geschichte des Abendlandes* [Contributions to the History of the West]. This volume, *Kaspar Hauser und das Schicksal Mitteleuropas im 19. Jahrhundert* [Kaspar Hauser and the Destiny of Middle Europe in the 19th Century] was dedicated to my wife because she had had a deep share in the work. The book came out in 1958, soon after my 70th birthday. For me, it represented the high point of my writing and a kind of crowning of my life's work. It linked on to all my earlier works, which it had as a foundation to a great extent, and out of which it grew.

Two decades after Heyer's death in 1964, in which year a second edition of the book was published unaltered by Verlag Freies Geistesleben, this literary crown of Heyer's life's work was really badly mauled and mistreated in the third edition of the book by the same publisher in 1983. In this third 'revised and improved' edition, presented to a new readership who could hardly have suspected the true extent of the 'improvements' indicated by an editorial comment that the text had been 'stylistically reworked in some places', entire sentences, even whole paragraphs were omitted in the most arbitrary fashion, individual sentences were cut up, adjectives and adverbs altered, words were even added which had never appeared in Heyer's text. It was an undertaking without parallel in the history of what professes to be anthroposophical publishing—comparable to those deceitful slanders which Kaspar Hauser himself had to experience after his death and until the present day,* and this time, as it were, repeating that abuse in what was the first anthroposophical work

* One can think of the pseudo-scientific genetic analysis published in 1996 in *Der Spiegel*, which was even taken seriously in certain anthroposophical circles, and which was intended 'scientifically' to do away with the notion of Kaspar Hauser as the Crown Prince of Baden once and for all. A sound analysis of this *pseudo*-analysis can be found in Rudolf Biedermann, *Kaspar Hauser: Neue Forschungen und Aspekte I—Von der Entzifferung des Dolches bis zur Genanalyse-Farce* [Kaspar Hauser: New Research and Aspects from the Deciphering of the Dagger to the Genetic Analysis Farce], Kaspar Hauser Verlag, Offenbach bei Frankfurt.

about Kaspar Hauser. We have already drawn sufficient attention to the details of this botched publication elsewhere.*

Aside from the facts of Kaspar Hauser's murder, the criminologist Anselm Feuerbach spoke of his case as 'a crime against the soul life of a child'. The third edition of Heyer's book could, analogously, be called a 'crime against the spiritual life of an anthroposophical author'. What was especially shocking in this instance was that this attack did not come from the usual camp of the opponents of Kaspar Hauser but from within a circle of people who considered themselves to be anthroposophical. Viewed symptomatically, nothing speaks more for the historic significance of Heyer's Kaspar Hauser work more than this destiny that emerged over a period of 14 years from such a group of people.†

This period corresponds approximately to the time in which Kaspar Hauser was incarcerated.

With the present fourth edition, the text of which is identical to the first two editions, the unworthy 'imprisonment' of the book, which hindered its full impact, has been ended. The hindering element of the third edition, however, still belongs to the peculiar destiny of the work and certainly cannot be ignored in any consideration of that destiny. It is precisely this element that can show how closely Heyer's work is bound to the destiny of Kaspar Hauser. Perhaps in the future people will say: the indisputable factual evidence for the spiritual weight of Heyer's Kaspar Hauser book is that it once had to experience such a falsified edition.

*

At the end of his Foreword, Heyer names three people to whom he feels obliged to express his gratitude for their help in various ways in supporting his work: Paul Michaelis, Ehrenfried Pfeiffer and Hermann Pies. Paul Michaelis, the

---

* *Der Europäer*, Vol. 1, No. 4, February 1997, p. 9ff.

† This circle of people are under no circumstances here accused of harbouring conscious, malicious intent. However, the objective irresponsibility of the matter remains unaffected by subsequent evidence of motives that were 'noble' and permeated, at most, by certain illusions. The writer of these lines had already, in his epilogue to Heyer's autobiography *Aus meinem Leben* [From My Life] in 1990, drawn public attention to the falsification; with regard to a correction of the falsification under publishing laws, the duped public, especially those in anthroposophical circles, showed in subsequent years an almost general 'indolence of the heart'. That this work has now been republished in its original form is due to the exclusive initiative of a single individual.

true friend and pupil of Ludwig Polzer-Hoditz, passed on to Heyer, amongst other things, information regarding Kaspar Hauser's heritage as Crown Prince as well as information about the occult opposition behind his incarceration and murder. Michaelis wrote a number of dramas, and among them, in 1943, one about Kaspar Hauser, prompted by communications from Rudolf Steiner which had been passed on to him from his friend Polzer-Hoditz. In the Foreword to this drama, which had developed under Polzer's eyes, as it were, and was fully approved by him, Michaelis wrote:

> On 3 March 1925, so just before Dr Steiner's death, Count Polzer had a very significant conversation with Dr Steiner. After they had spoken about certain difficulties within the Society, the conversation moved via discussion of Nero, Agrippina, and Seneca to Crown Prince Rudolf and then to the endeavours of Roman and western lodges, and in this context Dr Steiner emphasised with great seriousness that there were three problems to be solved which were of very special importance for the future: 1. The question about the two Johns, 2. Who was Demetrius [the Russian Czar Dmitrii, r.1604-1605]? And 3. Where did Kaspar Hauser come from? With all three problems it was especially important that one pay attention not to the deaths of those involved but to their births. Where did they come from and with what tasks? The individuality who was hidden behind the veil of K.H. was a being whose inspirations had worked into the Rosicrucian context from the very beginning and had then incarnated on 29 September 1812 as the first-born son of Karl, Grand Duke of Baden, and his wife Stefanie de Beauharnais. He had an important mission of esoteric Christianity to fulfil.*

Karl Heyer, who was familiar with Michaelis' Kaspar Hauser drama, took up an important part of what Michaelis had communicated about this conversation between Polzer and Steiner in his Kaspar Hauser book; it is on p. 124f.; Michaelis is not named, but this was probably in accord with his wishes.

---

* See *Der Europäer* magazine, Vol. 1, No. 7, May 1997, p. 17. Those who know my account of the conversations between R. Steiner and Polzer published in my biography of Polzer (T. Meyer, *Ludwig Polzer-Hoditz—ein Europäer* [Ludwig Polzer-Hoditz—a European] Basel 1994, p. 560ff.) will soon recognise that the core of Michaelis' statements, the authenticity of which has been repeatedly and sweepingly disputed, reappear in that biography. Whatever may be objected to in these statements will not be able to affect the above-mentioned comments by R. Steiner about Kaspar Hauser, which were written down in 1943 by Michaelis during Polzer's lifetime.

Heyer's gratitude to Pies is obvious; Pies had been the first researcher to have put together comprehensive documentation on Kaspar Hauser.

For a long time, Ehrenfried Pfeiffer's relation to this book remained a mystery, but this riddle too has since been solved. Pfeiffer had grown up in Nuremberg, which Steiner was aware of and which caused him to ask certain questions during a trip they took together from Stuttgart to Dornach one day. Pfeiffer spoke about this conversation on 31 January 1954 in a lecture in Spring Valley as follows:

> Then [during the journey] he began to speak about Kaspar Hauser and said: 'You grew up in Nuremberg and went to school there? What do you know about Kaspar Hauser? Have you seen the place where he lived?'
>
> I told Dr Steiner everything I knew about Kaspar Hauser, which really was not very much. Then I asked Dr Steiner: 'What was the mission of Kaspar Hauser?'
>
> This question may well seem peculiar to anyone who has read the outer story of Kaspar Hauser. But I asked it, and Rudolf Steiner answered: 'At the beginning of the 19th century there was the danger that the connection between the spiritual and the physical worlds—between the spiritual world and the consciousness of human beings—would be completely broken. There had to be a human being who lived in the physical world and yet who could have true and proper spiritual experiences. That was the mission of Kaspar Hauser—to maintain [lit. 'hold upright'—*transl.*] this connection between the spiritual and the physical worlds until an Age of Michael would come again in 1879. Kaspar Hauser was in fact the individuality who maintained the connection.'*

In the final chapter of his book Heyer held this comment to be 'well-authenticated' (see. p. 287).

Further to the aforementioned conversation, Pfeiffer spoke about another important comment by Steiner which should also be presented here, not least because in many places it is believed that the only source for the background to the Kaspar Hauser story that is spoken of there is Ludwig Polzer-Hoditz or Polzer's friend Michaelis, who is not regarded as creditable in certain anthroposophical circles:

> Then Dr Steiner said that certain occult circles—which belonged to the Freemasons and stood under Jesuit influence—used or abused Kaspar Hauser for an experiment.

Two years before his death Karl Heyer had an important addendum to his book published in *Mitteilungen aus der anthroposophischen Arbeit in Deutschland*

* See *Ehrenfried Pfeiffer—Notes and Lectures, Compendium II*, Spring Valley 1991, p. 20f.

[Communications from the Anthroposophical Work in Germany](Easter 1962), which complements the comments by Pfeiffer already mentioned but which was not included in either the second or the third edition of the book and which therefore should be reproduced here:

> An addendum has been made here to my book *Kaspar Kauser and the Destiny of Middle Europe in the 19th Century* (Kressbronn/Lake Constance 1958) in the form of an important comment by Rudolf Steiner. This comment, which comes with a sufficiently high degree of reliability, was first made known to me some time ago. It was communicated by Adolf Arenson.
>
> In view of Kaspar Hauser's violent death in 1833, when he was 21 years old, the question has often been raised why the opponents of the unfortunate youth did not already kill him when he was a child. There are several possible answers to this question. Rudolf Steiner's remark answers the question in a way that points to deep occult facts. He says: the opponents of Kaspar Hauser did not already kill him when he was a child because then he could have quickly reincarnated and the opponents involved *had known this*.

This comment must of course be set against the background of the whole, many-layered context which Heyer's book seeks to reveal. This context cannot of course be reproduced here, but it should be noted that a particular moment in time clearly played a decisive role. Kaspar Hauser would have had to become 'active' at a particular moment in world history, if one can express it in this way, if he was to be effective in the direction that his opponents wanted to drive forward. Later, (1833 and probably already in 1829), a rapid reincarnation would have been out of the question for them, and even his violent death, despite all the risks for them that were associated with it, may have appeared to them to be less dangerous in comparison with the more dangerous development in his consciousness which he had achieved in the meantime.

Heyer's addendum here casts a direct light on a central issue in his book: the confrontation with evil, and that means on the one hand also the confrontation with the activities of groups of people who have pledged themselves to the progress of humanity or a part of humanity more through a pact with anti-Christian powers than by working patiently with those spiritual beings who regard themselves as inwardly united with the human capacity for freedom. The reverse side of the confrontation with evil is therefore the confrontation with freedom: 'Through one's inner attitude to the phenomenon of Kaspar Hauser one can see what kind of human being one is', writes Heyer on page 95 of the book. These words can also apply to the most precious property of the human soul: the capacity for human freedom that is based on freethinking. For the destiny of Kaspar Hauser and also of Middle Europe is, in the most inward sense, also the destiny of the human soul that wills to grow and which is, in this urge to grow, repeatedly hindered. These hindrances of course can be found not only in the outer world but just as much within the human soul itself.

It was precisely in Middle Europe that the capacity for freedom germinated very powerfully; precisely here it was to blossom with full force; precisely here it was trodden down and mocked as nowhere else on earth, in that here the murder of an entire people occurred in the name of 'work' that would make one 'free'....

Heyer's book can therefore serve to orient us to everything that is related to German culture's true mission of freedom as well as to the true task of Middle Europe.

Even if the further fulfilment of this mission of freedom were to remain overshadowed at the beginning of the next millennium through the activities of dark internal or external powers or through the inattentive lack of judgement and illusions on the part of many people, as long as a number of people remain aware of the need for the fulfilment of this ideal, there will be hope that Europe will not be completely buried under the waves of internal and external hostility to the spirit and to freedom.

'The seed of the human being is called to the free spirit like the seed of the rose is called to become a rose', says Rudolf Steiner in his *Philosophy of Freedom*. Nothing, in the long run, will foster the individual's grasp of this seed more than familiarity with the hindrances which seek to hinder or entirely suffocate the growth of this seed. A real engagement with the destiny of Kaspar Hauser can lead to a new appreciation of the tender bud of freedom which wants to grow in each human soul. Such an appreciation of the life of Kaspar Hauser and of the work of the first person who sought to illumine Kaspar Hauser's life in a comprehensive anthroposophical way, was absent for a while. It is from this appreciation and not from fantasies of pan-European integration that a very direct path leads into the heart of Middle Europe's hope for the future, for to be a Middle European means to feel this spiritual seed of freedom within oneself.

This light-filled book of freedom crowned Karl Heyer's whole life's work; may this seed engender new life in every reader.

Thomas Meyer
Basel, 25 August 1999

Editor's Note: For this new edition, the bibliographical numbers of Rudolf Steiner's Collected Works (GA) have been added in the Notes section (p. 205.)

Foreword

What was true of all the earlier volumes of our *Beiträge zur Geschichte des Abendlandes* [Contributions to the History of the West] applies especially to this Volume IX: that it is for those readers who have a serious interest in hearing much that is essential that can be said on the basis of *anthroposophical spiritual science* about the subject of this book, the phenomenon of Kaspar Hauser, the mysterious foundling of Nuremberg and the wider context related to him.

More and more hearts and minds are occupying themselves with Kaspar Hauser. Increasingly, it is happening that when one speaks about him to earnestly striving people, it turns out in a remarkable number of cases that such people have a deep interest in him, or have had, often for decades already. It is something that goes deeply into the unconscious or the semi-conscious minds of many people, occupying souls in dreams, and the like. How much his memory lives on—more superficially of course, and yet ultimately from a deeper place—throughout society and how much the riddle of his life still captures people is shown in countless newspaper essays, reports and notices, in radio broadcasts, theatre plays, and film projects etc.

In this book we have made the attempt to look at much of the important material from the great quantity of facts that is known from the comprehensive corpus of Kaspar Hauser research and literature, from the perspective of the general and the more specific results of anthroposophical research. As with anything else, for the relationship of these two types of research, what Rudolf Steiner often said[1] in order to clarify how sensory and supersensory research relate to each other when seeking the full truth of a matter, applies here as well, if both types of research are pursued in the right sense. If a tunnel is to be built, then it can happen in such a way that the tunnel is driven into the mountain simultaneously from both sides. If the calculations are correct and the work is done properly, then the two drilled tunnels will meet somewhere inside the mountain.

We did not consider it our task to carry out 'Kaspar Hauser research' in the external sense, in order to increase still further the volume of facts which have been brought to light in infinitely painstaking work for far more than a hundred years now, but we wanted to try to throw some clarifying light from Anthroposophy onto these facts and onto some of the questions that have arisen from them.

To this end we were especially concerned to discover those statements made by Rudolf Steiner about this important subject, most of which were not made in lectures but in conversations. In doing so, we had to carefully check how far such statements were truly reliable. We generally preferred to leave unmentioned alleged statements which in themselves would belong to this context but the authenticity of which we could not establish with the necessary degree of certainty, even though those statements may have a high degree of intrinsic probability. Likewise, we have also preferred to leave out altogether important sections of the Kaspar Hauser story, if they could not be made sufficiently clear.

But even apart from this, it must be emphasised that we do not at all claim to cover all aspects of the great, many-sided, problematic riddle that Kaspar Hauser presents to the world, just as, on the other hand, we are by no means in a position to deal with *all* the aspects of this highly important subject that can arise from anthroposophical perspectives on its various levels and from the various possible points of view. What we believed we should hold to as our actual task was the attempt to situate the figure of Kaspar Hauser especially in those large historical and social contexts to which our work has been devoted for decades.

For this purpose, it was necessary, of course, first to gain a clear overall picture of his story, which is attempted in the first chapter, while the particular aspects of the social life and history of the 19th century and the destiny of Central Europe are elaborated in the second chapter. The nature of the subject matter means that many things cannot be presented in sharp contours, but can only be, as it were, touched upon.

This is connected with another important point. A presentation dealing with this subject must presuppose in the reader, to an even greater extent than was already the case in the earlier volumes of our *Contributions to the History of the West*, the readiness to think in a different, i.e. in a livelier and more active way than is expected and called upon in conventional works of history. Readers who do not have such a readiness will not be able to do much with this book or will be bound to misunderstand its character.

Of course, we could not presume that all my readers would know the facts and problems around Kaspar Hauser in detail, but on the other hand, we could not repeat in detail or refer to what can already be found in numerous other works—which vary a great deal in quality, by the way. We have therefore taken a middle course, by briefly mentioning the main facts in the relevant contexts to which they belong or into which they can be inserted. For the rest, we must of course refer to the Kaspar Hauser literature.

We would like to take this opportunity to express our heartfelt thanks to all those who have helped us in our work by providing information of various kinds and who have made this work possible in the first place! In particular, we would like to thank Paul Michaelis, Dr Ehrenfried Pfeiffer and Dr Hermann Pies.

The book is based on two lectures on Kaspar Hauser, which I was able to give at various locations in 1955/56.

Dr jur. et phil. Karl Heyer

1. The Being of Kaspar Hauser and his Appearance in the 19th Century

The Unwritten History of the 19th Century

Rudolf Steiner said of the true history of the 19th century that it had yet to be written. In all the published historical 'source' material and the superfluity of historical accounts of the 19th century, what they offer has the character of a 'fable convenue', an historical fable which people have agreed to think is true. It is unable to provide the deeper truth of the history of that century.

Highly significant processes played out 'behind the curtains' of external world history in the 19th century and they have to be included in any consideration of the events of that century if we want to penetrate with our understanding below the superficial 'maya' of outer processes.

A centrally important event in the 19th century, which underlies the entire configuration of the century is the struggle in the spiritual worlds which Rudolf Steiner spoke of[2] as a struggle waged by the Being known since ancient times as Micha-el (hereinafter Michael) against ahrimanic powers, which Steiner called the 'Spirits of Darkness'. This struggle began in the 1840s and led to a victory for Michael. The 'Spirits of Darkness' were cast down onto the Earth by him. There they burrowed themselves into human heads. This had a very strong impact on the human intellect. This intellect, which grasps only matter and is bound to the physical brain, underwent a great development in the 19th century. This is what directly brought about 'the full, impelling materialistic development'[3], a process which, of course, must not be judged in a one-sidedly negative way, as little as the materialism and intellectualism of recent centuries in general, which had their positive side that was part of the tragic necessities of human evolution, insofar as the achievement of human *freedom* is connected with them.

The turning point for this development, which strengthened all previous materialism and intellectualism in an unexpected way, is therefore the beginning of the 1840s.

The Appearance of Kaspar Hauser

Shortly before this point in time, 14 years beforehand, if one goes back from the year 1842, which was often mentioned by Rudolf Steiner, there appeared in Nuremberg a peculiar figure, who virtually represented the antithesis of everything that was soon to break in and triumph more and more in the form of the materialistic, intellectualistic impulses of the 19th century: *Kaspar Hauser*, a being who placed himself in every way as a *stranger* into the life of the Europe of that time.

He appeared in Nuremberg at Pentecost, (on a Whit Monday, 26 May 1828), and at the time of his death during Advent 1833 (17 December), he passed away in Ansbach after having been mortally wounded on 14 December. Thus, he lived only a little over 5½ years as 'Kaspar Hauser' among the people.

His life is now well over a hundred years behind us, and perhaps it is connected with this that today, at this great distance in time, many things want to, should, can and may be said about him.[4]

When he appeared in Nuremberg, he stirred a tremendous interest all over Europe and beyond. He became what today would be called a 'global sensation'.

The totality of his life amounts to a phenomenon full of the greatest riddles, incomprehensible to materialistic thinking and only really understandable, at least in its main features, on the basis of the ground of anthroposophically oriented spiritual science.

Rudolf Steiner's Reference to Kaspar Hauser, 17 June 1908

Rudolf Steiner spoke only once in any detail about Kaspar Hauser in one particular *lecture* (in another lecture,[5] he only mentioned him briefly). This first lecture was, understandably, held in Nuremberg, on 17 June 1908. It was a public lecture and significantly, was titled: '*Spiritual Science, the Gospels and the Future of Humanity*'. It immediately preceded Rudolf Steiner's lecture cycle for members of the Theosophical Society, also held in Nuremberg: 'Theosophy in the light of the Apocalypse.'[6]

We would like to take these statements of Rudolf Steiner about the phenomenon of Kaspar Hauser as the starting point of our own reflections.

First of all, we should make clear what the subject of this book will *not* be: it will not discuss the question of Kaspar Hauser's external origins and also the question of the manner of his death, i.e. precisely those two questions which generally—and certainly not without reason—occupy very much space in books and other published writings about Kaspar Hauser.

It is well-known today that many people, then and now, and some already soon after his first appearance in Nuremberg, regarded Kaspar Hauser as the heir to the Grand Duchy of Baden, born on 29 September

1812 in Karlsruhe, and supposedly removed for dynastic reasons, something that others have long denied and have tried to refute. Likewise, the question of the circumstances of his death has played an extremely important role in the extensive Kaspar Hauser literature: whether he fell victim to an attempt to murder him or whether he died as a result of a self-inflicted wound.

The Question of the Being of Kaspar Hauser

The primary concern of any investigation directed at the essentials of the phenomenon must obviously be that of Kaspar Hauser's *way of being*, of the '*qualitative*' aspect, if we may call it that, of this peculiar phenomenon. The question of whether he was the prince of Baden or not takes on a *deeper* interest only when we are somewhat clear about this 'qualitative' aspect of Kaspar Hauser. If a random, popular heir to the throne suffers the fate of being pushed aside by some criminal machinations and forced out of the succession, then this is certainly a process that can merit a certain human and political, perhaps also criminological interest, but it would be in any case a process that has taken place innumerable times in history and is of no special historical interest. The peculiarity in this case, however, lies more in the fact that such a case took place in the 19th century, i.e. in a time in which, at least in Germany, such means were no longer used in princely houses. This then would only have been a late example of practices which had been very widely employed in earlier times.*

A really deeper, spiritual interest in the princely status and nature of Kaspar Hauser thus depends entirely on the question of *what kind of human being* he was inwardly, and therefore we consider it useful, *to begin with*, to limit our discussion to this question.

In his public lecture of 17 June 1908, on 'Spiritual Science, the Gospels and the Future of Humanity', Rudolf Steiner speaks of the *development of the consciousness* of humanity. For example, that there was an ancient, pre-religious time on Earth in which people were so connected with the spiritual world and its beings that there was no need for *re*ligion, i.e. for a *re*-connection with that with which they were still connected in the old way. From such contexts the lecture then turns to Kaspar Hauser.

---

* Otto Flake (who affirms Kaspar Hauser's princely rank) writes in his book *Kaspar Hauser. Vorgeschichte, Geschichte, Nachgeschichte* [Kaspar Hauser—Pre-history, History, Post-history] Mannheim (1950), p.147: 'Things were Shakespearean in all princely houses, in the case of Baden, only somewhat later than in the others.'

The Text of Rudolf Steiner's References

In view of its fundamental importance for a spiritual scientific understanding of the phenomenon, we shall reproduce the passage here in full, in spite of its relative length, in order then to add to it our remarks and reflections.

In earlier ages, he said:

> the human being lived under other conditions and with other forms of consciousness. If we follow these back for thousands and thousands of years, we shall always find different ones. What today we call logical thought, intellect, understanding, has only evolved late in man's history. Much stronger were certain forces in him which today are already beginning to decline, such as memory, for instance. In an earlier age memory was far more developed than it is now. Due to the increasing intellectual culture of mankind, memory has stepped essentially into the background. If one looks at the world with alert, practical eyes, one can recognise that what spiritual science relates is nothing airy-fairy. People might say that if that were true about memory, then a modern person who remains backward in development due to some accident should be backward least of all in memory. They would also have to show that if one tried to induce intellectuality in a person who had been artificially retarded, then his memory would suffer.
>
> Here in this city, people witnessed a characteristic case of this very nature. Professor Daumer, whom one cannot esteem highly enough, observed this case very thoroughly. It was the case of that human being, so enigmatic for many people, who was once placed into this city in a mysterious way, and who, in just as mysterious a manner, met his death in Ansbach. An author, in order to indicate the mystery of this person's life, wrote that as he was carried out to burial the sun was setting on the one horizon and the moon was rising on the other. I am speaking, as you know, of Kaspar Hauser. If you disregard all the pros and cons that have been asserted, if you look only at what has been fully verified, you will know that this foundling—who was one day simply there in the street, and who, since it was not known from where he came, was called the Child of Europe—could neither read nor write when he was found. At the age of twenty, he possessed nothing of what is gained through the intellect but he had a wonderful memory. As people began to instruct him, as logic entered his soul, his memory disappeared. This transition in consciousness was accompanied by something else.
>
> At first, he possessed an incredible, entirely inborn truthfulness and it was precisely this truthfulness that went more and more astray. The more he nibbled, so to speak, at intellectuality, the more his truthfulness vanished. We

could study many things were we to enter deeply into this human soul, which had been artificially held back. It is not difficult for those grounded in spiritual science to understand the folk tradition, which educated people today do not believe, which relates that while Kaspar Hauser still knew nothing, while he still had no idea that there were beings of different form besides himself, he had a remarkable effect upon quite savage creatures. Wild animals humbled themselves before him and became mild; something streamed from him that made such beasts gentle, which would savagely attack anyone else.

As I said, because there was such a case, which can be understood by spiritual science, we could in fact penetrate deeply into the soul of this enigmatic personality, and you would see how everything that cannot be explained in terms of ordinary life is led back through spiritual science to spiritual facts. Such spiritual facts cannot be learnt by speculation but only through spiritual observation, though they are comprehensible to unbiased, logical thinking.

All this has only been said in order to show you that modern consciousness has evolved from a different, an ancient state of consciousness when man was not in direct touch with outer objects in the modern sense, but on the other hand related to the facts and beings of the spiritual world....

This is what Rudolf Steiner had to say about Kaspar Hauser in his lecture in Nuremberg on 17 June 1908.

These words, in all their reservation and 'sobriety' of expression, offer an extraordinary amount from which we can develop a more comprehensive understanding of the being of Kaspar Hauser. In what follows, we shall therefore proceed by taking the individual points in these remarks by Rudolf Steiner as starting points for what can, in a free way—it will not be a 'systematic' presentation*—be related to them, illumines them and is illumined by them:

Viewpoints that result from Steiner's References

1. Of central importance here is the fact that Rudolf Steiner deals with the phenomenon of Kaspar Hauser wholly in terms of the human *development of consciousness*, of which he refers to Kaspar Hauser here only as an example. This is the most essential viewpoint, from which one can gain an understanding of the being or, as we have called it, the *qualitative aspect*, of Kaspar Hauser. What is of great significance here is that this very point of

* The reader can find a certain substitute for this through reference to the index of names and subjects.

view was that of a number of important personalities of Kaspar Hauser's time who experienced him personally, knew him and observed him with sensitive understanding. Such personalities spoke of him, for example, as a '*paradisal human being*' who had preserved an earlier condition of humanity. The central viewpoint of Rudolf Steiner's spiritual-scientific observations of Kaspar Hauser is therefore in harmonious agreement with the wonderment, the sensing and thoughts of those important contemporaries of his. We shall return to consider in more detail such voices from Kaspar Hauser's environment in Nuremberg later on.

2. Kaspar Hauser's '*wonderful memory*', about which Rudolf Steiner speaks in the context of the evolution of human consciousness, was attested to by the various people who knew the foundling, especially in his first period in Nuremberg.

Such a witness, among many others, was Prof. Georg Friedrich *Daumer* (1800-1875), a high school teacher in Nuremberg, who was Kaspar Hauser's teacher in that decisive early period in the city and in whose house and under whose care Kaspar Hauser lived from July 1828 to December 1829.

In his book *Enthüllungen über Kaspar Hauser* [Revelations about Kaspar Hauser], Daumer writes about him, for example, '… In particular, his capacity for memory was incredible, and because of its wholly unusual strength, it appeared to be a true miracle….'[7]

Professor Daumer provides more details elsewhere, namely in his important book *Kaspar Hauser. Sein Wesen, seine Unschuld, seine Erduldungen und sein Ursprung* [Kaspar Hauser—His Being, His Innocence, His Endurance and His Origin], Regensburg 1873, pp. 208-209:

> Of almost everything that concerned him, he was able to state how many days and weeks ago it had happened. He knew how often he ate his soup, his chocolate, his milk porridge. Of the parties where he played chequers and chess* he could say how many games he had played with each person. Of the 5 games of chequers he played, he was able to tell the course of each one in turn. Of each of the many things given to him, he could tell who had given

* About 3 months after his appearance in Nuremberg, Kaspar Hauser, as Daumer writes,[7a] had grasped, among other things, the game of chess.

One of the astonishing things about this phenomenon is the rapid pace at which he grew into the civilisation of the time. 'His progress', wrote his fatherly benefactor and protector, Anselm Ritter *von Feuerbach* in a letter (dated 20 September 1828,[8] 'is extraordinary; what others take months or years to learn, he learns in days.'

> it to him; even of several pieces of money, he could tell from whom he had received them, because of the various marks or stains on them which they had. He knew the names of many hundreds of persons who had visited him or whom he had otherwise got to know .... In the first weeks of his stay in Nuremberg, he was told 48 names of people present in a public place, which he was later able to repeat without missing any of them. After 8 days he was still able to name (17 or 18) of these people who were again present in the same place. In all of these cases, he also remembered their designations of rank and office, such as actuary, officer, first lieutenant, adjutant, major, colonel, which for him were completely meaningless sounds ....

The human capacity of memory, which belongs to pre-cognitive development, was, as is known in anthroposophy, most strongly developed during the ancient *Atlantean* time.

To the degree that the power of human thought gradually developed, the power of memory receded, but remained very strong, especially in earlier, post-Atlantean times. Since the form it took in Atlantis, it has undergone many transformations up to the present day, about which we need not expand on here.[9] The *way* in which Kaspar Hauser's memory appeared certainly cannot be identified with the memory of the Atlanteans, which was an inter-generational, supra-personal (collective) memory, but in its enormous *strength* and in the way it preceded every stage of Hauser's intellectual development, it can certainly make one think of the Atlantean power of memory.

In this respect alone, a certain statement by Rudolf Steiner can therefore be very moving. He is well-known to have once called Kaspar Hauser a 'stray Atlantean'. This happened around 1905-06 in a conversation with a person from Nuremberg who asked Rudolf Steiner about Kaspar Hauser and whose own parents were close friends of Professor Daumer.[10]

In these words of Rudolf Steiner's is, apart from what one might otherwise find in them, at least also the fact that Kaspar Hauser exhibited essential traits that were possessed by the Atlanteans, and this applies precisely to the strength of his memory.

3. Of fundamental importance in Rudolf Steiner's text cited above is the value judgement he makes there about Georg Friedrich Daumer with the words: *'Professor Daumer, whom one cannot esteem highly enough, observed this case very thoroughly'.* This statement is confirmed a hundredfold by those who, without any prejudices born of materialistic thinking, study what Daumer wrote about Kaspar Hauser. This judgement by Rudolf Steiner is therefore of great importance in principle, because the opponents

of Kaspar Hauser, in order to devalue Daumer's testimony, which came from deep understanding, have repeatedly tried to cast suspicion on him in every way by portraying him as a fantasist, which has already been enough to convince some people because of Daumer's strong interest in homoeopathy (as well as in the phenomena of mesmerism, animal magnetism, somnambulism, etc.)[11] and the experiments that Daumer carried out on Kaspar Hauser with homoeopathic remedies, to which he reacted in an extremely strong way.

Georg Friedrich Daumer was in fact an important and interesting phenomenon in the cultural life and in the searching endeavours of the best minds of the 19th century. A sensitively written booklet was published about him in 1933 by the anthroposophist *Wilhelm Kunze*, who unfortunately died in 1939,[12] and there have been several essays by Professor Dr *Hans Wohlbold* in various anthroposophical journals. Especially important is his essay 'Georg Friedrich Daumer',[13] in which he describes the striving of this lonely spiritual seeker in the 19th century (including his errors and confusions), which is rooted in deep spirituality. He concludes his essay with the following lines, which deeply characterise Daumer and his endeavours, and which Daumer had written at the peak of his life:

> It is to break through the dull boundary we need;
> But not by God's gracious hand.
> To the bright spirits' fatherland
> 'Tis only work, deeds, and thoughts will lead.

Hans Wohlbold's essay '*Das eigentliche Problem Kaspar Hauser*'[14] [The Actual Problem of Kaspar Hauser] also contains much that is important about Daumer, his way of thinking and his spiritual development.

Striking for anyone who has had to deal with much of the opposition that arose in the 20th century *against Rudolf Steiner and anthroposophy*[15] is the similarity of *this* opposition to that other opposition that arose in the 19th century against Daumer and above all against Kaspar Hauser himself—striking in their similarity of attitudes and methods and the hostility of the spirit behind both.

Hans Wohlbold obviously realised this too and in his essay on Daumer[13] expressed it in his own way, including yet another motive:

> The dirt that was dumped on Daumer by some of his contemporaries came out of the same camp as the dagger thrust that finally struck at the foundling's heart. And ultimately, the opposition to Dr Steiner and to Anthroposophy flows from the same, dark source....

Obviously, it was a good thing in the difficult fate of Kaspar Hauser that he was placed in the care of Daumer for a good while soon after his appearance in Nuremberg. In such a context, it can make us sit up and take notice when we hear another, equally often-repeated statement by Rudolf Steiner: in one conversation (which, however, was about something quite different from Kaspar Hauser) he called Professor Daumer '*the last Rosicrucian*'.[16]

This too, of course, also sheds light on the deeper background of the malicious and hate-filled opposition to Daumer.

And on the other hand, how those words about Daumer being the last Rosicrucian resonate positively with what Daumer himself said in his old age, after a tragic life of seeking and struggling for the spirit in an age darkened by materialism, in January 1870, when from an intuition of and a deep yearning for the future founder of a new spirituality, he once wrote in a letter to his niece:

'I am at times inclined to think of myself as the unfortunate forerunner for another, for whom a better star will shine.'

4. In the text mentioned earlier from his 1908 lecture, Rudolf Steiner refers to a 'writer' who says of Kaspar Hauser—to indicate the mystery of his life—that 'when he was buried, it was a day when the sun set on one side of the sky and the moon rose on the opposite side'.

There can hardly be any doubt that this refers to Jakob Wassermann and his well-known novel *Caspar Hauser oder die Trägheit des Herzens* [Caspar Hauser or the Indolence of the Heart], which was first published in 1907/1908.[17] There the passage reads:[18]

> Two days later he was buried. It was afternoon and the sky was a cloudless blue. The whole town (Ansbach) was in motion. A famous contemporary, who called Caspar Hauser the Child of Europe, tells us that at that hour the sun and the moon were to be seen in the heavens at the same time, the moon in the east, the sun in the west, and that both shone with the same leaden light.

Whether the 'famous contemporary' introduced here by Wassermann really existed or whether he was a poetic invention of Wassermann's, and who it was if in the former case, I could not determine. The enquiries I have made suggest that the more probable assumption is that it was an invention of Wassermann's. That position of the sun and moon could not have been seen at the time of Kaspar Hauser's funeral, because it took place on 20 December (not two, but three days after Kaspar Hauser's death on 17 December) 'in the morning'. This is explicitly stated in a report of the magistrate of the town of Ansbach dated 22 December 1833.[19]

I have been assured that the sun and moon could not have been in the positions indicated at any of the times in question: neither on the day of Kaspar Hauser's fatal wounding (14 December), nor on the day of his death (17 December), nor at any time on the day of his burial, since the moon only became full on 26 December 1833.

The question is evidently without any particular significance when the position of the heavenly bodies is put down to a probable case of artistic licence by Wassermann in order to point up 'the mystery' of Kaspar Hauser's life. Yet a statement in one of Rudolf Steiner's lectures refers to this astronomical position. A question then remains here which anthroposophically-oriented astronomers or astrosophers could investigate.

5. From a methodological viewpoint, the following words of Rudolf Steiner's are important: 'When you disregard all the pros and contras that have been asserted in connection with this case, when you only look at what has definitively been proven....'

It stands to reason that one does well to approach this puzzling case in such a way. One gains a good basis for everything else if one first confines oneself to the Kaspar Hauser phenomenon which results from the facts and evidence that are also available in the outside world, and first puts aside the controversial questions.

In doing so, one soon realises that very much of what can be considered 'proven' for one with an unbiased and all-round view of the facts has been attacked from many sides, especially in the early days. For example, already during Kaspar Hauser's lifetime, the hypothesis was advanced, and then repeatedly defended over a long period, that Kaspar Hauser was *a fraud*. However, especially since 1924, the more recent Kaspar Hauser research, notably the work of the very commendable researcher Dr Hermann *Pies*,[20] has had a very clarifying effect. Given the present state of Kaspar Hauser research, it now requires a very unusual degree of blindness to the facts to still hold on to the fraud theory or related theories and in particular to push away all the now relatively accessible testimonies of people who experienced the Kaspar Hauser phenomenon, and which testify to its authenticity.

If one engages with all that has been asserted for and against Kaspar Hauser, it can become increasingly clear that behind the *opposition* to Kaspar Hauser there is ultimately a very specific *will* that (in the first place, deliberately) caused a clouding, so that, as Pies once put it, 'No matter how interested someone was in it in and of itself, the source material, complicated because of the strangeness of the case, became distorted and confused in the most hopeless manner.'[21] And for a long time this was extremely successful. The amount of hate and emotion expended in the process was characterised by another researcher with the words that Kaspar Hauser is 'not literature, but a battlefield'.[22] This itself is a key characteristic of the overall phenomenon. The nature of this hostility towards the unusual nature of Kaspar Hauser's appearance itself already indicates that something important and significant in a spiritual sense must be involved here, to 'warrant' so much effort being spent. It is very true that when views are expressed in the field of Kaspar Hauser literature, the case divides opinions in such a way that it soon becomes clear whose 'spiritual child' a person is. Daumer also clearly recognised this.

6. One of the most important aspects of the Kaspar Hauser phenomenon is only touched upon by Rudolf Steiner, when he speaks in that public Nuremberg lecture of this 'foundling who was simply and suddenly there on the street, and who, because people did not know where he had come from, called him *the Child of Europe* ....'

He was the 'Child of Europe' too, and this already leads us a little further into the depths of the story, in the sense that soon after his appearance (1828), he stirred the interest of the entire civilised world, and so very soon, the appellation 'Child of Europe' appeared and was applied to him.[23]

This phrase has a special meaning. A peculiar 'auric' element surrounds it—as, of course, does everything connected with Kaspar Hauser for those who have an ear for it. This 'aura' of the events surrounding Kaspar Hauser was felt strongly, especially among the common people.

What anthroposophy shows in general with regard to the experience of *history* applies here to a particularly high degree. Ordinary consciousness is not able to experience the course of history as wakefully as it can, for example, relate to modern natural science. History is experienced one degree less wakefully by the man of ordinary consciousness. 'What flows by as history is *dreamed* by humanity'; 'what governs history, people in the future will only be able to grasp with Inspiration, with inspired concepts'.[24] For our ordinary consciousness, history remains 'man's dream of the world'.[25] This plays an enormous role in the case of Kaspar Hauser, the Child of Europe.

It was precisely the common people who dreamt this 'dream' very strongly. They loved Kaspar Hauser. And that has had a very long-lasting effect. Pointing this out is one of the most important things to consider if one wants to understand the Kaspar Hauser phenomenon.

For example, a man wrote to me in 1953 of a time in his youth:

> ...About 25 years ago I spent some holidays in the countryside around Ansbach and I remember very well how vividly the personality of Kaspar Hauser was still alive in the memories of the simple country people. I was shown the grave and the memorial in the Palace Park [both in Ansbach] and I still remember well the shudder I felt at those places which for a long time thereafter always resonated within me at the mention of the name Kaspar Hauser.

Jakob Wassermann spoke similarly in the same period 1924;[26] he himself came from Franconia:

> ... In many places in Franconia it is still the same today as it was forty or fifty years ago: if you ask an old farmer in a village or an old master craftsman in the city about Caspar Hauser, a strange glow comes over his face and you have the feeling that a holy person is being spoken of. For three generations the picture is still unforgotten ....

Also in 1924, *Sophie Hoechstetter* wrote in her account 'The Child of Europe':[27]

> From Kaspar's first appearance until the present time, many voices have been raised against him and have sought to see in the tragic blamelessness of his life a poor story of deceit and to prove it with zeal or wit. He would have made a strange impostor indeed, for his fate has awakened an echo such as only the effect of an *illustrious spirit* can.

These words by Sophie Hoechstetter I would, in a certain sense, include among the most significant I have come across in the great body of Kaspar Hauser literature. They reveal something of a higher 'logic', namely, that significant effects (in this case: on people) do not come about without a significant cause.

Along the same lines is the experience of countless people who, once deeply touched by the Kaspar Hauser affair, repeatedly confess what one person expressed in the words: 'There is something about this story that will not let you go...'

From what are at first such purely psychological facts fruitful questions can emerge which challenge one's thinking. The question arises: What is all this about? What is the cause that produces such effects in so many sensitive souls?

In the phrase the 'Child of Europe' one can surmise, beyond what has already been said, a destiny that goes beyond the individual peoples of Europe, a task in the sense of an impulse of *the age*.

7. Let us return to that 'wonderful memory' in Kaspar Hauser's first period* in Nuremberg and what is connected with it! 'When they began to teach him,' says Rudolf Steiner in the text quoted above, 'when logic entered his soul, his memory disappeared.' Or, as Feuerbach, the aforementioned protector of Kaspar Hauser, and a leading criminologist, writes in his famous book published during Kaspar Hauser's lifetime (1832): *Kaspar Hauser. Beispiel eines Verbrechens am Seelenleben des Menschen*[29] [Kaspar Hauser—An Example of a Crime against the Soul Life of the Human Being]: 'This [power of] memory, however, diminished later on and, it seems, in the same proportion in which it had become richer *and his mind had had more work to do*.'[30]

'This transition in consciousness,' we hear in Rudolf Steiner's lecture, 'was also connected with something else. At first, there was an incomprehensible, almost innate truthfulness in him, and it was precisely this truthfulness that began to go more and more astray. The more he was allowed to nibble at intellectuality, the more it [his truthfulness] faded away.'

From here, a decisive light falls on the peculiar, disconcerting phenomenon of the untruthfulness testified to by many (even if it was judged very differently), which became noticeable in Kaspar Hauser after some time in Nuremberg and which plays such a large role in the Kaspar Hauser literature. Understandably, Kaspar Hauser's opponents have repeatedly exploited it and used it to deny Kaspar Hauser any credibility in what he said and, in particular, to portray Hauser's account of having endured imprisonment from his earliest childhood as a lie. Such behaviour, for example, was that of Julius *Meyer*, the son of Kaspar Hauser's teacher in Ansbach and one of the most active opponents of Hauser. (The fallacy of this argument was demonstrated by Baron Gottlieb *von*

* Kaspar Hauser was at that time not yet '20 years old', as we heard from Rudolf Steiner's lecture. When he appeared in Nuremberg, he must have been about 15, 16, or 18 years old.[28]

Tucher, who had been Kaspar Hauser's guardian in Nuremberg for a longer period and with whom Hauser had also lived for some time under his special direction.[31]

Witnesses who treated Kaspar Hauser with understanding, especially *Daumer*, saw the truthfulness of his story in a more correct light and judged it accordingly.

Daumer, for example, writes:[32]

> We have to distinguish carefully between two different periods of Hauser's life, as it lies before us, which opponents, in their own interests, always avoid doing. In the earlier one of these periods, qualities and phenomena of a very peculiar, even miraculous kind took place, which in the later period either disappeared completely or receded very much into the background and only revealed themselves in time and in part. In the first period, Hauser was an angelically pure human being with the finest sense of morality and the most rigorous love of truth; in the other period, he became accustomed to the ways of the world and of men in which he was almost constantly confronted with so much insincerity, untruthfulness and pretence,* and where he was even urged to use cunning and lies to defend himself, without which it was in fact often almost impossible to get by. The second of these periods already began in Nuremberg ....

Daumer also tells of a judgement by the Nuremberg city court physician Dr *Preu*, who immediately after Kaspar Hauser's appearance, was asked by the magistrate, to examine the foundling's state of mind[33] and 'who initially thought Hauser was a fraudster and had undertaken ... to expose him'. Preu 'spoke afterwards of the "*truly holy sense of truth*"' that was evident in this person. The unbelievable intrusiveness etc. of people towards Hauser induced him as [Daumer means here]

> to abandon the truth and to resort to all kinds of little tricks, excuses and untruths. It was self-defence, he could not do otherwise .... And after the world had succeeded in corrupting the initially so pure, innocent, even holy soul of this person to the point where he behaved as others did, it then turned into his accuser, blamed him for doing its own crim-

*This point of view is underlined by the fact that Kaspar Hauser also *imitated* people in their untruthfulness. It is well known that imitation plays a decisive role in children up to the age of seven. However, Kaspar Hauser continued to live at this age—as a result of his development having been artificially retarded—in many respects for a long time, as we will see more clearly later on.

> inal work and made him into a bad boy who had lied about his whole, terrible fate ....[34]

The Protestant pastor H. *Fuhrmann*, who gave Kaspar Hauser religious instruction in Ansbach and also confirmed him, expressed himself similarly in his book: *Kaspar Hauser, beobachtet und dargestellt in der letzten Zeit seines Lebens* [Kaspar Hauser—Observed and Portrayed in the Last Period of his Life]:

> Finally, I must say that I always found him quite open and sincere towards me. I did not easily perceive an untruth in him, and never a lie .... He may sometimes have told untruths to others,* but I see nothing else in it than that everyday phenomenon which is to be found in most, indeed—it is not too bold to assert—in all children of his mental age.[35]

All this can be regarded as quite true and correct, but it does not quite get to the core of the phenomenon, which only Rudolf Steiner's above-mentioned indication brings out. Seen in this light, Kaspar Hauser's development, with its suffering from *intellectuality*, appears to be a particularly stark example of the current general fate of humanity on Earth. From the sphere of a 'holy' truthfulness, Kaspar Hauser descended into the affliction of white lies, little acts of 'cunning' and the like. In the larger context of the overall Kaspar Hauser phenomenon, this process can be seen as a part of the *sacrifice* that brought this special kind of individuality to the 19th century.

8. In this context, the special nuance in Rudolf Steiner's words about Kaspar Hauser's '*nibbling*' at intellectuality deserves full attention. We can see in it an indication that Kaspar Hauser, as a special individual, had to be considered in a completely different way.

In 'Kaspar Hauser' we have to do with this unusual soul in which elements of an old human consciousness lived on. We are reminded of the 'stray Atlantean' (see above, p. 17). We can also think here of some of Daumer's remarks, e.g. things that he believed he could only put forward in his book of 1873—amidst the materialistic, intellectual thinking of the 19th century—in the following form, which at the same time speaks of Daumer's own spiritual isolation in his time:

---

* This is also reported, for example, by the above-mentioned Baron von Tucher, and indeed with a much sharper judgemental nuance. Cf. Pies, *Wahrheit* [Truth] pp. 180, 182, 184.

> If one did not have to deal with the literary and critical ragamuffins who persecute with their vulgar sneers anyone who even remotely hints at something unusual, one might dare to suggest something else. At times... it seemed as if Hauser was momentarily clairvoyant and thus read directly from the souls of others. At such moments, he was probably able to understand some of what was said to him without any knowledge of the language ....

The Nuremberg City court physician Dr *Preu*, mentioned above, points to something similar when he says of Hauser, apparently referring to the time after October 1828:

> Later, by chance, phenomena were discovered about him which obviously strayed into the area of animal magnetism and clairvoyance. Many [of his] prescient symbolic dreams belong to this ....[36]

Such a soul, according to the treatment it had received, should have gradually been led by a wise hand into contemporary consciousness, into the civilisation of the 19th century and its intellectuality, where, as we can perhaps already guess from what has been said so far, its mode of being could have had a beneficial effect.

Something *along these lines* can also be found in the following words of Dr Preu:

> Hauser had been deprived of all the effects of daylight through many years of confinement in an underground room. The solar sphere of the human organism had been suppressed in him, kept asleep; the telluric principle had become the dominant and only ruling principle, and he himself had become a nocturnal person. Therefore, suddenly being removed from the constant darkness surrounding him, the powerful effect of the stimulus of light, of the warmth of the sun, and the prolonged daytime waking caused by both, must necessarily have had no less of an adverse effect on his body than the replacement of the years of dull languishing in a lonely, grave-like silence by the noise of the lively bustle of life in the city.... If at that time [i.e. at the time of his appearance in Nuremberg—K.H.] one had even a faint inkling of his earlier destiny, it would have been easy to lead him, *methodically and gradually,* from his night existence to a life in daylight, just as we know how to arrange the transition of new-born children from the night, in which their mother's womb kept them enclosed, to the bright morning of their daily existence.[37]

Of course, Preu here only takes into account those peculiarities of Hauser that have resulted from his artificially retarded development or else those which Preu attributes to it; in a broader sense, however, these peculiarities also latently contain, as it were, those that this special kind of soul had already 'brought with it' into earthly existence. (We will have more to say about this difference later).

Were there people in the 19th century—we may ask—who could have recognised this soul at birth, received it and led it into the outer world in a meaningful way? People who were certainly ready to receive it in the environment in which it was born? I only want to raise this question here and can only later try to answer it at least tentatively.

What actually happened to Kaspar Hauser was, in any case, the exact opposite of what would have been sensible treatment: first, he was imprisoned—by whoever might have done that—and completely shut off from the outside world, but then he was drawn into intellectuality by means of a normal contemporary education and this unprepared soul was made to 'nibble' at it.

Feuerbach had at least something of this in mind when he wrote in 1832 in his famous book:

> One of the greatest blunders in the upbringing and education of this person was indisputably that instead of giving him a common human education appropriate to his particular nature, he had been sent to the high school for a few years and, on top of that, had been allowed to start in a higher class. This poor, neglected youngster ... suddenly had to rack his brains with Latin grammar and Latin exercises. Forced into rigid Latin-based schooling ..., his spirit now suffered its second imprisonment, as it were. Like his earlier cell walls, the dusty walls of the schoolroom now shut him out from nature and life.[38]

These sentences by the perceptive Feuerbach are certainly still far from grasping the depth of the whole problem that was at stake here, but at least they clearly indicate the central *pedagogical* aspect of the Kaspar Hauser phenomenon.*

---

* This aspect inspired the well-known 19th-century novelist, Karl Gutzkow, who wrote his three-volume novel *Die Söhne Pestalozzis* [The Sons of Pestalozzi] in 1869, 'in which he used the story of Kaspar Hauser as an archetypal human being for the material basis in his novel for solving the problem of education'.[38a] Gutzkow adopts many details from the fate of Kaspar Hauser, but treats everything in a rather external way, without going into depth.

This pedagogical aspect was addressed by Johannes E. *Hohlenberg* in his Danish-language book *Kaspar Hauser, eine Seelentragodie*[39] [Kaspar Hauser—A Soul Tragedy] of which the decisive final chapter has also been published in German translation.[40] Hohlenberg very aptly explains here, for example, how Kaspar Hauser's fate provides 'confirmation upon confirmation of spiritual-scientific insights': how, for example, all the descriptions from the early days of Kaspar Hauser's life after he appeared show the essential picture of a child before the seventh year; how at the same time, however, he also exhibited the characteristics of an older child, so that the two otherwise separate phases were abnormally conflated in him; but at the same time, he was also in certain respects an adult;[41] which must have increased confusion to an extreme.

At the end of his book, Hohlenberg says:

> In the course of his destiny, the figure of Kaspar Hauser is virtually representative of the mythos for the struggle of our time for individual spirituality. It is this alone that is still able to arouse people's engagement with his mysterious life and death. This engagement appears as spontaneous empathy with the nature of his fate, which we all intuitively feel to be our own....

In discussing the treatment of Kaspar Hauser, depicted by Anselm von Feuerbach as a 'crime against the soul life of the human being', the curative pedagogue *Karl König*, in an essay on curative pedagogy, characterised the case of this human destiny by saying that the figure of Kaspar Hauser appeared like a transfiguration on the mountaintop, 'in order to illumine—as a sign and symptom—the first awakening of curative pedagogy'. He asks: 'Does not each of the so-called difficult-to-educate, retarded children come into life in a similar way to Kaspar Hauser? Poor, unknown, a riddle and yet a blessing wherever open hearts meet him?'[42]

But in addition to the nibbling at intellectuality and its effect on Kaspar Hauser's initially wonderful memory and on his inherent, holy sense of truth, there is another important factor which led many of Kaspar Hauser's qualities—about which we will hear more later—to disappear. This came about when *meat* was introduced into his diet.

At first, as Daumer describes it, Kaspar continually showed the 'strongest aversion to all food and drink, except dry bread and water' (which had been his only nourishment in his captivity.*

'Not only the taste but even the mere smell of our normal fare caused him to shudder or worse....'[43] Only gradually, through many intermediate steps, was Daumer able to get him accustomed to 'normal' food, including the eating of meat. But with this was deeply connected the great change in Hauser that then occurred, as Daumer's eminently illuminating observations and arguments bear out.[44]

'The unusual abilities,' writes Daumer,

> which Hauser manifested at first, such as the remarkable, quite peculiar sensitivity and delicacy of his whole nature was obviously connected to his pure and innocent food. ... he lost this, however, when he got used to eating meat, which ... had a noticeably dulling and debilitating effect on him .... Unfortunately, amongst other things, his great powers of understanding and memory also disappeared....[45]

Daumer noted similar nuances:[46]

> The spiritual forces of the foundling were uncommon and extraordinary only *until he got used to eating animal products*, which is a strong dietary indication and proof of the view that this diet is not only physically but also spiritually disadvantageous for human beings. Hauser's decline in the moral sense at the same time can also be ascribed to this. His fine feeling for the truth in the beginning, when he did not want to allow an untruth even in a joke or an excuse, in order for example to avoid meeting annoying visitors, likewise became dulled....

---

* According to Daumer (his 1859 book pp.148-9), this bread was 'not the usual rough black bread..., but a finer, strongly seasoned kind of so-called starter bread....' Anyone who doubts the possibility that the boy could have been nourished exclusively by bread and water, may first reflect that in the second and third decades of the 19th century bread was still substantial and full of life and had not yet become the degraded and deadened bread of the 20th century. Many other deeper viewpoints could obviously be drawn from this.

And the water, of which Hauser could not easily get enough? This may lead us to think, albeit far from in an external way, of a time once on earth, in ancient Atlantis—we recall the 'stray Atlantean'—of how the waters, for human beings, meant waters filling the air in which 'wisdom itself' still lived and sounded to human beings from the waters.

> ... his moral faults, apart from the social circumstances that influenced him, were also not insignificantly related to the dietary change which he so long resisted and to which he was nevertheless led in the end, a reproach that I unfortunately have to direct at myself.

It can be deeply instructive to note these two points in Kaspar Hauser's case: that he was allowed to 'nibble' at intellectuality and that he was 'seduced' into *eating meat.* Both together caused his original abilities and qualities to melt away, and in both—*pedagogy and diet*—he demonstrated in a symptomatic and, as it were, in an archetypal way, the most important factors that will be of profound, general human significance at a time when new spiritual forces are seeking to awaken in mankind.

'There is no longer anything extraordinary about him,' wrote Feuerbach[47] in 1832 in his famous book on Kaspar Hauser, which ended with these words: 'except for the extraordinary nature of his fate and his indescribable goodness and loveableness.'

9. In his public lecture of 17 June 1908 Rudolf Steiner describes Kaspar Hauser as a soul '*which was artificially retarded*'.

This happened precisely because of Kaspar Hauser's many years of imprisonment and isolation, as cannot be doubted by anyone willing to take account of all the testified facts with an open mind. Of course, many of Kaspar Hauser's opponents—for whatever reason—were obviously not so willing, and so it is precisely this imprisonment of many years that has been disputed, and in its place various hypotheses have been suggested or desperately constructed.

For example, that Kaspar Hauser was a vagabond peasant, a tramp or the like. In the beginning, of course, justified doubts could arise before the circumstances were known in detail, or in the absence of a personal impression of Kaspar Hauser. One assumption, for example, was based on the fact that Kaspar Hauser soon developed great skill as a horseman in Nuremberg; it was suggested that he was perhaps a young English horseman who had run away from his gang![48]

Against all this, *Feuerbach,* the significant criminologist pointed in his 1832 book to the essential fact about the crime that had been committed against Hauser:

> Even about the story of the deed we have for the time being no other information than the account of the person against whom it was committed; but the truth of the account is hidden from us by the personality of the

> narrator, on whose body, mind and spirit ... the deed itself is visibly and clearly written. Only someone who has experienced and suffered what Kaspar has suffered can be like Kaspar; and someone who shows himself to be like Kaspar must have lived in the conditions Kaspar has told of himself.[49]

Hermann Pies rightly writes about this passage: 'This, in my opinion, is the central point of the whole matter.'*

In other words, countless established facts about the Kaspar Hauser phenomenon can easily be explained if one essentially accepts the captivity (of course, this need not apply to all the details, some of which are highly problematic) as Hauser narrated it—initially as a 'working hypothesis'—whereas otherwise, those same facts would appear completely inexplicable in their entirety.†

Such facts include above all those which exist independently of any deliberate influence by Kaspar Hauser. Thus, for example, about Hauser's first days in Nuremberg, Daumer writes in a report submitted at the beginning of September 1828:[51]

* On the other hand, Professor Dr Ivo Striedinger, Director of the State Archive in Munich, one of the more recent 'anti-Hauserians', is very wrong when he describes these two sentences of Feuerbach's (from 'Only someone' until 'has told of himself') as a 'circular argument'.[50] They are not; they are two parallel sentences, neither of which serves to define the other.

† In 1956, Pies, in *Wahrheit* [Truth], p. 287, states in the same sense on the basis of witness statements which he exhaustively reproduced and worked through: 'All these testimonies by eyewitnesses compiled in the foregoing about the impression Kaspar Hauser made on them at his appearance and during his first days in Nuremberg, about his clothing, how he looked, his physical condition, namely his complexion, body posture, gait, feet, hands, muscles, other physical anomalies, his mental habits, namely his lack of concepts and words, and finally his strange diet, are easily understandable if Kaspar Hauser had experienced the fate he described. It is also understandable that Kaspar Hauser's development in Nuremberg, as observed and described by witnesses, was in complete harmony and consistency through all stages, from infancy to adolescence, without him—as "Hiltel" (Hauser's guard in Nuremberg during Hauser's very first time in police custody there) once put it—"going out of control".

All these observations of Kaspar Hauser, recounted as facts by eyewitnesses, are, however, unbelievable if Hauser was a swindler....'

In the course of our further explanations, we will encounter most of the facts referred to here in their relevant contexts.

> His hands and the soles of his feet were previously so soft, free of callouses and vulnerable that one could clearly see his unfamiliarity with walking and working. When he was handed over to me, I could still find significant traces on his feet of the many sores he had received from unaccustomed walking.

The above-mentioned guardian of Kaspar Hauser, *Baron von Tucher*, a lawyer (later a member of the Upper Appeal Court Judicial Council), mentioned something similar and also pointed out, for example, the 'unusually broad and large liver, which was found during the autopsy, as in animals that had been deprived of the opportunity to move freely'.[52] (We will come back to this later.)

This 'artificial retardation' was thus inflicted on a soul that was already living out a primordial human life (we will get to know the essence of the 'stray Atlantean' at other important points). He was artificially prevented from living into the culture of his time, so that in addition to what, as an exceptional being, he had already 'brought with him', this retarded character was, as it were, confirmed and intensified in an unhealthy and violent manner. This could be called an '*adequate*' process in a diabolical sense.

10. As we have heard, Rudolf Steiner says of Kaspar Hauser: '*We were able to study many things* when we delved into this soul which had been artificially retarded....'

It must be pointed out here briefly at least, but emphatically, that an important *task* arises from this multi-layered phenomenon, which 'speaks' so very much when it is perceived and understood in the right sense. It needs to be understood in the most diverse fields, namely by a spiritual-scientific study of man in the broadest sense: by doctors, psychologists, psychotherapists, medical psychologists, priests, sociologists, historians, and above all, through their interaction.

In addition, of course, lawyers would be very much engaged, especially criminologists, who would be more interested in Kaspar Hauser because he appears as the victim of a crime committed against him by unknown perpetrators or the victim of a whole complex of crimes.

The latter point of view was also the main concern for the famous criminologist *Anselm von Feuerbach* who, in addition to all his deep human compassion and understanding, was at the same time an eyewitness to the phenomenon. In a letter of 15 May 1830 to the well-known Berlin criminologist Hitzig, he calls the Kaspar Hauser case 'the most remarkable of strange criminal cases, the like of which has probably not been seen once in thousands of years'.[53] The title of Feuerbach's above-mentioned book *Example of a Crime against the Soul of the Human Being*, is also completely in line both with general human and criminological interest.

In the 20th century, a criminological interest in the 'case' became the leitmotif for one of the most zealous and accurate Kaspar Hauser researchers, namely the Hamburg criminal lawyer *Adolf Bartning*, who unfortunately died prematurely in 1929 in the midst of his Kaspar Hauser research, at the age of 53.

In addition to the more soul and spirit aspect of the Kaspar Hauser phenomenon, there is also the more *physical and psychological* aspect, which we have only touched on occasionally thus far, and which is naturally connected with him in the most intimate way. We shall at least look into some of this here, always in the sense that it applied primarily only to the first period after Kaspar Hauser's appearance in Nuremberg, while later on, the phenomena increasingly diminished.

We already mentioned above (p. 18) how Kaspar Hauser reacted extremely strongly to homeopathic remedies. This went so far that the strongest effects often occurred even when he was not given the remedies but only allowed to smell them.

Daumer described such experiments and experiences in detail in his *Mitteilungen über Kaspar Hauser* [Information about Kaspar Hauser], published in 1832. Likewise, in a homoeopathic journal, *Dr Preu*, a municipal court physician from Nuremberg whom we have mentioned several times already, describes his own experiments in his essay '*Der Findling Kaspar Hauser und dessen ausserordentliches Verhältnis zu homöopathischen Heilstoffen*' [The Foundling Kaspar Hauser and His Extraordinary Relationship to Homoeopathic Remedies], where he says that through Kaspar Hauser, the teachings of Hahnemann (the founder of the homoeopathy) 'were not only fully confirmed', but at the same time also 'far surpassed all human belief'.[54]

A famous passage in Preu's writings relates to 'the almost supernatural quality, sharpness and refinement of all his senses' (Feuerbach)[55]. 'At a distance of a hundred paces,' testifies Dr Preu[56], 'he could count the individual berries on an elder tree, could distinguish in complete darkness dark brown from dark red etc.'

He was able to find metals lying on a table, covered up so that he could not see them, and correctly indicate which metals they were. 'Of all the metals, mercury had the strongest effect on Hauser' (Daumer[57]).

He had an extreme reaction to grape juice. In September 1828, Daumer reported:[58]

> In September 1828 Hauser tasted a few drops of freshly pressed (i.e. *unfermented*!) juice from grapes and presented the perfect image of a drunk. He staggered about, his speech was heavy, and he laughed continually; the little finger of his left hand was moved a great deal, as it did whenever he was much excited, and soon afterwards he had to go to bed.

Something quite similar was reported by Baron von Tucher:[59]

> I witnessed that when a champagne bottle was opened 3-4 steps away from him at my father-in-law's table [his father-in-law was the philosopher Hegel—*Ed.*], he showed the signs of drunkenness without having drunk any champagne himself—he did not enjoy any kind of alcoholic beverages at all—so that he became drowsy and woke up after more than an hour's sleep with a severe headache.

This effect of drinking a few drops of unfermented grape juice on the one hand, and the mere smell of champagne on the other, is particularly striking if one thinks of Rudolf Steiner's words about Kaspar Hauser as a *'stray Atlantean'* and of what is expressed in the well-known story of the 'drunkenness of Noah', i.e. the man who led humanity from the Atlantean period into the post-Atlantean cultures, the 'first wine drinker',[60] i.e. the one who first gave mankind the drink of fermented grape—wine which would lead human beings much deeper than previously down into the world of matter—the role which alcohol was to play in the growth of the human I as a personal being separated from the spiritual world and everything related to that.

11. 'Not at all unjustified', said Rudolf Steiner in his lecture of 17 June 1908 (cf. p. 30 above) 'for those who stand on the basis of spiritual science, is the folk tradition which the learned people of today do not believe, which tells that Kaspar Hauser, when he still knew nothing at all and had no idea that there were beings of different types apart from himself, exercised a remarkable effect on wild animals when they were brought to him. They crouched down and became quite gentle; something emanated from him which caused such animals, which had attacked others angrily, to become gentle.'

A 'folk tradition' (which educated people do not believe): here again we have the motif that it was precisely the common people who had an inner soulful understanding of Kaspar Hauser which somehow penetrated deeply into their being (cf. p. 22 above), an understanding that was lacking precisely in 'educated people' with their mere cleverness.

The extent to which Kaspar Hauser really had such experiences with animals 'historically' is not settled, and how far he would have had them does not seem quite understandable in the sense of that 'folk tradition', before he knew that there were beings of different types apart from himself, for in his cell he certainly had not encountered animals of the kind indicated, and in Nuremberg he soon learned that there were other people apart from him (whom he called 'Bue'—boys—whether man, woman or child) and that there were animals, all of which, including birds, he called 'Ross' [horse]—after the wooden horses he had had with him in his cell and with which he had played during most of his time there.*

Jakob Wassermann describes such a scene in his Kaspar Hauser novel:[61]

> Another day there was a great noise in the neighbour's garden. A violent dog had broken its chain and, foaming at the mouth, raced around in wild spurts, knocking over a child, bit into the flesh of a servant who was chasing it and jumped against the fence of Daumer's garden. A lath cracked under the impact, the animal slipped through and turned its bloodshot eyes wildly towards the small company sitting under the lime tree. Daumer himself, his mother, the mayor Binder and Caspar. They all stood up fearfully, Binder raised his stick, the animal made a few moves, but suddenly stopped, sniffed, trotted towards Caspar, who was sitting pale and still, wagged his tail and licked the youngster's hand which was hanging down. It looked at him with a passionate but uncertain gaze, almost full of surrender, expecting tenderness, and as if asking for forgiveness. Caspar had the same uncertain and devoted expression in his eyes; the dog was whining at him, and he didn't know why. It was said that Daumer had wept after this incident.

Perhaps Wassermann was inspired by that 'folk tradition' to write this account. Or perhaps he created it entirely from his artistic imagination. In any case, it is important to be clear about the fact that Wassermann's novel, although it is based in outer historical reality in many essential points and in innumerable details, not only supplements that reality in some places

---

* In the beginning, writes Daumer (in Pies, *Augenzeugenberichte* I [Eyewitness Accounts] 158/159), Kaspar only called *white* animals horses, 'because his toy horses were white; he denied, for example, that brown horses were horses, but white geese and oxen he considered to be horses'.

through the author's artistic licence but also deliberately departs from it in that it describes things that, while 'untrue' in an outer historical sense, may at times reveal the deeper reality all the more truthfully. The most blatant case of this kind is the 'correction' that Wassermann makes in his novel to the fate of the shady figure of Lord Stanhope, Kaspar Hauser's suspicious 'foster father': he has him end his life by suicide (he hangs himself) while Kaspar Hauser is still alive (1833)[62], whereas in 'reality' Stanhope did not die until 1855, and peacefully, in his bed.

In the same vein is, for example, the undoubtedly fictional letter that Wassermann has Stanhope write to a recipient, 'the Grey one', as Wassermann calls him and who remains unknown to the reader, with an effective, imaginative bluntness.[63] This is Stanhope's report, invented by Wassermann, to the one who had given Stanhope his task and who is imagined to be active behind the scenes. Not a word of this is to be found, of course, in the 'sources' on record.*

So, to take this opportunity to introduce a methodological remark here, it is in principle never appropriate to use Wassermann's novel unseen, for example, as a source for investigating the external historical facts about Kaspar Hauser! Rather, these must be drawn from other testimonies or representations.

In these more scholarly sources or accounts, which lay claim to external 'correctness', it is nowhere possible to find a source for Wassermann's story of that angry, vicious dog. Nevertheless, something at least *along these lines* is reported by Daumer, under the heading: 'Striking Relationship to a Cat':[64]

> Before he learned to eat meat (1828), Hauser had a relationship, which could not be explained in the usual way, with a cat that was fed in my house. Indoors, this cat allowed itself to be touched and carried, but never by anyone when it was outside. As soon as Hauser came into the garden, however, it ran up to him, let itself be picked up and carried about by him, and chased around the garden playing with him. This cat enjoyed nothing else but meat and milk. From Hauser's hand only would it eat a great deal of rye bread and

*This is confirmed above all by *Marianne Thalmann* in her essay '*Wassermanns Caspar Hauser und seine Quellen*' [Wassermann's Kaspar Hauser and its Sources] (in the journal *Deutsches Volkstum* [German Folk Culture], Hamburg 1929, No. 3, pp. 215/216), in which she writes about Wassermann's 'artistic qualities' that he (who otherwise draws much from documentary 'sources') 'systematically lays out the series of disguised figures and strangers', 'who, as emissaries of a hostile camp, besiege Caspar and in Stanhope have their trivial and deceptive leader'.

> even fruit, even when it was not very hungry... etc. Hauser claimed that this animal had only begun to bite at him, as it did to others, when he began to tolerate eating meat.

This motif of Kaspar's unusual relationship to animals, be it from folk tradition, be it from poetic fantasy, be it from the sober world of facts, is also strongly reminiscent of primitive humanity and of an age even closer to 'paradise', when man and animal were still close to each other, when animals still trusted human beings instead of fearing them as they came to do later. (Humans were not yet meat eaters!)

But one can also think of the figure of Orpheus, of whom it is said that he tamed the wild animals by playing his lyre with its seven strings.[65] Orpheus was the son of Apollo, the divine being in whom[66] the Greeks worshipped that primordial human being who dwelt in higher worlds, who had never entered into an earthly incarnation until the events in Palestine at the Turning Point of Time, but who had a harmonising effect on human souls in the spheres of the seven planets.

12. As the last of the motifs from Rudolf Steiner's lecture, following on from our previous considerations, we would like to touch on the motif which is so important for an understanding of the most ancient times of human development, namely, that these were '*pre-religious*' times in which the human being was still so strongly connected in the old dreamlike clairvoyance with the beings of the spiritual world, with the gods, that there was no need for a 're-connection' (*religio*) with them, which only became necessary and possible to the extent that the ancient real spiritual connection with them had faded away.

From this point of view, it would seem understandable if a human being, in whom very old states of consciousness strongly resonated and who, like Kaspar Hauser, had initially been held back from the outside world and from an organic living into it, was, to begin with, able to muster little sense for 'religion', religious instruction, for a concept of God grasped in thought, etc.

And this was precisely the case of the stranger in the first period after his appearance in Nuremberg! A bright light shines from his primordial human nature on the long and futile efforts—about which Feuerbach says: 'There was not a tiny spark of religion, not even the smallest speck of dogmatic dust to be found in his soul',[67]—of well-meaning people to approach him—to introduce religious concepts and ideas to him. These made no sense to him; he could do nothing at all with the very concept of God and rather, made very naive primitive, rationalist objections against it—Feuerbach even speaks of 'his crude materialistic conceptions',[68]; these of course very soon developed after his appearance 'in the world' in the intellectual thinking that was so new to him.

Of course, rather than this negative aspect of his relationship to religious ideas, which was quite obvious and repeatedly noted by observers, it is much more difficult to penetrate into those deeper layers of Kaspar Hauser's consciousness in which the positive counterpart of this negative aspect must be sought, and to grasp what ancient connection with a spiritual fullness of life there might have been under the threshold of his newly acquired intellectual consciousness. One would come closer to this if one knew his dreams better, some of which Daumer reported.[69] He also says of the time about one year after Kaspar Hauser's appearance in Nuremberg, very strikingly:

> On the whole, he appeared to be a sober person, with very little poetry and imagination; but he had very poetic dreams, and sometimes even in his waking hours strange images would appear in his mind.

Hans Wohlbold rightly said of these dreams that they 'clearly have the character of Imaginations'.[70]

But what were the times in the development of humanity in which 'all human beings still had more or less direct experience and perception of the suprasensory', 'in which human beings lived in the spiritual world itself, which they experienced at all times like humanity today experiences the sensory world', in which 'human beings ... still lived with their gods' so that 'there was no need for religion', as Rudolf Steiner put it?[71] Those were the times of ancient *Atlantis*![71]

And so this too serves to substantiate further the description of Kaspar Hauser as a '*stray Atlantean*'.

★

'Afterwards,' writes Daumer,[72] 'when his spirit became dulled and his power of understanding and comprehension sank due to his getting used to animal food, he also fell in with the usual religious ways of thinking about things.' More comprehensively, we can say that Kaspar Hauser's relationship to religion changed as he became ever more consciously integrated into the earthly world, and as he became more and more detached from the inner world in which man is connected in ancient ways with the being of sustaining divine powers.

Within the framework of a consciousness limited to the senses, a conventional religiosity developed in Kaspar Hauser, but it had a seriousness, purity and depth that were very moving. This was also felt by the above-mentioned Pastor Fuhrmann, who gave him 5-7 hours of religious instruction a week in Ansbach from October 1832 to May 1833 in preparation for confirmation, and who says of these sessions that Hauser's good, innocent soul, so eager for religious instruction, made these lessons 'true hours of joy', 'beautiful, blessed hours'. On 20 May 1833, Pastor Fuhrmann confirmed Kaspar Hauser in the St Gumbertus Church, with many of the people of Ansbach in attendance. Through Kaspar Hauser's behaviour and the whole course of events, the ceremony produced an extraordinary effect of deep emotion in the whole congregation.[73]*

What Fuhrmann reports about the way in which Kaspar Hauser took in the mystery of the teaching of redemption and similar teachings (contrary to what Feuerbach had expected) seems particularly significant: 'It was precisely here that Hauser expressed the most sublime feeling, precisely here that he showed such emotion and zeal that would have enraptured everyone who saw him, as I did. His tears flowed continually at the telling of the story of Jesus Christ, his words and his gestures expressed the deepest reverence, the holiest veneration for the suffering Redeemer.'[74]†

Deeply moving also were the religious feelings Kaspar Hauser expressed on his deathbed ....

But there is something else that comes into consideration. Daumer tells how Kaspar Hauser, in this respect quite different from other children (with whom he otherwise had so much in common), did not accept anything on the authority of adults but 'wanted to understand everything'. That is why the religious instruction he was initially given tormented him; 'in it he was

---

* From this, light is cast on a peculiar similarity between Kaspar Hauser at the level of development here indicated and certain phenomena of *Chinese culture* (which in itself can be traced back to the ancient Atlantean nature).

† These last comments by Pastor Fuhrmann are in harmony with something that Rudolf Steiner is supposed to have said about Kaspar Hauser and which, because we have not been able to ascertain its authenticity with complete certainty, we would have left unmentioned, but these comments by Pastor Fuhrmann seem to provide a certain support for Steiner's remark. Rudolf Steiner is supposed to have said that besides Christian Rosenkreutz Kaspar Hauser had the greatest empathy for the sufferings of Christ .... (From another direction, these words, in so far as they compare Kaspar Hauser to Christian Rosenkreutz, are supported by what was said earlier about Professor Daumer being 'the last Rosicrucian', as well as by other things which we shall mention in the second chapter of this book.)

referred to mere faith, which went so much against his nature, and was urged not to investigate and ponder on the darkness in such mere faith'.

Hauser complained about the religious instruction he was given by a Protestant clergyman in Nuremberg, saying that 'it revealed nothing and every time he wanted to understand something, he was told to take it on faith'. Daumer himself was able to help him successfully in that he brought his pupil to an understanding of the existence of God through reasoned thoughts, which the boy gladly accepted.[75]

So when one takes all this together, one sees how this strange child who had come into the earthly world, as it were, recapitulated the developmental path of mankind in the five short years of his life 'in the world' also in respect to religious life: from a pre-religious stage to that of religious feelings and sensibilities and ideas, and then as the fruit of rationalistic thinking, doubt pushed its way in, a disinclination to mere 'belief', but then also—a very important motif pointing to the future—the endeavour to understand what he was being led to believe; this was a seed of the post-rationalist stage in the spiritual and historical development of humanity. Here a transformed, spiritualised thinking already made its appearance in a new form as spiritual *science,* and that which had once been the object of *faith* and rationalistic thinking alone had necessarily to be rejected. It also seems deeply meaningful, especially with regard to the latter point, that Kaspar Hauser was led by his good karma to *Daumer,* the 'last Rosicrucian', the deeply spiritual seeker for a new spirituality in the middle of the 19th century. Broad perspectives can open up for us here. We can, for example, recall *Lessing's* striving to transform the old 'truths of revelation' into 'truths of reason'—Lessing, who himself was inspired by an important Rosicrucian source.[76]

The Kaspar Hauser phenomenon needs to be placed in the broad context of human spiritual history and the development of consciousness. From there we can begin to sense his significance, in order to gradually understand it ever more clearly.

A Necessary Distinction

It is already clear from our previous considerations that it is important to distinguish strongly between the following two things in Kaspar Hauser's life, which nevertheless obviously merge into a unity:

1. He entered earthly life through birth as a being of particular provenance in soul and in spirit.

2. What *became* of him as a result of the treatment he received: the incarceration and isolation he experienced for many years under very specific circumstances, about which we will have more to say, then his education, upbringing and other living conditions in the 'world' in Nuremberg and Ansbach.

As far as the former point is concerned, what is of profound significance is that which, in a nutshell, as it were, lies in the characterisation of Kaspar Hauser as a 'stray Atlantean', as we have already seen in various ways previously. In addition, however, there is another very important statement by Rudolf Steiner, the authenticity of which, according to what I have been able to ascertain, cannot be doubted: namely, that in 1924 Rudolf Steiner was asked by someone about the karma of Kaspar Hauser and that this man—the next day—received the answer from Rudolf Steiner that *he had not been able to find a previous incarnation of Kaspar Hauser.*

To the already highly significant nature of this reply must be added the peculiarity that it bears the closest resemblance to various versions of the statement made by Rudolf Steiner about *Napoleon*: he had not been able to find Napoleon's soul anywhere in his researches (see a more detailed account of this in my book, *Die Französische Revolution und Napoleon* [The French Revolution and Napoleon] 1953, p. 271). So here, for the first time and in this strange way, we find ourselves mentioning Napoleon in connection with the fate of Kaspar Hauser. As we shall see, this will not be the last time.

It is becoming increasingly clear from what has been said so far that in Kaspar Hauser's case we are dealing from the outset with a particularly individual character.

Furthermore, he was subjected to what was, similarly, very particular treatment. (Already here, therefore, the question may arise in us whether this special treatment of Kaspar Hauser is intrinsically connected precisely with the fact that he was such a special individual.)

One thing, at any rate, can be clear to us from what has been said so far, namely, that it cannot be the case that the 'Kaspar Hauser' phenomenon, as the world has come to know it (with the exception, of course, of those opponents of Kaspar Hauser, who, through their prejudices and blindness, have prevented themselves from really seeing the phenomenon) is based solely and exclusively on *the particular way Kaspar Hauser was treated*, but only on the fact that *this particular individual* was treated in this way. Or, to put it another way: it is not the case that *any* person born in the 19th century, if they had been treated the way Kaspar Hauser was treated, would have presented the same phenomenon.

As far as we have been able to observe, this is, understandably, not seen in the Kaspar Hauser research and literature of a non-anthroposophical nature, i.e. in almost all Kaspar Hauser research and literature. The latter, understandably, has to do only with the phenomenon of the Kaspar Hauser who experienced this particular treatment. It must be a misapprehension on the part of such research and literature when it assumes that Kaspar Hauser essentially only became what he did become as a result of this treatment.

The situation becomes decisively different only on the basis of a way of looking at things which has learned to reckon from the outset with the pre-existence of human souls, which enter into earthly existence through birth, and to feel inwardly the question of the 'how' and the 'where from' of individuals. And without such a questioning attitude, even here, one cannot easily expect answers either.

Walking, Speaking, Thinking

The treatment that Kaspar Hauser received in his cell for many (10-12[77]) years was such as to artificially prevent the development in him of those three main abilities that must normally be developed in the childhood and early youth of all human beings, and which are central to the human growth and distinguish the human being as the bearer of an ego from the animal[78]: *walking* (the upright posture), *speaking* and *thinking*. This seems to have been, objectively, the most important function of Kaspar Hauser's incarceration and complete isolation.

1. The unfortunate child was prevented from assuming an *upright posture* and from walking. The details of how this happened (shackling or the like)—as described in the Kaspar Hauser literature)*—are difficult to ascertain with complete certainty. *That* it happened, however, cannot be doubted according to the phenomenon as a whole, if one only lets it speak. Further proof given by Kaspar Hauser's later physical condition that he must have spent many years constantly in a sitting position with his legs stretched out flat on the floor was the way in which, according to a forensic doctor's statement in Nuremberg, as late as 1830, when sitting in this way on the flat floor, the backs of Hauser's knees (contrary to what is possible with all

* Daumer (in Pies, *Augenzeugenberichte I*, p. 153) writes for example: 'Hauser, sitting up in his prison, felt that something prevented him from leaning forward even slightly towards his knees; he was not even able to lie completely on his side, only lying on his back and sliding slightly to his left side was possible.'

other people) rested so firmly on the floor that 'not even a sheet of paper could be pushed through'.[79]

That Kaspar Hauser's own account given in Nuremberg that his guardian taught him to walk (or more likely, retaught him) only shortly before his release from prison, is confirmed by the condition of the soles of his feet already mentioned above (p. 32), and by the clumsy and swaying gait he had when he arrived in Nuremberg, and the efforts he had to make to walk during his first time there.

'His gait,' writes Feuerbach (quoted in Pies, *Augenzeugenberichte I*, p. 40), 'similar to that of a child making its first attempts on a treadmill, was not so much a walking as a waddling, swaying toddling, an awkward movement between falling and standing upright.'

2. Due to the complete isolation in his cell, where, according to Kaspar Hauser's account, his circumstances were arranged in such a way that he himself never got to see his gaoler, he did not learn to *speak* (or unlearned it again, if he had already been able to speak in his earlier childhood). In this respect, he was comparable to the hypothetical human being who grows up alone on a desert island without any language, since speech only develops in human company with (at least one) other human being.

It was only during his very last period in the cell, before his release, that his gaoler seems to have spoken to him and to have taught him to walk and to speak individual sentences, which Kaspar Hauser, without understanding the meaning, parroted and repeated again and again in Nuremberg after his arrival, e.g. the sentence 'I want to become a rider, just like father is'[80] and which he repeated in all kinds of situations, even those in which it was completely meaningless. His speech was still 'laboured and difficult' even after some time in Nuremberg.[81]

3. Only by speaking does a person learn to *think*. During his time in his cell, Kaspar Hauser was kept away from everything that would have enabled him to learn to think. There must have been very little light in the cell. No sunlight penetrated into it that could make things appear in clear, sharp contours, which in turn are the basis for thinking in clear, sharp contours. (Thus, in the course of the development of mankind, it was generally only to the degree to which the masses of mist that had once filled the whole atmosphere in ancient Atlantis disappeared, that the sun became visible on earth and made things appear clearly defined, and that the physical preconditions for the rainbow came into being, in the sign of which, in the biblical sense,

Noah (for post-Atlantean mankind) enters into the new covenant with God, etc.) In such contexts, we can again be reminded in a most peculiar way of Rudolf Steiner's words about Kaspar Hauser as the 'stray Atlantean'.

It can also be regarded as certain[82] that Kaspar Hauser was often given *opium* in his drinking water in the cell, which put him into a deep sleep, especially during the times when his gaoler physically attended to him, changed his washing, emptied his toilet pot, etc. This opium also seems to have been given to Kaspar Hauser in larger amounts, so as to keep him in his dull, dreamlike state,—a procedure deemed 'suitable' for him in the same diabolical sense as we noted in a more general way above (p. 32).

Daumer speaks of Kaspar Hauser's 'childlike soul that had been bound by imprisonment, bondage and opium'.[83,84]

Thus, the unfortunate child—who in a *subjective* sense evidently seems not to have felt himself to have been unfortunate at that time—lived in an inner and outer twilight. In the relatively more awake hours of this twilight life, he played with his little wooden horses—it was his main activity—which had been given to him in the cell (along with a little wooden dog), by decorating them with coloured ribbons, feeding them (as he believed) from his bread, etc.).* There is something deeply moving and touching in what he later said about this.

Autopsy Findings: Brain and Liver

The fact that Kaspar Hauser did not learn to *think* in the decisive years of his childhood or, in other words, did not use and develop his brain in a normal way, is also proven by his physical condition, which was revealed by

---

*The role played by the *horse* in Kaspar Hauser's life seems to be strangely symbolic or suggestive of deep connections: in his cell, the very small horses which led to his calling all animals (at least all white ones) 'Ross' at the beginning in Nuremberg (see above p. 35); then the sentence he learned in which he repeated that he wanted to become a rider, i.e. to join the Light Horse cavalry like his father (something similar was also written in the safe conduct letter he was given to take with him to Nuremberg and which he handed in to the cavalry captain von Wessenig in Nuremberg); and finally, the fact that in Nuremberg itself he very soon developed 'a peculiar talent for riding'[85] (even if he did not become a soldier!). However, as is well known in the field of spiritual science, it is precisely the development of human thinking, of intelligence, that is connected with the horse (see, for example, the imagery of the myth of the Trojan horse, etc.) and which Kaspar Hauser had been kept from for so long.

the forensic autopsy: his underdeveloped *brain*. This—as a bodily clue to the retardation of his development in the cell—naturally needs to be looked at together with, for example, what has already been briefly mentioned above (p. 32) about his unusually large *liver*.

In view of the great importance of this matter, we would like to quote something from an essay by the Ansbach general practitioner, Dr *Heidenreich*, who was Kaspar Hauser's physician and who was present at the court-ordered autopsy. The essay '*Kaspar Hausers Verwunderung, Krankheit und Leichenöffnung*' [Kaspar Hauser's Wounding, Sickness and Funeral] was published in 1834 in a medical journal. There it says, among other things:

> The liver was very large and hypertrophic. The district court doctor, who had to give an expert opinion,[86] could not deny that this enlargement and hypertrophy could be related to Hauser's previous incarceration, in that even animals that are allowed little exercise in cramped conditions develop large livers.

Dr Heidenreich also writes the following in this connection:

> In relation to the relatively small lungs, I also find the enlargement of the liver quite natural, since these two organs are physiologically dependent on each other as organs for the excretion of carbon; in the foetus the liver functions for the lungs and becomes more prominent in animal species the more the lungs retreat.
>
> If the lungs were able to develop only a little with minimal movement, and in the dull air of the cell the lungs could only develop a little, the burden must then fall on the liver.*

---

* Regarding the liver and lungs, Rudolf Steiner's lecture in Berlin of 6 January 1908 should be mentioned:

> The *Saturn* forces have a strong and intensive influence on the *liver*. Therefore, the human being, because he is increasingly developing beyond all things Saturnian, must grow beyond the forces that are anchored in his liver. In the time before and immediately after birth, the liver expands the most in comparison with the rest of the body, but then becomes smaller and smaller in relation to the rest of the body. The organs that are the opposite of the liver in a way are the lungs. Etc.

The phenomenon of the hypertrophic development of the liver in Kaspar Hauser and the small size of his lungs also seem to accord with the fact that he—completely given over to the human *birth*-pole—was strongly re-living conditions of human prehistory, which furthermore were artificially preserved and intensified by the external treatment (imprisonment, etc.) which was imposed on him.

Dr Heidenreich also makes statements about the condition of Kaspar Kaspar Hauser's *brain* (for example, about the 'smallness of the brain in general, the relatively small mass of the large brain and the significant size of the small brain', with further details), which could certainly become more significant if anthroposophic medicine were to attempt to shed light on the Kaspar Hauser phenomenon. All the findings 'seem to me', explains Dr Heidenreich, 'to point to the defective development of the brain'. Indeed, he writes:

> Incidentally, during the examination of the brain, I could not suppress the feeling, and as I write this now also cannot suppress the words, 'formation similar to the animal'.

'In this case,' continues Dr Heidenreich:

> it was not the mental development that was inhibited by the insufficient formation of the brain, but the brain was retarded in its development by the lack of all mental activity and stimulation. For it is a law of nature that every organ and structure which remains unexercised and unused does not reach the full degree of its potential, or shrinks back from it and becomes diminished. By the seventh year, the material development of the human brain has more or less finished ....
>
> If Hauser spent his time before his seventh year in a dark hole, in a dull slumber, without all the intellectual activity and mental stimuli which are necessary for the development of the human brain, his brain formation would also have to remain at the animal level, as he himself had only lived in an animal condition.
>
> But if the autopsy really showed signs of such an undeveloped formation of the physical brain, then that condition is also sufficient proof that Hauser must have been placed into the circumstances in which he had to remain for so long, some time before his seventh year.
>
> However, if his youthful years had been lived in this condition and his brain had completed its physical formation at this low level, what had been missed out on could no longer be replaced ....
>
> This explains the rapid progress and astonishing capacities which Hauser achieved at first, because his brain was already mature enough for them, which in children must first be physically formed; but it also explains why his progress soon stopped at the limit of the mediocre

and the ordinary, because his brain could no longer be remodelled for a higher intellectual life.[87]*

'Manifestations of Higher Spiritual Powers'

Here, then, insofar as Heidenreich, for example, speaks of a 'higher mental life', we are speaking of that thinking which is bound to the physical tool of the brain, that is, of the body-bound thinking which, in the course of more recent centuries and especially the 19th century, was developed ever more remarkably, but also ever more one-sidedly. Yet one does not see the phenomenon of Kaspar Hauser fully, indeed one sees it in a negative, one-sided way if one looks only at the 'deficiency' that results from the underdeveloped brain, and then overlooks the other side, which seems to 'rhyme' so badly with this one, as Daumer, for example, expressed it. He once pointed to 'Hauser's

---

*What Dr Heidenreich notes about the brain of Kaspar Hauser, the 'stray Atlantean' (according to Rudolf Steiner), can appear in a very special light in developmental terms if one takes into account how Rudolf Steiner describes the formation of the brains of the ancient Atlanteans:[88] they still had small forebrains (and an even more receding forehead), but a much stronger ether body. The physical head was only small and embedded in the etheric head. The functions that humans now carry out with the help of the forebrain were carried out by the Atlanteans with the help of organs in the ether body. It was not until the last third of the Atlantean period, from the time of the so-called Proto-semites, that the etheric forebrain developed the (physical) forebrain. This gave man the capability of the brain, the mind, power over the physical and mechanical. (For this, he lost his power over plant growth, which he had previously been able to exercise by means of the etheric head.) 'He now had to begin again with many things' (from the Proto-semitic race onwards). 'Then he was still like a child, awkward and maladroit...'. (Doesn't this last nuance also touch one inwardly, related to the phenomenon that Kaspar Hauser, the 'teenage child', presented in the first period after his appearance in Nuremberg?)

In view of all this, may we not perhaps assume that the brain formation which Kaspar Hauser, the 'stray Atlantean', brought with him through birth was from the outset an abnormal one in the direction indicated? Here, too, it would have been the case that instead of leading over organically into present earthly conditions what he had lived through as an echo of an ancient human past, he had been artificially held back through a kind of life in which he was held in his childhood and early youth, so that the attempt was made to bind him to the past, as it were—the very person from whom, as we shall see more and more, important impulses for the *future* should have emanated.

manifestations of higher spiritual power and vitality', 'which, even if they were still so spontaneous and short-lived, at least elevated him for the moment to the rank of a highly gifted poet and thinker', and opined—very understandably in view of the way of thinking of the 19th century—that these manifestations rhymed badly with Hauser's 'brain, which had remained at an animal-like and foetus-like level'.[89] The two certainly did not rhyme. Rather, the manifestations of higher spiritual power indicated by Daumer are quite obviously something that, without the tool of the physical brain, shone out from this stranger to the earth from what he was 'actually', in his true individuality, that is, from his spiritual and supersensory being. This is why he was granted important 'lightning-like' insights, and it is of decisive importance to look at these if one wants to learn to understand the being of Kaspar Hauser.

For this reason, the following important statements by Daumer[90] may also be mentioned:

> Hauser had moments when a sudden enlightenment and revelation seemed to come to him and when symbolic images full of deep meaning appeared before him in a visionary manner. Such was the case once in the winter of 1830 to 1831, when he felt a great urge for knowledge. Then, he said, everything suddenly became clear to him through an image that presented itself to him, the meaning of which he immediately understood completely. It seemed to him 'as if everything was one, humanity together with nature', but in such a way 'that humanity actually made up the whole'. The image he saw was a kind of tree whose branches had moved and formed all kinds of figures which were no longer clear to him, for he had been disturbed in his contemplation and then sickened by the smell of camphor; then that clarity had become dulled for him and it seemed to him as if there were a veil over it.
>
> But he still remembered the following: opposite branches had moved in and out of each other and it seemed to him as if the whole emerged through this movement. The tree had stood on a base, on something solid, which he no longer knew how to describe; from below upwards there was a kind of pole, on the top of which was a little crown with a red berry in it; it seemed to him as if that was the main thing.

In her well-known book,[91] the sensitive author *Klara Hofer* writes of Kaspar's vision that 'he saw the Tree of Life'. Daumer himself seeks to translate Kaspar's 'speculative [i.e. visionary—*transl.*] thoughts', as he calls them, more into concepts; he emphasises that Hauser was completely unfamiliar with philosophical systems: 'such images and ideas as those described came to him entirely from within himself and in a way that makes one think of Jakob Boehme'. In 'what he said about that vision, there was no mention of God nor of evil, while he nevertheless affirmed that at the time of that vision and his contemplation of it everything that otherwise had been troubling him was perfectly clear to him, and the solution of the difficult riddles that had been making him anxious seemed quite easy; "if only it would happen to him again!" '

Doesn't it seem quite palpable that we are dealing here with the lighting up of a spiritual individuality through the maya that was 'Kaspar Hauser'? And with a lack of the 'rhyming' together of his light-filled, visionary thinking in pictures with body-bound and brain-bound thinking? Doesn't Daumer's reference to Jakob Boehme also seem to be revealing with regard to the spiritual 'provenance' of Hauser's visions?*

Rudolf Steiner often spoke about the three capacities of the human being as such or the three forces on which they are based: the upright posture and walking, then speech, and finally thinking, and the development of these in this order throughout childhood and their relation to human I-consciousness.

In addition to this, we may also briefly refer to a special aspect of these three forces which Rudolf Steiner speaks about in his lecture of 9 April 1918: he shows there how these three forces have a significant function even after the earthly life of the human being, and how it is they which, after death, carry our I-consciousness and its outer image, the material particles of our body, out into the wider world. (In the context of this same lecture, Rudolf Steiner also mentions how certain occult truths—which obviously include the ones we are talking about here—are still held back and closely guarded by people who have always known them, which, as has often been pointed out, has to do with the fact that the exclusive possession of occult truths signifies a factor of power for their owners.[92]

Blurring the Traces

In Kaspar Hauser's case, the phenomenon that he suffered the most severe damage precisely in relation to these three forces due to his forced retardation and isolation can be seen quite clearly, and all the more effort seems to have been expended to blur precisely this phenomenon. Characteristic of this are, for example, the efforts of *Lord Stanhope*, Kaspar Hauser's 'foster

* See the indication by Rudolf Steiner from his lecture of 1 Feb. 1920 in Dornach: 'What comes from Jakob Boehme is still noticeable today at the basis of Middle European [spiritual] endeavours',—even if it is fading.

father' and, after his foster son's death, his open opponent, who then endeavoured to portray Kaspar Hauser as a fraud.

'In the course of these machinations directed against Hauser,' writes Hermann Pies[93] about Stanhope:

> he also sought out people who earlier had somehow been involved in the Hauser affair, in order to obtain material against Hauser from them. The material thus obtained, statements of the first witnesses to Hauser's appearance, he asked to be sent to the Ansbach court of enquiry, which arranged for the witnesses named by Stanhope to be questioned again in Nuremberg.

This is how the statements of these witnesses came about, in which, in 1834, after Hauser's death, the witnesses very substantially modified their earlier statements about his appearance. These modifications referred to precisely those things that reveal Hauser's radical lack of development with regard to walking, speaking and thinking. His gait, his speech and his ability to think in concepts were made to appear much less underdeveloped than they actually were according to the earlier statements of the same witnesses.

Dr Julius Meyer, the opponent of Hauser, then published these statements—which had been twisted in this way, and without drawing attention to how they had been twisted—in his *Authentische Mitteilungen über Caspar Hauser* [Authentic Infomation about Caspar Hauser], (Ansbach 1872), which had a strong effect for over 50 years, because people believed in their authenticity and objectivity, until 1926, when Hermann Pies earned the merit of revealing their true character that had distorted the facts.[94]

The threefold elimination of upright posture or walking, of speaking and of thinking in Kaspar Hauser's case over a period of many years could have had no other effect than to prevent his ego from taking possession of his body in a normal way. This is the highly important fact, which—at least in its full clarity—can probably only be grasped from the anthroposophical study of the human being, since in fact, as far as I can see, the significance of it is not nearly enough recognised in the Kaspar Hauser literature.

The Disrupted Development of the I

Feuerbach probably came closest to Pies here, as the title of his famous book *Kaspar Hauser, Beispiel eines Verbrechens am Seelenleben des Menschen* (1832) [Kaspar Hauser: Example of a Crime against the Soul Life of the Human Being] shows, in which he writes, for example, 'that it is principally the criminal interference in the soul life of this human being, the sacrilege against his higher spiritual nature, which is the most outrageous aspect of the way he was treated....'[95]

This shutting out of the I, to which the manner of Kaspar Hauser's treatment in his cell led, was of course (as only an inadmissibly great naivety could doubt) not an accidental and unintentional effect, but obviously all-too intended and deliberate. In view of such an intention, however, it has to be said that the way Kaspar Hauser was treated was very expedient and sensible. It was carried out with real 'expertise' and great prudence, whoever the perpetrator or perpetrators may have been. In terms of their spiritual and moral 'quality', they are characterised by their deeds, by their conscious actions. We will encounter them later.

The effect which the incarceration of the unfortunate youth was intended to produce in him was evidently brought about consciously. Along these lines may lie the sense of what, for example, Emil Bock called a 'reckless, magical educational experiment', which was felt and suspected by some in the 19th century.[96]*

The blocking of Kaspar Hauser's I from his body during his incarceration also makes observations understandable such as those, for example, by Feuerbach and Daumer during the first period in Nuremberg.

Feuerbach writes:

> At that time, his face was very common and, when at rest, almost without expression; its lower part protruded somewhat, which gave it an animal appearance. Also, the fixed gaze of his blueish, clear, bright eyes had the expression of animal dullness. After a few months, the formation of his face changed completely: his gaze took on expression and life, the protruding lower parts of his face receded more, and his former physiognomy was hardly recognisable....[98]

Similarly, Daumer:

> When I first got to know Hauser, his face, when it did not show any emotion, appeared to be common, and the lower parts of the face protruded, which

* But then, *Johannes E. Hohlenberg* did not grasp the actual facts when he wrote in the final chapter of his book:[97] 'Kaspar Hauser was the victim of an experiment in destiny that no human being could have intended or even less wanted to carry out ...'. (Hohlenberg sees the meaning of this destiny experiment in the sense that Kaspar Hauser's life can appear to be an attempt to 'have a person fight for a place in life without any tradition and without any basis in experience, solely through the forces of a completely isolated free personality unbound by any attachments to the past'—an attempt which failed.

> might have been due to the long period of underdevelopment of his mental development; this facial formation changed completely later on. His crying was very unpleasant to see: he opened his mouth wide at such times, but his laughter, in which the lower parts of the face receded, his mouth opened, his eyes lit up and the whole person came into the liveliest movement, had an indescribable charm; an expression of pure childlike joy such I have never seen anywhere else. It was like the laughter of a small child ....[99]

Kaspar Hauser Speaks about Himself. His Death

We see how the I—significantly, when laughing!—gradually intervened. But for some time, the 16-year-old continued to speak of himself in the third person—as children do before the awakening of ego-consciousness—e.g. 'Kaspar very good' instead of 'I am very good.'[100]

'When he came to Nuremberg,' writes Baron von Tucher, 'his mind was really like a *tabula rasa*, which quickly and easily absorbed everything that was presented to it with the most marvellous receptivity and retained it with a quite extraordinary memory.'[101]

'Such a complete ... lack of words and concepts', we read in Feuerbach,[102]

> such a complete unfamiliarity with the most common objects and the most everyday natural phenomena ..., and at the same time such extraordinary peculiarities in his whole mental, moral and physical being that one could believe oneself forced to choose whether one should take him for a citizen of another planet* who had by some miracle descended to earth or for that

*This sounds remarkable in view of Rudolf Steiner's statement (see above p. 41) that he had not been able to find a previous incarnation of Kaspar Hauser!

Incidentally, in his well-known book *Caspar Hauser, nicht unwahrscheinlich ein Betrüger* [Caspar Hauser, Not Improbably a Fraudster], published in Berlin in 1830 (p. 13), Police Commissioner Merker quotes the following sentence from a letter of *Anselm von Feuerbach* of 15 May (1830) to Criminal Police Director Hitzig in Berlin, which gives another special twist to Feuerbach's words above:

'... If there were human beings on Saturn and, by some miracle, such a Saturnian were suddenly transported to the middle of the large and free imperial city of Nuremberg, then the question: where is he from? What are his origins? etc. would certainly pose no greater riddle than these same questions have been up to now with Caspar Hauser ....'

Here, then, Feuerbach, of the 'planets' mentioned above, focuses specifically on *Saturn.* Surely, he meant this only figuratively. Nevertheless, it again sounds strangely in harmony

> man of Plato's who, born and brought up under the earth, only at the age of maturity ascended to the upper world and the light of the sun.

The unbelievable sensitivity of Kaspar Hauser's senses, which has already been emphasised above (p. 33 f.), always went along with an almost incomprehensible lack of development of the ability to think. We could also express it like this: while his capacity for *perception* was extremely strong, he lacked concepts to an unimaginable degree.

Feuerbach tells how, during a visit to Kaspar Hauser about a month after the latter's appearance in Nuremberg—Hauser was then held in police custody 'on the Luginsland at the Vestner Gate'—he told Kaspar to look at the window, pointing to the large, expansive view of the beautiful countryside resplendent in its summer finery, and asked him if what he saw outside wasn't beautiful. He obeyed, but immediately turned away in visible disgust, exclaiming: 'Nasty! Nasty!' He then pointed to the far wall of his room and said: 'Not nasty there!'

With Feuerbach, Daumer and others, one can sometimes have the impression that in the words they chose to speak about Kaspar Hauser, they were saying more spiritually concrete things in those words—as if out of inspiration from what was before them—than could otherwise have lived in their conscious thoughts at that time.

It was only a few years later that Kaspar Hauser was able to explain his behaviour to Feuerbach:

> ...When I looked out of the window, it always looked to me *as if a store had been set up right in front of me, and on this store a painter had splashed all kinds of colours with his brushes white, blue, green, yellow, red, one after the other.* I could not recognise and distinguish individual things on it, as I see things now. It was quite horrible to look at; I felt anxious because I thought they had closed the window with the brightly coloured store so that I couldn't see out into the open....[103]

In his essay '*Das eigentliche Problem Kaspar Hauser*' [The Actual Problem of Kaspar Hauser],[104] Hans Wohlbold rightly demonstrated that this story by Feuerbach shows that 'in the early days Hauser's perceptions were not permeated by concepts; he saw things only as images and thus only two-dimensionally. Like small children, he had no conception of space'. (The phenomenon of Kaspar Hauser therefore confirms at the same time that 'pure perception, which occurs in images, precedes thought').

---

with what we said above, p. 45, footnote *), about the connection of the liver with Saturn forces, a connection which is considered real from the point of view of spiritual science.

Hauser was therefore also unaware of perspective at first. 'Distant objects seemed to him to be very near, only smaller than nearer ones.' (von Tucher[105])

Likewise, at first he was unable to recognise *dreams* as such (which he first had in Nuremberg, since at Daumer's house, he slept in a bed, i.e. not only on a bed of straw as before). He told his teacher that they were real experiences, 'in that he only learned later to differentiate between waking and dreaming'.[106]

Since Kaspar Hauser, when he appeared in Nuremberg, had almost no concepts and was virtually incapable of speech, and interrogations of him by the police and others faced nearly insurmountable difficulties, it is therefore not possible to determine in some respects how much in his alleged statements was 'asked' or 'questioned' or 'talked' into him and how much he really meant and wanted to say himself.[107] This is a reason for the opacity that certainly plays an important role, especially in the famous, very detailed official 'announcement' of 7 July 1828, which was issued by the first Nuremberg mayor *Binder* and in which Kaspar Hauser's story was told with the intention of obtaining statements through which the crime committed against the unknown youth could be clarified. It is understandable that Kaspar Hauser's opponents would have taken advantage of this opacity to cast doubt on *everything*. But we have already seen repeatedly that the main points of Hauser's historical account have also been confirmed by external criteria. It is precisely his extreme poverty of concepts and his inability to speak that are such criteria.

Gradually, Kaspar's I took more and more hold of his body. As early as the summer of 1829, he was able to begin to 'set down his memories of his life into a written essay in accordance with the wishes of his superiors' (Feuerbach), and it soon became known to the public through newspapers and pamphlets that Kaspar Hauser was working on his biography. '*It is very likely*,' Feuerbach says, 'that this very rumour brought about the catastrophe that was intended to bring his short life to a tragic end soon afterwards, in October of the same year (1829).' This catastrophe refers to the assault on Kaspar Hauser in Daumer's house in October 1829, in which Hauser was wounded in the forehead (relatively lightly) and which is very controversial in the literature. Feuerbach clearly regarded it as an assassination attempt on Kaspar Hauser, who was writing down his autobiography, an attempt which, for the secret criminals against Kaspar Hauser, may have seemed like 'a kind of self-defence'.[108]

After this terrible experience, Kaspar Hauser's development continued in the sense that he became more and more a relatively 'normal' person. In the following four years of his teaching, his I took more and more possession of his bodily sheaths—such as they had become through everything that had happened to him.

It is in this context that one will perhaps also have to see the (futile!) efforts, known from the literature,[109] that Stanhope made in order to get hold of the diary that Kaspar Hauser had kept. Daumer suspects that it contained information about Stanhope that was disadvantageous to him, and that he therefore wanted to take the diary for himself so that no one else would see it. But beyond the interest in the content itself, it might ultimately also have promised insights into the extent to which Kaspar Hauser's memory had revived at all.

Apparently, Kaspar Hauser's 'incarnation process' progressed as he approached the age at which a person normally experiences the full birth of his I: the age of 21.

Soon after that time had come, in the Ansbach Palace Garden (Hofgarten) on 14 December 1833, the unfortunate Kaspar was the victim of a serious stab wound from an unknown person and died of the wound at 10 o'clock[110] in the evening of 17 December—all of this surrounded by profound riddles.*

Many of the words spoken by Kaspar Hauser on his deathbed seem as though spoken by his higher self.

On the morning of 20 December[111] he was buried in the cemetery in Ansbach with a very large crowd of people attending. 'Thousands of people ... were present at the church and crowded about his grave', reports Pastor Fuhrmann, who held the funeral service.[112]

On his gravestone are the words:

Hic jacet
Casparus Hauser
Aenigma sui temporis
Ignota nativitas
Occulta mors†

---

* Daumer (in his 1859 book, p. 278) suspected that certain people, for whom his growing memory was becoming ever more dangerous, had found it necessary to have the young man fall to a bandit's dagger—a suspicion along the same lines as that which Feuerbach had expressed with regard to the first attempted murderous assault (17 October 1829). Also along the same lines is what Daumer wrote elsewhere (op. cit. p. 101) : when he saw Hauser for the last time, in Nuremberg in October 1833, the young man had told him of his plan to come to him (Daumer) as soon as he (Hauser) was free and under Daumer's supervision, to write a book 'about himself and the circumstances of his life'.

† Here rests Caspar Hauser, the riddle of his time, his birth unknown, his death hidden.

How the Foundling Experienced the People Around him.

We come ever closer to Kaspar Hauser's way of being when we hear how, especially in the early days in Nuremberg, he affected those people who, with an unprejudiced mind and a feeling human heart, were impressed by his way of being and testified to it. Because of their great importance for all that is to come, it is precisely these voices that we need to hear in relatively greater detail. From there we can try to deepen our view and approach the larger contexts in which this individuality appears to be placed.

First of all, there is the public announcement by Mayor Binder mentioned earlier. One may argue with the way this unusual announcement was made, but it is certainly genuine in its reflection of the impression that the foundling made on people in Nuremberg, especially on the man who made the announcement—Mayor *Binder*. The sheer exuberance of his diction shows how greatly he was gripped by the human phenomenon of Kaspar Hauser. The powerful sensation that was caused by his appearance is certainly echoed impressively in Binder's announcement. In it, after a long recounting of Hauser's arrival in Nuremberg, his behaviour, his manner and outward appearance, his background (as far as could be surmised from what had been or was believed to have been extracted from him)—we find the moral impression of Hauser characterised as follows:[113]

> His pure, open, innocent gaze ... , the broad high forehead, the highest natural innocence, which does not know, does not even suspect any difference in gender, does not even suspect it, and has only now learned to distinguish people only by their clothes,* his indescribable gentleness, his cordiality and good-naturedness, which attracts all those around him, ... his devotion, sincere as it is

---

* This asexuality of the 'young child', as he was sometimes called, was also emphasised again and again. Daumer,[114] for example, writes: 'Hauser's nature was for a long time completely indifferent to sexual relations, and his sexual capacity had sunk into a deep, unawakened slumber.' 'Nothing was more abhorrent to him than love stories.' Von Tucher[115] speaks of his 'total indifference to sexual life for at least 2-3 years after his appearance in Nuremberg'. This trait of Kaspar Hauser's is also consistent with the fact that he was somehow living in the original state of human development. Again, we can think of the 'stray Atlantean'. We may refer here, for example, to Rudolf Steiner's lecture of 19 March 1912 in Berlin, where he speaks of ancient reproductive relationships (not yet between man and woman) and says that 'these relationships played a role right into Atlantean times, and that actually, the present form of the development of humanity did not appear until the second half of the Atlantean period'.

> touching, to all those with whom he has frequent dealings and who show him kindness, and his trust also in all other people, his sparing of the smallest insect, his aversion to anything that could cause the slightest pain to a human being or an animal, his unquestioning obedience and willingness to do good, as much as his freedom from all bad habits and vices, combined nevertheless with an inkling of what is bad, and finally his extraordinary eagerness to learn....

Hiltel, Hauser's warder during his stay 'in the tower' in police custody in Nuremberg, speaks similarly about him:[116]

> His whole behaviour was, so to speak, a pure reflection of the innocence of childhood; there was nothing false in him; whatever he had in his heart, he spoke it out, so far, that is, as his grasp of language allowed.

With deep understanding, Feuerbach describes Kaspar Hauser's being in such a way that we can increasingly surmise his origins:

> In his soul there was a childlike goodness and gentleness which made him incapable of harming a worm or a fly, let alone a human being, and which in every respect proved to be as spotless and pure as the reflection of the eternal in the soul of an angel.

Even in 1832, when Feuerbach wrote his book about him, he described Hauser as 'incapable of hurting an animal, compassionate towards the worm he fears to step on, fearful to the point of cowardice ....'

'In a moral sense,' Feuerbach wrote in a letter on 20 September 1828, barely four months after the foundling's appearance, 'Kaspar Hauser is a *living refutation of the doctrine of original sin.* The purest innocence and goodness of heart* showed itself in everything he did and said, although he had not

---

* In a highly significant way, this trait of life in the *heart* forces which permeated Kaspar Hauser's entire being, can also, in addition to everything else that he tells us, again evoke the motif of the 'stray Atlantean': Rudolf Steiner spoke (in the lecture of 28 July 1924 in Dornach—my emphasis in what follows) about how during the *Atlantean* period what he called the 'cosmic intelligence' had 'taken possession of the human *heart*'. It was not until many millennia later, at the beginning of the 15th century after Christ, that it also took possession of human *heads*. Both times it was the work of mighty deeds of the highest hierarchical powers. (For more details, see the above lecture.) Summarising, Rudolf Steiner says: 'Man used to be a being of the heart [*Herzensmensch*]; man has since become a being of the head [*Kopfmensch*].' Kaspar Hauser's pronounced heart-being nature was obviously also a part of his Atlantean-ness.

the slightest idea of right and wrong, good and evil.... Nothing of passions or bodily inclinations has yet emerged in him, except for the vanity which has now awakened.'[117] 'His physiognomy has nothing distinguished about it, and especially when he speaks, the whole left half of his face goes into unpleasant convulsions, yet the form of his face exudes an irresistible charm through the innocence and goodness of heart that is expressed in it. Anyone who approaches him, warms to him immediately.'

We experience Kaspar Hauser's 'character and manner' even more impressively in the descriptions of the sensitive, profound and spiritual *Daumer*:[118]

> When Hauser emerged from his seclusion into the world, his soul was the mirror and reflection of a heavenly purity and innocence such as had never been seen or known before. It did not remain so. ... But that it once was so, that this rarest and most remarkable of all moral phenomena did really appear and was observed amongst us—that is a fact. The most valid and consistent testimonies exist for this, even apart from *my own* relations [with Hauser—*Ed.*]. Indeed, it is demonstrable that Hauser, although during the rest of his life in the world he fell into a certain wavering ... he was, nevertheless, until his last breath, on the whole such a good, noble and lovable person that mankind would have to congratulate itself if all or only most people were like him.
>
> It was not only the romantic strangeness of his fate and appearance that attracted and captivated people, it was the quite unique childlikeness and sweetness of his nature and the flawless beauty of his soul that exerted such a wonderful charm ....

The 'Archetypal Human Being from Paradise'

I have already reported on the remarkable nature of his soul, as it appeared in the early days, in my *Mitteilungen* II ['Information'] p. 7 ff.

> The most stirring image of the purest goodness, which his appearance afforded, surpasses everything of this kind that the imagination could invent, and no description can express its vividness. He felt every pain and every suffering

---

In this way, too (cf. p. 39, footnote), he proves to be related to that which lives in *Chinese* culture—which indeed goes back to the ancient Atlantean nature. Chinese culture is inherently a 'culture of the heart', as *Hermann Pundt* sensitively explains in his essay '*China—Kultur des Herzens*' [Culture of the Heart] (in the journal *Die Drei*, Stuttgart 1958/3, pp. 123-137). In this context, Pundt also refers to that inaugurating act of the highest powers in ancient Atlantis.

> that happened to others, or only seemed to happen, entirely as his own. He could not be brought to strike a blow at anyone, even as a joke; *that would hurt himself too much*, he said.* The cold, hard-hearted isolation of human selfhood and prudence, *this true fall into sin, had not yet appeared*[122] [in him—*Ed*.]; a *paradisal, original human being*[122] in the moral sense was there before our eyes, an adorable miracle in a deeply degenerate human world that was sunk in an abyss of selfishness and wickedness.... Even if partial modifications and deviations continued to occur, the noble and loving foundations of his nature remained so unshakeable that they were noticeable to the end and filled the hearts of those who had sense and understanding with emotion and affection....

How much these impulses of Kaspar Hauser's nature also cause something to resound in us of the great *Parsifal* motif, as Richard Wagner conceived it:

> The pure fool, understanding through empathy, ...

Kaspar Hauser's real compassion was revealed in a number of his remarks which are quite touching. Daumer recounts,[119] for example, the following comment by Hauser from October 1828:

> He also does not like to think back to his incarceration, because he imagines the fear in which the unknown person who held him captive must have lived. This man had probably always hoped for his [Kaspar's] death, which had not taken place, and so [Hauser] believed that the unknown person had lived in the most agonising anxiety until he was rid of him, which hurt [Hauser] when he imagined it.

---

*This repeatedly witnessed trait in Kaspar Hauser's being brings to mind a verse that Rudolf Steiner gave at the beginning of the First World War (e.g. in his lecture of 1 September 1914 in Berlin),—like a kind of inner remedy against the hardships and catastrophes of the time. Rudolf Steiner said that Christ's blood flowed on Golgotha to ensure that the pain that lives in the other does not avoid us, but goes on within us. This sentiment lives in the words of the verse that was given at that time, 'which one speaks entirely as if to oneself':

> As long as you feel the pain / Which I am spared/ The Christ, unrecognised / Is working in the world / For the spirit remains weak / When it can only feel suffering/ In its own body /.

(These words also refer to a characteristic trait of the sixth post-Atlantean cultural epoch—which today is to be prepared for—or of those people who will stand at the peak of that epoch). For more details, see Rudolf Steiner's lecture in Dusseldorf on 15 June 1915.

Daumer remarks on this:

> In Hauser's case at that time, such feelings were neither based on upbringing and education at all, nor particularly by religious influences; they arose purely and independently from his untarnished original human nature, which life in the world soon forced to fall away from itself.

(The absolute opposite of such sentiments or impulses, to which reference will be made here, for deep inner reasons, even if in a somewhat anticipatory manner, in order to characterise the present in all its crassness, we find, for example, in the following words of *Hitler*, as reported by Rauschning from the autumn of 1933—words which were verified through countless infamous deeds and which have become history on a grand scale. They refer directly to concentration camp atrocities attributed to Hitler: ' ... Terror is the most effective political instrument.... Whoever is such a wimp that he can't stand it when someone next to him has to endure pain, let him go to the churchy types, but not to my party comrades.'[120]

It is symbolic that Kaspar Hauser's last act in life was an act of mercy: he gave alms to a poor woman shortly before his last walk into the Ansbach Palace Garden, where he received his fatal wound. Klara Hofer[121] rightly draws attention to this trait.

Even in the introduction to his book written in 1873 (p. XVIf.), Daumer refers to Kaspar Hauser as the 'heavenly appearance of a soul that is as gentle and pure as an angel' and expressly asks that this should not be regarded as a poetic exaggeration or effusiveness.

The much more sober *Baron von Tucher*, lawyer and Kaspar Hauser's guardian in Nuremberg for a certain period, also writes:

> As I found and described this man, with his natural purity and *lack of self-consciousness*, he presented to the utmost degree the image of *the first man in paradise before the fall of man.* [123]

Hans Wohlbold, in our 20th century, must also have received an impression very similar to these characteristics of Hauser when he wrote the significant words about Hauser in his essay on Daumer in 1930, already mentioned above (p. 53):

> In him was once again placed before humanity something like *an image of the first Adam*, as God had created him *before the Fall*. But Hauser could not consciously take hold of what was there for him, the gift of God, through the power of his I and form himself into a new man. Little by little, he lost his

> higher faculties, and through the influence of the environment he became like other people. In a small way, like the original human being, the fall into sin, the entanglement in the earthly world, was repeated in him....[124]

Here, it seems to us, Professor Wohlbold comes very close to something very important.

But of this 'first Adam before the Fall' there was that part which is also called the pure 'sister soul' of Adam who passed through the Fall, about which Rudolf Steiner spoke in a new way, especially in his lecture cycle on the Gospel of Luke (1909). He showed how this 'sister soul' had been held back in the spiritual world and had not entered the earthly world until it first embodied itself in the boy Jesus from the priestly, Nathan line of the House of David, of whom the Gospel of Luke tells us.[125]

This great soul is characterised in anthroposophical spiritual science in such a way that we can be reminded of it 'qualitatively', i.e. in kind (but not in degree, of course), if we now allow those descriptions to work upon us which—independently of all anthroposophy—have been given by unprejudiced, sensitive people about the nature of *Kaspar Hauser* and which we have come to know. It is as a reflection of that soul that—despite all the great distance and all the differences in rank between beings—we can then feel in a certain respect the soul of Kaspar Hauser, related to it in its way of being, and as though coming from the same sphere of the world.

The Child of Humanity and the Child of Europe

Let us therefore hear even more how Rudolf Steiner spoke about the boy Jesus in Luke's Gospel, whom we remember especially at Christmas, which celebrates his birth, where the warmest feelings of deep, intimate love arise. We may call this child of Bethlehem, says Rudolf Steiner, for example,[126] '*the child of humanity*, the human child' in the most beautiful sense. For in him a being came to Earth which had not been on Earth before, which had not shared in the earthly development of humanity, which had been held back in the innocent state before the luciferic temptation, and 'which had come to Earth as a *childlike* human soul' in a much higher sense; how should one not recognise this human soul as 'the child of humanity'? It appeared on Earth at the beginning of our reckoning of time, in the very infancy of man on Earth. This child grew up as if it contained, concentrated in its own being, 'all that in love and the capacity for love which, in a certain sense, all human souls together could muster. And the great geniality of love was what lived in this child.' It could not learn much from what human culture has achieved on Earth. But everything it touched from its earliest, tenderest childhood was touched by the most perfect love. 'All the qualities of the soul, all the qualities of feeling, worked as if heaven had sent love to Earth, so that in the winter time of the Earth a light could be brought in, which shines in the darkness of the human soul ....'

The Christmas Motif

This is the profound *Christmas* motif that resounds for us from this soul, from this soul at whose birth the *shepherds* appear, the simple people who are close to nature, who take deeply into their feelings the human event in which they are being allowed to share, and who offer their gifts to this child.

This child, as Rudolf Steiner described in another lecture,[127] represents neither wisdom nor power; powerless, it is cast into a 'corner of the world', into a stable in Bethlehem. But love lives in the child. It speaks to the heart. The simplest person can feel a kinship with it.

Because it points to the origin of humanity in that pristine time before the Fall, it also has nothing to do with all that later came to differentiate people according to gender, status, races or nations, nothing to do with what makes for strife and dissonance among human beings. Rather, it represents the original human power, the original peace and love nature of humanity. As Rudolf Steiner says, the beings of all earthly kingdoms bow down before this divine origin of man. Thus, the wonderful image of the manger shows us how the animals bow before the original human being, who was born in Bethlehem as an 'exceptional human being'. 'In this boy Jesus we have before us the whole of humanity at the stage of its infancy.'[128]

Can one not, as we have said, despite all the great distance and difference in rank, clearly and deeply feel the similarity of essence that exists between all these traits of the two 'exceptional human beings', the boy Jesus in the Luke Gospel and the stranger to earthly life who appeared in Nuremberg in 1828? The childlikeness of the nature of both; the primordial human nature of the 'stray Atlantean', of whom Rudolf Steiner could find no other incarnations, related to the human soul that had never been embodied before the events of Palestine? The life in the cell comparable to the birth in the stable of Bethlehem? The lack of earthly cleverness and earthly experience they both brought with them, and their participation in the achievements of the historical evolution of humanity on Earth? The heavenly goodness and purity, the 'angelic gentleness' and innocence of Kaspar Hauser's soul, which, as we found, was witnessed by many? The radiation of deep impulses of love and compassion which, together with the childlike innocence, speak to people's hearts and which in turn lead the hearts of well-meaning people to turn intimately towards the one boy as well as to the other? Even those simple people like the shepherds, who came to Jesus, the divine child, in Luke's Gospel? We even saw the motif of the difference in animals' behaviour towards Kaspar Hauser.

Can we not have the feeling that the foundling of Nuremberg is hierarchically related to the high individuality of the boy Jesus of Luke's Gospel, as the 'Child of Europe' is to the 'Child of Humanity'?

The Christmas motif resonates strongly in all this. And as if to reinforce it, Kaspar Hauser left the earthly world during Advent, seven times twenty-four hours before Christmas Eve: on 17 December 1833, at 10 o'clock at night.

The writer *Helene Hirschmann*, for example, felt this Christmas motif in a sensitive way when she wrote her little story 'Kaspar Hauser's First Christmas'.[129] She clearly created the little story entirely out of her imagination, which often comes so much closer to deeper truths than all 'documented' external research. This is particularly true of the figure of the Child of Europe, which, by its very nature, is most closely related to people's real feelings and sensibilities (as the organ of knowledge that is, as it were, suited to them). Helene Hirschmann has Kaspar celebrate his first Christmas with Daumer, his revered teacher, and with Daumer's mother and sister, around the lighted Christmas tree. Towards the end, Kaspar looks out of the window once and has an impression that brings up in him the old fear of something unspecific stalking him. He quickly closes the window and returns to the warmth of the Christmas room. 'The candles were all burnt out; only one was still lit and its bright glow fell directly on the small ribbon among the branches that read: Peace on earth and goodwill towards men.' This moves Kaspar deeply and warms his anguished soul: 'Peace on earth and goodwill towards *all* men...'. Kaspar falls deeply asleep. Daumer and his mother and sister see him like this, an astonishing expression of purity and peace on the child's face, only around the mouth a slight tug of pain. Daumer, greatly moved, says to his mother: 'Mother, I will dig up the roots of this life and make its branches blossom, and then I want to hold up a mirror of untarnished humanity to a world that has become dull ...'. 'Peace on earth and goodwill towards men'....

Kaspar Hauser can be found in another special 'relationship' with the being that lived in the Luke Jesus boy besides the similarity of which we have just spoken—namely, if one takes into account certain results of spiritual-scientific Christological research. We can only briefly hint at these results here so that our considerations do not stray too far. Rudolf Steiner, as many know, also described from his research certain effects which that high Being—long before his first incarnation at the Turning Point of Time—exerted from spiritual worlds in earlier epochs of human development for the healing of humanity. These effects had different aspects. The aspect of immediate importance for our considerations here was given in a lecture given by Rudolf Steiner in 1914.[130] There he says that Lucifer and Ahriman would already have disturbed the development of mankind in very ancient times and would have brought it into disorder, if a healing counter-action had not emanated from the very being that was later embodied as the Jesus of the Gospel of Luke. This counter-action consisted in the fact that this being permeated itself with the Christ three times in different ages (the Lemurian and Atlantean periods) in spiritual worlds. These are the three spiritual preliminary stages of the Mystery of Golgotha. In this way, a threefold healing process was brought about for humanity, which countered the luciferic and ahrimanic impulses that sought to cause disorder.

Walking, Speaking, Thinking: Reprise

The first of these beneficial counter-effects led to the human being becoming an *upright* being in the right sense. 'We therefore look rightly at a developing human child,' says Rudolf Steiner, 'when, at the moment that the child rises up from its crawling, sliding, unhelpful state and stands or walks for the first time, we then say: this can only happen rightly and for the salvation of humanity because the first Christ event took place in ancient Lemurian times ...'.

The second healing counter-effect was related to *speech*. It prevented speech from becoming 'thoroughly ignoble' through the luciferic and ahrimanic influence, which would have meant that man 'would only have been able to express in a poor, mumbling manner ... what egoistically causes him pain, joy, pleasure and lust'; 'what goes on in the organism as bodily processes', through which the whole of language would have become nothing but a series of interjections and exclamations. Through the second event, human beings became capable of grasping objective events and phenomena with language.

The third event, the third healing counter-effect against the luciferic and ahrimanic influences, led to the fact that the words of language can be 'proper signs for external things',—a means of understanding what the external environment is.

The fourth Christ event, in which the pure soul of the human participated who had not passed through the Fall of Man and took part in the form known from Rudolf Steiner's Christology as Jesus of Nazareth—an event which did not take place only in the supersensory world but also on Earth, was the Mystery of Golgotha itself.

Rudolf Steiner says of this, in the context we are concerned with here, that it prevented people's thinking from having a disordered effect on the I, so that human thinking could, rather, become thinking with a 'healthy sense for truth'.

Thus, in the sense of these indications, the healthy development of man's *upright posture* (or *walking*), the healthy development of *language* (in the twofold sense characterised above) and, finally, the healthy development of *thought* are all owing to the wholesome action of that being of whom we have been speaking and his permeation by the Christ (and at the fourth stage, here in the earthly world).[131]

It therefore appears highly significant, and here we think we can sense deep connections and background factors relating to Kaspar Hauser's martyrdom, when we see how his unfortunate treatment for many years in the cell was suited (and obviously intended) to *disturb* or *prevent* precisely this threefold normal formation of genuine human capacities, which otherwise takes place in the childhood development of every human being, as we have seen above (p. 42 f.).

The 'Child of Europe', we must say, was *deprived*, as though from profoundly based intentions, of those very fruits of the spiritual deeds of that high being who, after aeons of activity in supersensory worlds, appeared on Earth at the Turning Point of Time as the 'Child of Humanity'.*

The Motif of Persecution

But in addition to the relationship between the Child of Europe and the Child of Humanity, there is another very important motif that cannot be understood in terms of the similarity between these two 'children'.

---

*We could approach another, related remarkable fact if we were to set the 'experiment' carried out on Kaspar Hauser (see, for example, above p. 51), both analogously and, at the same time, in its abysmal difference alongside something else. Rudolf Steiner spoke about this 'something else' in his lecture cycle (No. 10) about the Gospel of Luke, held in Basel in 1909—in the 4th lecture (18 September). He spoke there of a 'hypothetical life experiment'. But to go into this would mean straying beyond the scope of our book. We therefore thought that we should at least briefly mention it.

Certainly, we can draw a parallel between the 'stable' in Bethlehem, in which the Child of Humanity was born in an obscure 'corner of the world', and the cell into which the Child of Europe was put. But at the same time, there is also a completely different motif here, namely, that of the *persecution* to which important people are so often exposed in their youth. The Luke Jesus boy was not persecuted, (for what is told in the Gospel of Matthew does not refer to him, according to spiritual-scientific Christology,[132]) but to the other Jesus boy, about whom the Gospel of Matthew tells us.

Rudolf Steiner spoke about this motif of persecution especially in connection with the story of the great *Zarathustra*, from whose childhood the legends tell of such persecutions.

'It is the fate,' says Rudolf Steiner:[133]

> of divine, spirit-filled personalities, that they grow up as strangers, that their environment has no sense and no feeling to understand them properly. . . . If one now clairvoyantly observes such a child as Zarathustra was, it turns out that he had within himself sensations, abilities, powers of thought and will which were quite different from what was developing all around him ....Above all, it turns out ... that the environment knows nothing of the true nature of such a child, but feels quite instinctive hatred towards such a person, and does not like the fact that he is growing up.
>
> This is the sharpest conflict that confronts one with clear-sighted eyes: that such a child, who is actually born for the salvation of humanity, unleashes storms of hatred all around. This must be so. For it is because the child is so different that great impulses come to humanity.

Rudolf Steiner then goes on to recount the legends of the persecutions of Zarathustra, against whom there was a kind of King Herod in the region where Zarathustra was born.

Similar things are told, for example, of the great *Cyrus*, the founder of the later Persian Empire. His grandfather, the Medean king Astyages, ordered his daughter Mandane to kill her son Cyrus, the fruit of her marriage to Cambyses. But Harpagos, the minister, saved the child, which later led to the adult Cyrus deposing his grandfather from the throne (560 BC). This is explained by Sigismund von Gleich,[134] who also thinks it probable that Cyrus, the renewer of Zarathustranism, was initiated into his tasks by the Chaldaean Zarathas (in whom the ancient great Zarathustra had reappeared).

The same motif of persecution is known from the stories of *Romulus* and *Remus*, the founders of the city of Rome: how they were abandoned but miraculously rescued from the waters of the Tiber, which had burst its banks, and so on. Such people suffer something like a 'betrayal by the homeland' and thus the fate of homelessness, as Rudolf Steiner has shown in connection with Romulus and Remus.[135,136]

The motif of persecution is also known from many ancient stories! The greatest example is the destiny of the Jesus boy from the Solomon (royal) line of the House of David, the boy in the Gospel of *Matthew*: how he was persecuted by King Herod, who ordered the child murders in Bethlehem because of the boy, but how he was saved, through the urging of the angel, by his parents' flight with him to Egypt. He too therefore also suffered the fate of homelessness, not to mention all the other profound connections that played in here. This Solomonic Jesus boy of the Gospel of Matthew, however, was, as Rudolf Steiner's Christological research shows, none other than the reincarnated, great Zarathustra himself.

So we are moving here in the 'other' stream that accompanies that of the Nathan Jesus described by Luke. While there we are dealing with the priestly line of the House of David and with the 'shepherds', here we are dealing with the royal line and the great 'spiritual king', the reincarnated Zarathustra, to whom the Three Wise Kings from the Orient, the Magi, are drawn.

In Kaspar Hauser's destiny, as is only too clear, this motif of persecution *also* worked very strongly: something was to be eliminated. And his fate was, in a more extreme sense than with any other historical character, that of homelessness: he grew up in such extreme circumstances that he lived without any awareness of his homeland, his origin, his family, his father and his mother, or the name of his inheritance. In this respect, then, he appears, not in his own nature, but in his destiny, as if he were included in the dynamics or the drama of the other stream of the 'wise heads of kings', the stream of Zarathustra and Solomon.

Is it not symptomatic here that (for whatever motives!) he was given the name 'Kaspar'?* Did the wise powers of destiny intend to weave him, who

---

* *Caspar*, whose day according to the '1912/13 Calendar' (Philosophisch-Theosophischer Verlag, Berlin 1912) is 3 January (like 2 January that of Melchior and 4 January that of Balthazar), is described in a lecture by Rudolf Steiner on 30 December 1904 in Berlin as representing the third 'root race', i.e. the Lemurian, Moors and Africans among the three kings, and as offering myrrh (the 'symbol of the death of

in his nature was similar to the Luke stream of the Nathan Jesus and of the shepherds and their 'poor shepherds' hearts', into the fate and tasks of the 'kingly' stream?

This would already cast a mysterious light onto the motif that emerged soon after his appearance in Nuremberg (see above p. 12) and according to which he was supposed to be a scion of a German princely house, indeed a Crown Prince of this house, thus actually someone called on to rule.

And then this whole destiny would be in line with the fact that, from a world-historical point of view, the two currents characterised thus far seek to flow together, unite and intermingle. This happened in an archetypal way in the union of the Nathan and the Solomon Jesus boys, through which, in the sense of Rudolf Steiner's Christology, the Incarnation of Christ was directly prepared.

The 'Shepherds' and the 'Kings'

This union would henceforth be an essential factor in later world-histor-

---

the lower life and the resurrection of the higher life'). (Likewise, Balthasar as the representative of the fourth, i.e. the Atlantean 'root race' as an Asian and offering incense; and Melchior as a white, as a European, representative of the fifth, i.e. the post-Atlantean 'root race' and offering gold).

In a deeper sense, therefore, the meritorious Kaspar Hauser researcher *Adolf Bartning*[137] is very much in error when he writes: 'Since the beginning of the world, no monarch has ever been called Kaspar' (this in connection with the question of whether Kaspar Hauser was that prince from the House of Baden who is mentioned in history as having died without a name because he had not yet been properly baptised).

With another writer concerned with Kaspar Hauser, however, we find an indication in the imagery of which we can see something of a moment of truth: *Otto Flake* writes in his Kaspar Hauser book:[138]

'He bore the name of one of the three holy kings; but the star under which he stood glowed a malicious red from the first day to the last of the twenty-one years allotted to him.'

If, incidentally, Hauser was given the name Kaspar by those who imposed upon him his tragic fate, the motive could have been to make him an object of laughter (*Kasperl*?) ['clown' in German—*transl.*]. Of course, one could then think it possible to find a deeper, 'symbolic' meaning in this 'clown': in the 'Kasperl Theatre' [puppet theatre], the clown (like all the figures) is moved from the outside: as a marionette hanging from wires or by the skilful fingers of the puppeteer who moves him.

ical events. In our essay on the spiritual origins and later fate of the social ideals of the French Revolution—freedom, equality, brotherhood—we ourselves were able to trace this in detail by means of examples[139] how this ideal appears as a confluence of the impulses of the 'kingly' stream of leaders, i.e. the impulses of freedom, with those of the 'shepherds' stream', i.e. the impulses of equality and brotherhood. This can be seen in numerous metamorphoses throughout the 18th century—e.g. in the juxtaposition of the two infinitely influential representatives of that century: Voltaire and Rousseau—right up to the events immediately preceding the French Revolution.

In other contexts,[140] we were able to show how this threefold ideal of the French Revolution, on the other hand, is to be understood as a reflection of what was celebrated in great imaginations in spiritual worlds at that time as the 'cosmic cultus' setting its goals for the age, of which Rudolf Steiner spoke. The impulse contained in that 'cosmic cultus' for the social life of human beings, seeks to be realised in our present time as the threefolding of the social organism.

For all this, the united action of the two great streams and their specific forces which come together in the Christ is required, and in addition to the effectiveness of the wise 'heads', the rejuvenating force of the shepherds' stream is also required, which reaches, as it were, back to the pure, original forces of humanity.

Rousseau

In yet other contexts, when we spoke of figures and events before the French Revolution[141], we were able to see the figure of Rousseau in the light of such ideas and show how his famous call—'*retour à la nature*'—was ultimately followed by the search for the original human being, for original innocence and purity, even though this search was not really understood correctly by Rousseau himself, but appears luciferically distorted and externalised. In Rousseau we were able to show precisely the impulses of *equality* and *brotherhood* as being intrinsic to him. It is precisely because of this that he turned his gaze back to the past, and ultimately to humanity's paradisal state.

The enormous effect that Rousseau had on his contemporaries can only be understood if one realises that his 'gospel' sounded tones that corresponded to the deepest longings of Western humanity in his time, that there was something profound behind it, which admittedly appeared in a very inadequate and distorted form in his work in the 18th century.

These Rousseau impulses resounded—or sought to resound—from the world of the 'shepherds' into the sphere of the 'kings' in the 18th century, when, like a trivialised, playful reflection, it became normal in royal courts to play at being shepherds (e.g. Queen Marie-Antoinette in France). Kings played at 'shepherds'.

In truth, Europe longed for something like a *rejuvenating force* in social life, something from the 'Tree of Life' to add to what existed one-sidedly from the 'Tree of Knowledge'—in the sign of the Fall.... Only when seen in such a light does the mysterious figure of Kaspar Hauser, the 'man from paradise', appear placed in the larger historical context in which it belongs. Only in this context does it become understandable in a deeper sense.

This is when little things start to gain symptomatic interest, e.g. certain statements from the writer *Klara Hofer*. In her book *Das Schicksal einer Seele. Die Geschichte vom Kaspar Hauser* [The Fate of a Soul: The Story of Kaspar Hauser], she tells how she discovered a hidden prison cell in the castle she lives in, Pilsach (near Neumarkt in the Bavarian Upper Palatinate), which she is convinced, and she substantiates her conviction with many facts, that it is the room in which Kaspar Hauser was held captive for many years. (We will come back to this book and its effect on Kaspar Hauser research in another context.) She also relates[142] how one of the many visitors to the prison cell in Pilsach drew her attention to the 'hypothesis of an experiment in accordance with Rousseau's theory'. This means, of course, that this visitor had the idea that Kaspar Hauser had been imprisoned for so long for the purpose of determining 'experimentally' whether Rousseau's theory was confirmed in Hauser, namely, the theory of the original purity and goodness of man, who had only been corrupted by the later influences of civilisation, and so on.

The idea was that this original human nature must reappear if a sufficiently young child were, artificially, to be kept away from all influences of civilisation. We can see, then, that the ideas of this visitor, in the question he raised, revolved around the very things that can indeed be arrived at from very large contexts with cogent, spiritually deeply grounded reasons when faced with the Kaspar Hauser phenomenon. (Klara Hofer, however, says in her book that the visitor's hypothesis is 'not without reason and perhaps conceivable under certain conditions', but she believes that under the circumstances prevailing in Pilsach in Kaspar Hauser's time, the character of the owner of Pilsach castle at the time, etc., it is out of the question; her view, incidentally, has already been rightly rejected by Wilhelm Kunze as inadequate.[143] It goes without saying, for example, that the owner of the castle at most could have been a tool of the organisers of such an 'experiment'.)

Rousseau, whose great ideas were based on an all-embracing experience of inspiration that an initiate had stimulated in him,[144] was searching, we can say, for the same spheres of the primordial human being from which Kaspar Hauser's whole way of being originated.

'Since Rousseau, there has been a social conscience in Europeans' consciousness', wrote Karl Vossler, the well-known scholar of Romance languages and cultures.[145] Prominent *social* impulses—not social 'demands', but real social qualities of soul—lived (see above p. 59f.) in Kaspar Hauser: empathy with other people. Did such impulses seek to have an effect through him in the sense of a force for renewal in the social life of his time?

The Mercurial Element. Kaspar Hauser and Napoleon

Repeatedly, and for a long time now, the '*mercurial*' element in Kaspar Hauser's life has been felt by people whose thinking is informed by anthroposophical spiritual science—in contrast especially to everything martial.

To put it in a semi-figurative way, we could perhaps say: if Feuerbach (see above p. 52f.) felt that Kaspar Hauser was like 'a citizen of another planet who had been transported to earth by some kind of miracle', then we would think of this planet (far more than Saturn!) as '*Mercury*'.

Is it mere coincidence that, as Daumer remarks (see above p. 33), mercury—i.e. the metal mercury—had the strongest effect on Hauser? 'Mercurial, not martial': in Kaspar Hauser's human, all-too-human nature, as it had become under the fate he had suffered, it looks like this:

'Unable to hurt an animal, compassionate towards worms ... , fearful to the point of cowardice' (Feuerbach, see above p. 57). 'Hauser was fearful . . . if one came at him with a knife or any weapon at all, one could drive him wherever one wished; pleading and imploring and ... with really fearful gestures and movements, he would draw back...' (Pastor Fuhrmann[146]).

'Nothing,' said Otto Flake in 1950,[147] 'is as real in Kaspar Hauser as the fear that hounded him. He saw shadowy hands grasping at him, and he was right to do so.'

'He would have liked to become an army officer,' he himself once said, as his doctor Dr Heidenreich remarked,[148] 'as long as there was no war and he wouldn't be wounded or shot dead'!

'As long as there was no war...'. One can hardly express the opposite of everything martial more radically!

Both positively and negatively, Kaspar Hauser appears as *the opposite pole to everything of a martial nature,* which had raged violently in Europe in the decades before his birth, above all through *Napoleon*, the great martial genius and the bringer of materialistic impulses in the 19th century.[149]*

For a long time therefore, people have felt that Kaspar Hauser, as *the opposite pole to Napoleon* and as the bringer of impulses of love, was called to create a balance against the entirety of the destructive, untransformed martial forces that had their effect on Europe through the great conqueror and despot.

Incidentally, many contemporaries in their own way associated Kaspar Hauser during his lifetime very tangibly with Napoleon. Already in June 1830 an officer by the name of von Pirch, who himself had visited Kaspar Hauser, remarked: 'A favourite notion of the public' (who had been allowed access to Kaspar Hauser at the time of his appearance in Nuremberg) 'which was often expressed, was: Caspar Hauser is Napoleon's son.'[150] Some even claimed to see a physical similarity between Kaspar Hauser and Napoleon.

The apparent polarity between Napoleon and Kaspar Hauser† seems to be very remarkable and profoundly grounded, as we have already noted here. It says much about both of them, and contemplating it deepens one's thinking to an unexpected degree when one considers what we ourselves were able to bring forward in our book *Die Französische Revolution und Napoleon* [The French Revolution and Napoleon] about Napoleon's 'forgotten task',[151] which was itself of a 'mercurial' nature. We shall return to this very important point later.

---

* Here too, incidentally, we find a strong point of contact between Kaspar Hauser and *Rousseau*, for whom 'the sword of war caused shuddering and revulsion' and for whom 'iron' was alien. See the chapter about Rousseau, p. 196 in my Vol. VI.

† See the following noteworthy comments in the essay 'Die Frage nach Kaspar Hauser' [The Question about Kaspar Hauser] by *Wilhelm Kunze* in the supplement to the *Stuttgarter Neue Tagblatt* No. 47, 9/10 December 1933:

> Bonaparte had risen to the highest position attainable in this world—the imperial throne—entirely through his own forces and capabilities. His fortunate destiny had enabled him to become the ruler in this world of the senses. This is exactly the opposite picture of Kaspar Hauser, who seems to have taken on himself all the misfortune of mortal man. In his dreams of mastery, Napoleon had gone so far as to conceive of Europe as a political union; his life was a struggle for power. Kaspar Hauser, who was soon called the '*Child of Europe*', was the very embodiment of vulnerability. Napoleon and *Kaspar Hauser are absolute opposites, like Mars and Venus, like spirit and nature.* (But Venus is essentially related to Mercury.)

There is a profound justification in thinking of the polarity of Napoleon—Kaspar Hauser in terms of the old reversal of the words 'Roma—Amor'.[152]

At this point in our considerations therefore, we can approach a centrally important aspect of what may now begin to dawn on us as the 'actual task' of Kaspar Hauser, and which we hope to elaborate ever more clearly in what follows.

The Task of Middle Europe

The *mercurial* element, especially the mercurial, therapeutic element is intimately related to the true *task of Middle Europe*.

This was profoundly expressed, for example, in the first Goetheanum Building, which was burned down on New Year's Eve of 1922/1923. The pillars which bore the large dome represented, amongst other things, the various 'planets' and at the same time, certain larger populations of Europe. The Mars pillar, for example, was also the 'British' pillar, the Moon pillar was the 'French' pillar. In the Mercury pillar was expressed the task of *Middle Europe* in the broadest sense (it was by no means only that of the Germans). This was visible, for example, in the staff of Aesculapius, which pointed to this therapeutic mission of Middle Europe.

Along the same lines is something from a very different context (also related to European cultures), namely, the three kinds of occultism in the way they are arranged in the world: opposite 'eugenic occultism', which has to do with the secrets of birth and which is 'at home' in the East of the globe, is the predisposition in the West to mechanical 'occultism', which works with occult methods in mechanical forces. Between these two is '*hygienic*' or 'therapeutic occultism', which is bound up most deeply with the task of the being of the '*Middle*', between East and West.

Impulses, tasks and predispositions of such a kind therefore live especially in the true *folk soul of the Germans*, from which with good reason one may accept that the German folk soul is deeply connected to the power of the—mercurial—being of the *Buddha*.[153]

We therefore understand why an entity like Kaspar Hauser incarnated in Middle Europe and especially in *Germany*, and suspect that his task had to do with the true mission of that region.

We also therefore understand why such bitter opposition arose against him, which tried to *prevent* him from becoming effective.

The 'Child of Europe' must have been something that, starting from Middle Europe, could have had great significance for Europe.

Hence the tremendous attention evoked by Kaspar Hauser's appearance, his life and his death, gripping the people's feelings in the strongest possible way.* People felt gripped deep down in their souls. They *felt* something that they could not understand in a conscious way. This can only be understood in our present time through the cognitive approach provided by anthroposophical spiritual science.

Kaspar Hauser's Appearance in the 19th Century

Kaspar Hauser incarnated a few decades before the beginning of the 1840s, that is, before the onset of the impulse of mere intellectualism of which we spoke earlier in this book (see p. 11 above) that was related to the 'Fall of the Spirits of Darkness'.

As Rudolf Steiner once said,[154] 'In the middle of the 19th century there was a kind of materialistic high tide within the evolution of humanity', which had not existed before. In a certain sense it was foreseen by the Swabian theosophist *Johann Albrecht Bengel* (1687-1752) and his apocalypticism.[155] In his calculations, he came to the year 1836 as a particularly important year in the development of humanity. As Rudolf Steiner explains it, Bengel was out by 6 years, which was due to his mistaken notion of the year of the foundation of Rome (apparently 753 instead of 747 BC). What Bengel had meant in his calculation was the year *1842*, the year of the 'materialistic crisis'. 'It was a new day for the ancient wisdom!'

It is certainly significant that a being like Kaspar Hauser was born about 30 years before this year 1842. Obviously, something was to emanate from him that was to have acted along the lines of a kind of balance or counter-

---

* 'Hauser's story caused incredible excitement in its time, even among those who were completely uninvolved in it.' (Daumer 1873, p. 347.) 'Already at the time of his appearance' Kaspar Hauser had 'achieved the greatest popularity and fame'. 'It is no exaggeration to say that around this time' (after the first attempt to murder Kaspar Hauser, on 17 October 1829) 'the whole civilised world was gripped by a real shock'. 'Even more famous ... than his birth and the attempt on his life' did the little foundling's death become, 'which spread the name of the victim into every nook and cranny of the civilised world.' (Adolf Saager, *Das Rätsel Kaspar Hauser* [The Riddle of Kaspar Hauser], Ansbach 1911, pp. 35, 39.)

weight to this merely intellectual development—to which Kaspar Hauser was the perfect counterpole. It had been prearranged in good time.

Perhaps, however, he had already worked spiritually in *this* way, through his mere existence or his presence.* Looking at him with the right spiritual empathic understanding can be important not only for a deeper comprehension of the 19th century, but also for what is the appropriate further development into the future. We find this more or less indicated in the title of Rudolf Steiner's only lecture, in which he included the relatively more detailed explanations of Kaspar Hauser which we have mentioned above and from which we have proceeded in our reflections; the title of the lecture is: 'Spiritual Science, the Gospels and the Future of Humanity'.

Many have felt the special moment of time with regard to the mystery of Kaspar Hauser: that the ancient lived on in him ... that perhaps the future was latent in him ... how he was not accepted in the present ..., the suffering he experienced in connection with it ... and that he should be remembered.

This also comes to life in an impressive way in the concluding verse of a poem by *Paul Verlaine*, which a French diplomat, writer and Kaspar Hauser researcher placed at the beginning of a large work of his as a kind of motto.[156] The poem is entitled 'Gaspard chante' [Kaspar sings]. Here is this key verse, which is often quoted in Kaspar Hauser literature:

Suis-je né trop tôt ou trop tard?
Qu'est-ce que je fais en ce monde?
0 vous tous, ma peine est profonde;

---

* In this sense, for example, can be cited what the medical doctor *Ita Wegman*, following a conversation with *Rudolf Steiner*, shared (in the magazine *Natura* II 3/4–September/October 1927—pp. 94/95, in an essay on the phenomena that had occurred in Konnersreuth with Therese Neumann:

'And so I recall a conversation that I was once able to have with Rudolf Steiner, in which he spoke about the significant events that occurred after the mysterious appearance of Kaspar Hauser, which also at that time occupied everyone' (clearly, Ita Wegman had in mind the case of Therese Neumann von Konnersreuth in our time). 'He indicated that the essential point in such a mysterious occurrence is that people's feelings were drawn to investigate such a thoroughly unusual event which could not be understood in terms of daily life.

'It was an attempt of the spiritual world to remind people in the midst of the most materialistic era that there is something else besides what philistine thinking lets itself dream there is.'

*Priez pour le pauvre Gaspard!**

Was I born too early or too late?
What in this world is my part?
Oh everyone, my hardship is great,
Say a prayer for poor Gaspard!

People around Kaspar Hauser

At the end of this chapter on Kaspar Hauser's being and his appearance in the 19th century, a few reflections should be added that are not so much directly related to Kaspar Hauser himself, but rather to some of the people who have become important in connection with him in one way or another.

If the destiny of a person is a part of himself that cannot be disregarded, then it is certainly important to look at the circle of destiny that formed around Kaspar Hauser, above all during his lifetime, of course, but in a broader sense also in the following decades up to the present day—and both in very opposite senses.

Wilhelm Kunze,[158] for example, also aptly pointed to such connections when he wrote:

> That it was precisely Daumer to whom Kaspar Hauser was entrusted in 1828 when he had emerged from obscurity speaks just as much for the hidden deeper layer of the situation as it does for the mysterious providence that, as a consequence, Hauser mostly came into contact with people who, through the way they lived their lives, had the capacity to understand the phenomenon that presented itself in Kaspar Hauser—people such as the criminologist *Feuerbach*, or Baron *von Tucher*, or even Lord *Stanhope*, whose later† behaviour

* *Richard Dehmel*[157] translated this verse into German as follows:

Kam ich zu früh, kam ich zu spät
In diese Welt, was soll ich hier?
Ach Gott, ihr lieben Leute ihr,
Sprecht für den Kaspar ein Gebet!

† However, Kunze's words do not express a sufficiently deep understanding of the role that Stanhope played in the Kaspar Hauser affair. *Daumer*, in particular, gave much serious thought to this from his own experience. Half of his book which was published in 1859 was directed against Stanhope. He believed that in Stanhope's appearance he had come to the point 'where the whole Hauserian problem could

> was not exactly unimpeachable but in whom there were characteristics that predestined him, as it were, to a relationship with Hauser.

Besides Daumer, Feuerbach, von Tucher and the dubious Stanhope, the Mayor of Nuremberg, *Binder*, should also be mentioned here, whose public announcement, already mentioned above, which made the Hauser case world-famous, bears witness to much of the sympathetic understanding that Binder also otherwise displayed.

It says a great deal in terms of destiny (cf. p. 17 above) that Kaspar Hauser came under the care and supervision of the very same Professor *Daumer* whom Rudolf Steiner called 'the last Rosicrucian'. Wilhelm Kunze's fine booklet on Daumer (cf. also p. 76 above) bears the significant title: *Georg Friedrich Daumer und die Fortführung der Reformation* [Georg Friedrich Daumer and the Continuation of the Reformation]. The last words of the book point to an important motif in Daumer's endeavours: the continuation of the Reformation.

> The Reformation, as Daumer explained [as Hans Kern writes in his above-mentioned small work,][159] got stuck at the outset. ... The spirit of the Reformation was the spirit of seeking knowledge and the unconditional freedom of thought. It is in the nature of the Reformation to go beyond itself and to prepare a spirit of the age, which of course will only appear 'within the Christian worldview itself'.

---

be grasped at its roots. . .'; again and again, he believed he could show that Stanhope must have acted from quite different motives than those he openly revealed to the world; there must have been a secret involved, a secret reason for Stanhope's behaviour, etc. (his 1859 book, pp. XXI, 159-162, 168). *G. Friedrich Kolb* (*Kaspar Hauser*, Regensburg 1883, p. 104) saw Stanhope's behaviour as leading to the hypothesis 'that he was, if not from the beginning, at least subsequently, a tool in the hands of Hauser's enemies, and knowingly worked for them'. (Cf. also what the author Jacob Wassermann wrote in his novel, above p. 36.)

Hans Wohlbold's thoughts moved in a similar direction when he wrote (in his above-mentioned essay 'Kaspar Hauser' in the Stuttgart monthly *Anthroposophie*, January/February 1932, p. 156): 'Perhaps of all those who publicly opposed Hauser, only Earl Philip Stanhope knew what was at stake.' Indeed, Wohlbold believed (p. 159) that, as in Daumer he saw the representative of the powers of Light, so in Stanhope he saw the representative of the power of darkness in the Hauser affair.

And yet in a certain sense, Wilhelm Kunze may well be right to see in Stanhope one of those who (to a certain extent) could 'understand' the Kaspar Hauser phenomenon.

Here, too, Daumer seems to be related to certain efforts of Rosicrucianism, which are indicated, for example, in the Rosicrucian writings from the beginning of the 17th century.[160] Kunze's booklet also shows on almost every page to what extent and in how many respects Daumer, the noble spiritual seeker, was a forerunner of the spiritual science of our time. ... 'Daumer was waiting for something new that was coming', writes Wohlbold.[161]

It is also interesting that Daumer, as a high school student, was for a time a pupil of none other than *Hegel*, who had been headmaster at the Nuremberg Aegidian Grammar School since the autumn of 1808. In Daumer's spiritual strivings, he went down the most diverse paths, including those that he himself described as 'terrible aberrations'.[161] But even during his polemics against what he understood by Christianity at that time, he had a small volume of poems published under a pseudonym, which he had written in praise of the Virgin Mary. It was especially the veneration of the Madonna that led him to join the Catholic Church in 1858.[161] He wrote about this in his book *Meine Konversion* [My Conversion], which was published in Mainz in 1859 (a significant year historically, in terms of other spiritual events).

After all this, it is no wonder that the idea of *repeated earth lives* had also taken root in Daumer. Emil Bock describes this in more detail in his important book, '*Wiederholte Erdenleben. Die Wiederverkörperungsidee in der deutschen Geistesgeschichte*'[162] [Repeated Earth Lives—The idea of Reincarnation in German Spiritual History]. There, Bock also characterises in a beautiful way the great and benevolent humanity of Daumer and the inner world that this inward and sensitive spirit built up.

Daumer (as mentioned by Wilhelm Kunze[163] and Emil Bock[162]) had a pupil: the writer Amara George, as she called herself (1835-1907). Her real name was *Mathilde Binder*. She was an (illegitimate) daughter of the Nuremberg mayor Binder, who was so positively concerned for Kaspar Hauser. In her novel *Dissonanzen und Akkorde* [Dissonances and Accords] (1879), we again find the idea of reincarnation.

Can one not tangibly grasp what kind of spiritual impulses lived in this connected circle of people who were bound by destiny?

The idea of repeated lives on earth was something that had been trying, out of a *Rosicrucian* inspiration, to penetrate the spiritual life of the Occident since the 18th century, first appearing in Lessing's writings on the education of the human race.[164]

Thus, everything comes together, and so the great spiritual contexts in which we must also think of the figure of Kaspar Hauser himself increasingly dawn on us. We shall have more to say about these later.

Jakob Wassermann

Among the numerous German writers of later times in whose works the idea of reincarnation is more or less clearly sounded, we also find *Jakob Wassermann* named in Emil Bock's book.[165] Bock says of Wassermann that in him we 'repeatedly encounter the idea of repeated lives on earth'. Jakob Wassermann (1873-1934) was probably the early 20th-century author whose writings did the most to bring the figure of Kaspar Hauser closer to countless people in an intimate, positive sense through his widely read novel *Caspar Hauser oder Die Trägheit des Herzens* [Caspar Hauser or the Indolence of the Heart], which was first published in 1907/1908.[166] For many people, this book was their first encounter with the mysterious stranger, an encounter that deeply touched many hearts, stimulated many minds* and often had an effect on people that lasted for decades. The reader senses that Wassermann's literary imagination has in many respects come very close to the deeper truth of things and to Kaspar Hauser's real being, the genuine phantasy which proves itself, to borrow a phrase from one of Rudolf Steiner's Mystery Dramas, to be the child of 'the father of truth'.[167] The fluid element of spirit and soul that fills this novel can only be understood in terms of a certain inner closeness of Wassermann himself to the soul of Kaspar Hauser.

A significant light is shed on all this when we hear from Wassermann what he tells us autobiographically about his own destiny in relation to the subject that gripped him and us, and how he fared with it—Wassermann, who was born in Fürth, in the immediate vicinity of Nuremberg and grew up in the province (*Land*) of Franconia (and who, incidentally, died almost exactly 100 years after Kaspar Hauser—on 1 January 1934).

In his essays '*Akten zur Verteidigung Caspar Hauser*'[168] [Records for the Defence of Caspar Hauser] there is a long section titled 'My personal

* The important Kaspar Hauser researcher *Hermann Pies* (*Wahrheit* [Truth], p. 337), for example, tells us that he first became acquainted with the material through Wassermann's gripping novel, which prompted his research that then led to all his important works.

experiences with the Caspar Hauser novel', from which we shall reproduce at least a few important passages. Wassermann writes:

> ... it is about the salvation of a noble name and an extraordinary being from a hundred years of unhappiness, frosty malice and slander, and even more, it is about the final redemption of an unatoned German guilt.*
>
> The figure of Caspar Hauser was a decisive youthful experience for me, a vision since the awakening of my consciousness almost. I lived in his landscape, old people spoke of him with emotion, my grandfather had known him and spoken to him,† the scene of his suffering and his death was the scene of my own development. When we were shown the Vestner Tower[169] at the castle, we knew that his first stay in human society had been within its gloomy walls....
>
> My first decision to write about Caspar Hauser dates back to my seventeenth year, but fifteen years would pass before it was realised....

Wassermann was often close to giving up hope and dropping the plan. He describes how, in December 1905, his Caspar Hauser vision became wedded to *the idea of indolence*: 'the tragic lawfulness of a soul unsullied by the world and how the world passes it by dully and without understanding'.

'... In Caspar Hauser's case, the purity of his appearance is the prerequisite and the absolute. His guiltlessness lies in his fate, is revealed in it and is virtually a part of it ...' The Caspar Hauser figure: 'a human miracle, no more and no less....'

The 'idea of indolence' is the important motif in Wassermann's novel: the 'indolence of the heart'. It is essentially the counterpole to the original human being, who was all heart and soul, and the opposite of love and

---

* The redemption of a German guilt: here too Wassermann shows his sensitive feeling for the relationships in which Kaspar Hauser was mysteriously placed. What he writes in his autobiographical work *Mein Weg als Deutscher und Jude* [My Path as a German and Jew] (Berlin 1921, pp. 78 and 83) is also significant: he says that he 'imagined', with his Kaspar Hauser novel, that he had 'given the Germans an essentially German book, written from the soul of the German people', but the German public did not think it could be true 'that a Jew wrote such a peculiarly German book....'

† His grandfather 'spoke of him as of a very mysterious person. Others, the most simple and sober people, always spoke of him as something very mysterious, of which it was bad to speak too loudly.' (*Mein Weg als Deutscher und Jude*, p. 76.)

compassion, as they lived in him, most intimately related to the teachings and the impulses of the great Buddha rejuvenated in a Christian context.

From this 'indolence' it is only a step to direct opposition. It is significant how Wassermann tells of the attacks and hostility he experienced because of his novel.

'I had,' he wrote in 1924,[170] 'the unavoidable impression that a definite order had come from somewhere, a command that one had to behave in such and such a way if the dangerous and unwanted effects of the book were to be avoided. I could not help but suspect that certain instructions were emanating from a certain place, and that this tactic was already a long-established one....'

Whatever may have been the objective basis of Wassermann's impression, it hardly suffices *in itself* to explain why in his novel Wassermann identifies Kaspar Hauser with the Prince of Baden born in 1812.

Kaspar Hauser's Opponents

The opposition to Kaspar Hauser is an integral part of the whole Kaspar Hauser phenomenon, like the light of the shadow, or—we could also say—like Herod's hostility to the baby Jesus in the Gospel of Matthew.

The deeper root of this hostility that is known from the Kaspar Hauser story lies in the fact that one does not want to admit to oneself—although the subconscious mind nevertheless suspects it—that there *is* something like the being that is concealed under the name of Kaspar Hauser, i.e. that something of such qualities has entered into earthly existence, something that calls the human being to self-knowledge and that through its existence demands of us to work on the transformation of our own sunken being. It is precisely against this that elementary impulses of hatred rise up, impulses of hostility, even the will to destroy.

Daumer was very close to such insights and he expressed them in a way that really hit the mark: how, in people's behaviour with regard to the phenomenon of Kaspar Hauser, we are really dealing with the '*struggle of faith with unbelief*', unbelief as regards the unfamiliar, the unique, the spiritual.

'By *faith*,' writes Daumer,[171]

> I understand the recognition of the extraordinary, even if it contradicts the world of common concepts; devotion to the fact that presents itself and can only be dismissed in a crude way; to the deep, inner connection of things that is attested thereby; to that which is not obvious, which cannot be grasped and explained materially and mechanically, and yet which is true and real, but

> which the common materialistic mind so antipathetically opposes, and which it so passionately seeks to do away with at all costs and by every possible means. On this faith rests not only all religion, but also all *culture* in the full, human sense of the word....

This really points us to the decisive issue. What is of interest in a human sense about the phenomenon of the actual opponents of Hauser (of course we are not talking about those who honestly seek the truth) is therefore not so much what they put forward in terms of content (and which, of course, often also contains quite bona fide facts or indications), but rather their inner motives, which live in people's subconscious, in the nature of their *feelings*—we have already pointed out how, especially in the case of a figure like Kaspar Hauser, it is very important to have *feeling* as an organ for finding the truth, such as in the case of hate-filled passion from a hidden, sometimes barely concealed spiritual enmity. All of this shows in a striking way the deep affinity of *this* opposition, as we have already mentioned in this book, with that which arose against *Rudolf Steiner* in the 20th century. (We are disregarding here certain external motives which more or less also played a role with some of the opponents and about which there is still much to be discovered by Kaspar Hauser researchers.)

Only from this point of view does a book like the two-volume work of the Wiesbaden archivist *Antonius von der Linde*,[172] 'full of distortions and lies',[173] take on a deeper interest: what is it that lives in the depths of such a man's soul so strongly that he is able to write such a work?

At the same time, through the medium of this kind of literature, one experiences once again the power of the *lie*: for decades [in the 19th century—*Ed.*] and of course afterwards as well—it has been able to obscure the image of Kaspar Hauser. Finally, however, 'the sun' does 'bring it to light', and Pies was able to note as early as 1925[173] that the work of A. v. der Linde, for example, is today universally dismissed.

The opposition to Kaspar Hauser, as well as to Daumer, etc., is of a certain interest from a more *methodological* perspective: as some opponents, for example, invent hypotheses or 'explanations' in the name of 'common sense', which make the hair of all people of common sense stand on end. For example, the hypothesis that a man as intellectually undeveloped as Kaspar Hauser could have composed and written down the famous 'letter of introduction' which he was holding when he appeared in Nuremberg, or that someone with soles such as Hauser's was a 'tramp'. In the same vein is the amount of dissimulation which some opponents ascribe to Kaspar Hauser,[174] and which goes beyond anything humanly possible. Precisely such hypotheses show how blind their originators were to the phenomenon of Kaspar Hauser and how deaf they were to the language of facts—because these did not fit into their materialistically preconceived habits of thought. This is what constitutes the 'unbelief' of such people in the sense meant by Daumer.

This is ultimately also the case with an anti-Hauser figure who has come forward more recently—Archive Director *Dr Ivo Striedinger* in Munich; we have mentioned him already (p. 31, footnote). He published an essay about Kaspar Hauser as well as a long critique of recent writings about him.[175] In these works Kaspar Hauser appears as a 'poor sick person' suffering from the kind of 'hysterical illness' which specialists call '*Pseudologia phantastica*', not just a systematic fraudster, but an hysteric who was compelled by the circumstances of his environment and his lack of understanding of them onto the precipitous course of his continuous fraud, from which there was no turning back.[176] Certainly, these writings by Striedinger greatly surpass those of A. v. d. Linde and also those of the literary historian Eduard Engel. But what Daumer (see above, p. 81) calls 'unbelief' and the lack of any sense for a qualitative human dimension, for the deeper nature of things, which can result from a holistic viewpoint—these also underlie Striedinger's thinking and mode of research.

As the case of Striedinger[177] is of a certain symptomatic interest, we shall consider it in rather more detail.

What Striedinger, like many others, seeks to do with the story of Kaspar Hauser is to explain it in terms of what is 'natural and rational', to characterise Striedinger's approach with the words that he himself often uses.[178] But the case of Kaspar Hauser has nothing at all to do with 'natural and rational' in the sense, basically, of a need for comfort!

In principle, this was recognised very correctly in 1829 by the Nuremberg Municipal Court doctor whom we have already mentioned several times and was expressed by him during an interrogation when he emphasised that the phenomena associated with Kaspar Hauser were 'quite unique and no criteria used for other people can be employed to judge them',[179]—words that agree with what Feuerbach (see above p. 33) wrote about the quite unique nature of this *legal* case and which applies very generally in the most comprehensive sense to the whole case.

In the face of this unique phenomenon, the normal professional historical method on which Striedinger repeatedly bases himself as a 'professional historian',[180] in the way he applies it, must necessarily fail. Certainly, it should not be denied that some of his criticisms of some Hauser research are valid; but what he himself brings forward shows the inadequacy of the usual historical method faced with something like the appearance of Kaspar Hauser. Here that method proves to be a thoroughly blunt tool, which itself would first have to be transformed and refined in order to be able to 'get to grips' methodically with things in which the spirit plays a role so fully in an unusual manner, as in the case of Kaspar Hauser.

(Perhaps this feeling is one of the reasons why historians have always been so reluctant to deal with the Hauser case.)

Because Striedinger is convinced from the outset that there could have been no such phenomenon as Feuerbach and Daumer and other eyewitnesses described in the most careful and credible manner the Kaspar Hauser phenomenon to be, he takes the Hauser researcher Hermann Pies, for example, to task for the fact that in his work *Augenzeugenberichte* ... [Eyewitness Reports], which we have also referred to time and again, Pies placed first and foremost the reports of Feuerbach and Daumer, these truly classical witnesses, 'precisely such statements by which', as Striedinger writes,[181] 'the whole confusion has been caused'! Elsewhere,[182] he reproaches Pies in a similar sense for presenting 'much literature and few official records'. By 'literature' is meant here what living, educated and discerning people wrote about the Hauser case as witnesses who experienced it from the inside, i.e. precisely the most valuable statements that there can be. The director of the archives values them much less than what are, as everyone knows, the more derivative and dead 'official files' from the archives, (valid and important as they too are, of course).

This one-sided 'archival attitude' tends to transfer the well-known saying '*quod non est in actis, non est in mundo*' (what is not documented does not exist) more or less from the legal sphere to that of historical method.*

Such views and attitudes contributed greatly, especially in the 19th century, to the emergence of the kind of historical science from which the living element of history, its soul and spirit, have receded. The most grandiose and tragic effect, as has often been shown by spiritual science, has been in the field of theology where, with this scientific and especially historical method, all the research and study, all the infinite effort

---

* With regard to this whole context of historical method, Rudolf Steiner's lecture of 12 April 1924 in Dornach, may be referred to here, in that, amongst other things, it deals with the famous 19th-century historian *Leopold von Ranke* and his concrete karmic antecedents.

that has been expended, was ultimately bound to lead to the fact that the central figure of Christianity, the source of life and the actual spirit working in *history*, slipped away more and more through the fingers of this scholarship.

Destiny Relationships among the Opponents

It can be of deeper human interest to observe how certain destiny relationships and encounters also occur in the camp of the opponents of Hauser,—as we saw, on the other hand, in the circles of Hauser's friends. A significant example of this kind may therefore also be mentioned here.

Stanhope had Kaspar Hauser taken to Ansbach in December 1831[183] and placed in the care and under the instruction of the teacher *Johann Georg Meyer*, a 'schoolmaster' in the very worst sense of the word, who was most unsuited to understanding the character of his unique pupil, and who was to the greatest degree—to put it mildly—guilty of what Jakob Wassermann in the twentieth century indicated with the phrase the 'indolence of the heart'. Life with Meyer became a torment for Kaspar Hauser. Meyer wrote very detailed notes about Kaspar Hauser,[184] which characterised his own desolate 'schoolmasterly' soul far more than his unhappy pupil.

J. G. Meyer had a son, *Julius Meyer* (1835-1913), whom we have already mentioned several times, and who was a lawyer and one of the most active opponents of Kaspar Hauser. As Court Assessor in Ansbach, in 1872 he had an Ansbach publisher bring out a 611-page book, *Authentische Mitteilungen über Kaspar Hauser ... zum erstenmale aus den Gerichts- und Administrativ-Acten zusammengestellt und mit Anmerkungen versehen* [Authentic Information about Kaspar Hauser ... compiled for the first time from judicial and administrative records, with notes] in which he sought to do away with Kaspar Hauser 'documentarily', as it were.

Fortunately, *Daumer* was still alive at the time. Meyer's book stimulated Daumer to respond in his fine work *Kaspar Hauser—Sein Wesen, seine Unschuld, seine Erduldungen und sein Ursprung...* (1873) [Kaspar Hauser—His Nature, His Innocence, His Sufferings and His Origin], which we have often cited. In this book he characterised Meyer's writing as typical of the materialism common at that time and Meyer himself as a 'malevolent and dishonest man'.[185]

Decades later, in addition to what Daumer himself had said in his book, Hermann Pies confirmed that Daumer's sharp characterisation of Meyer was not unfounded when he analysed Meyer's 'Authentic Information....'

and the method used in it. Pies compared the book with the documentary material (unavailable to Daumer) on which Meyer had built his case, and was able to reveal the thoroughly dishonest, tendentious method that Julius Meyer employed in publishing the documents.[186] Pies was able to state very aptly that 'this publication of documents by Meyer is anything but "scientific" and cannot be used for scientific purposes'.[187]

Towards the end of 1883, Dr Julius Meyer (in connection with his Kaspar Hauser research) visited Mrs Henriette Feuerbach (1812-1892), the daughter-in-law of Court President Anselm von Feuerbach, and the (step-) mother of the painter, Anselm Feuerbach. It is certainly of objective interest how this distinguished, important and sensitive woman perceived the author of the 'Authentic Information…'.She wrote to her nephew, the staff physician Anselm Feuerbach, on 5 February 1884, that 'Mr Meyer is an extremely narrow-minded person, disgusting and crude. I have seen nothing more of him. I have the feeling that I was rather off-putting towards him, which was quite proper....'[188]

When the archivist *Antonius von der Linde* brought out his two- volume book of abuse about Kaspar Hauser (which we have already mentioned, p. 82 and briefly characterised) in 1887, he placed in it the inscription: 'Dedicated in friendship to the Royal Bavarian District Judicial Counsellor Herr Dr Julius Meyer in Ansbach'.

At the beginning of the 1880s Julius Meyer sent a copy of the new edition he had had published of his father's aforementioned book about Kaspar Hauser to *Eduard Engel* (1851-1941), writer and literary historian, who was at that time the editor of the *Magazin für Literatur* (Journal for Literature). It was a book that Engel very much appreciated.[189] Other publications by Hauser-opponents (1876 Mittelstädt, 1887 Antonius von der Linde) had made a strong impression upon him and had convinced him, for example, that the Kaspar Hauser case was only a matter of 'an unimportant police case'. The actual question became for him, as he wrote, one of ascertaining who was to blame for turning such a case into 'a German, a European riddle?'

In 1912, Engel became personally acquainted with the retired district court director Julius Meyer in Ansbach. Engel vividly recounts how he was able to visit him in the evening, how Meyer had beer served and how he (Engel) was able to talk 'with Kaspar Hauser's foster brother about Kaspar Hauser until midnight'.

They talked about questions such as: What might the tramp have been ...? From where did he come to Nuremberg? Julius Meyer (like his father) was of the opinion that Kaspar Hauser was a peasant farmer's lad from Franconia who had run away when he was about 16 years old.

'We talked,' Eduard Engel continues, 'about Wassermann's novel, which was very famous at the time, and we laughed a lot....' (Engel, the literary historian, calls Wassermann's novel a 'penny dreadful'[190]—literally, a 'back-stairs novel'—*transl.*)

This is an image that deserves to be kept in mind: how Julius Meyer, about 77 years old, and his kindred spirit, Eduard Engel, were sitting over beers in Ansbach in 1912, exchanging their pearls of wisdom about Kaspar Hauser and 'laughing out loud' about Wassermann's novel.

In 1931, when he was already 80 years old, *Eduard Engel* himself wrote a book about Kaspar Hauser, one of the most scandalous books in the whole Kaspar Hauser literature.[191] A boundlessly superficial, indeed downright narrow-minded book, which—again!—ignores the most important facts of Kaspar Hauser's life. Engel's main thesis is that Kaspar Hauser was neither a prince nor an actual fraudster,* but a runaway lad, 'a very ordinary Bavarian peasant boy', 'an average young rascal', 'a pitiful young little swindler',[192] who was only encouraged to tell his fraudulent tales by the great 'fools' in Nuremberg and Ansbach (namely Mayor Binder, Feuerbach and Daumer).†

Engel repeatedly insults these three in particular in the most unheard of manner. He sees them as the 'generators and nourishers of the most ridiculous swindles in German history'. It is incredibly significant for him that in such a context, in order to justify his invective against them, he comes up with the words: 'Binder, Daumer, Feuerbach have long been dust, and it does them no more harm what and how one speaks of them.'[193] (Wilhelm Kunze[194] draws attention very properly to some words from *Stanhope*, which he uttered on a visit he made to Daumer after Hauser's death, 'where Daumer's mother implored him' (Stanhope) 'not to cover the ashes of the unfortunate one with insults and disgrace'. What did Stanhope say? '*It won't hurt him any more'*.... !)

---

* Police Comissioner *Merker* (see above) had wanted to see Kaspar Hauser as a fraudster, just as later (1857), the Danish university professor *D.F. Eschricht* saw him as an idiot, and in the 20th century (see above) Striedinger saw him as a hysteric.

† Feuerbach, Daumer, Binder (and von Tucher) are the men whose names *Karl Röttger* placed on a 'Table of Honour' at the beginning of his documentary novel, *Kaspar Hauser's Last Days* (Berlin-Vienna-Leipzig 1938, p. 5).

'The monster stronger than I'

The main argument or 'document' that Engel thought he could produce in his book in order finally to dismiss Hauser as a fraud was immediately proven to be completely untenable by Kaspar Hauser researchers,[195] so that the book which was launched with much publicity has become a great humiliation for the author.[196]

The most interesting thing about this book, in a deeper sense, is the *How* of it: the way in which it sneers at and offends all those who think differently, its cynicism and its frivolity, combined with an insufferable arrogance, so that here too one wonders: from what kind of hate-filled soul depths does such a turbid tide arise?

Of course, Julius Meyer, Antonius von der Linde and others, and finally also Eduard Engel, were only something like the literary auxiliaries and enforcers, latecomers and ultimately, the rearguard of those impulses, originating in a dark will, which had prepared Kaspar Hauser for the fate which he suffered in the 19th century.[197]

This power was evidently in the dying man's mind when he spoke words[198] such as: 'Many cats, the mouse [is] dead' or, as if already removed from earthly consciousness, as if looking back on his life from beyond the threshold and drawing the conclusion of his effort in the 19th century: 'The monster (was) stronger than I.'

II. The Destiny of Kaspar Hauser and the Destiny of Middle Europe

People always take note only of what is,
and do not pay attention to what is not.
Rudolf Steiner[199]

'History which did not come about'

One of the most fundamental things to recognise if one is really to understand history is that the course that history has actually taken should in no way be considered as *necessary*, as if everything *had to* be as it has been.

Rudolf Steiner once emphasised, for example, in a seminar on world history:[200] spiritual science shows that things could have been very different. What would have happened—he asked—if, for example, Dante had died as a five-year-old child?

Dante is in a very different sense a prime example of how completely differently history could have developed if certain things had come about. We can only touch on this here: if Dante, Rudolf Steiner once said on another occasion,[201] had not been driven from Florence, he would have had an extraordinarily important political career there. Indeed, as supreme head of the city of Florence he would have been followed by a series of significant people. Something grandiose would have developed, the effects of which would still be felt today; seven centuries would have passed very differently. Obviously, there would have been no *Divine Comedy*, for which the world has to thank the fact that Dante was exiled and could not engage in that significant political activity.[202]

External historiography tends in many respects to disapprove of hypothesising about history ('What would have happened if....?'). It is felt, probably with a certain justification, that such questions in many cases are posed more or less playfully or arbitrarily and that it makes no real sense to think out intellectually what would have happened or could happen if this or that had turned out other than it did. Yet such building of historical 'hypotheses' can be undertaken meaningfully and can in corresponding cases be fully justified: only 'for the purposes of understanding', as Rudolf Steiner once expressed it,[203] for which it can contribute a great deal.

Rightly understood, this applies even in a very universal sense:

> ...one can not understand history when one only takes note of what shows itself; for one will never come to a real, proper appreciation of events , when one only looks at what is manifest. It is precisely because people only pursue sensory and intellectual science and never ask what could have happened, that they cannot judge events in their true reality.[204]

This is especially the case when certain impulses from the spiritual world existed and wanted to be realised, but did not come about, when therefore what did not happen was precisely something that was wanted by the spiritual world, and so historical development took a very different course from what it could have done and—perhaps precisely in the sense of the beneficent spiritual powers—'should' have done.

An Indication by Rudolf Steiner

Behind the scenes of history are, according to spiritual science, the beings of the Third Hierarchy: Angels, Archangels, Archai, i.e. the spiritual powers who as Angels lead individual human beings, who as Archangels lead peoples, and as Time Spirits lead whole ages of time. 'No one,' said Rudolf Steiner,[205]

> knows something of the reality of the historical life of humanity, who has no idea that what history actually is, is not in reality made by human beings, but by the beings of the Third Hierarchy.... Outer external historical life, which conventional history describes, is essentially a *fable convenue*, it is only an image of inner historical life which in its course is made by the beings of the Third Hierarchy.

But as well as the normal progressive spiritual powers, there are also the retarding powers, and one 'only has to become aware that there is design in world history [and] there is also design on the part of the evil powers' (Rudolf Steiner[206]).

History is not to be understood as the outflow of what necessarily proceeds from a single spiritual direction (as, for example, Strindberg thought[207]), but as the result of the dramatic collaboration and opposition of impulses and counter-impulses which proceed from very different powers in whose service human beings align themselves in accordance with their individuality.

For a deeper understanding of history, it therefore does not suffice to stick to 'merely showing how things actually were',[208] as the famous words of Leopold von Ranke put it, i.e. merely recording and presenting the sensory facts of history. Rather, in addition to this, one also has to consider the history which 'has not happened'.[209] It is precisely from this direction that the first light is shed on the history that actually happened, which represents the 'alternative' to it, so to speak. Often, in the history that has 'not happened' live those impulses which, just because they have not been realised, remain as unfulfilled tasks for the future in which they will actually be realised (even if in a metamorphosed form). Knowledge of these impulses can become a force which may be employed in the ongoing struggles of history. That is their real meaning for the *future*.

All this is extremely important for a real understanding of the historical phenomenon of *Kaspar Hauser*, which at first seems so mysterious, i.e. an understanding of what was wanted and prepared by this being for the course of historical development in the 19th century.

The Question of Kaspar Hauser's Family Origins

For the destiny of Kaspar Hauser in connection with his whole character it is deeply significant that many traits appeared in his life which as well as being real biographical facts (or at least represented as such) have at the same time a *mythical* or 'fairy-tale' character: the destiny of being abandoned as a child who suffered homelessness in the most extreme way; the fact of having been persecuted in early childhood (cf. above, pp. 65-68); the motif of the prince under a spell who was placed in demeaning circumstances, held prisoner on bread and water etc. Many people have keenly sensed this mythical element. As late as 1922 one writer was speaking of how in Franconia, the story of Kaspar Hauser went around 'almost like a fairy tale',[210] another called Kaspar Hauser 'the mythos of the district of Ansbach'.[211] The story was perceived most powerfully and essentially by *Wilhelm Kunze* in his book *Mythos, Gestalt und Schicksal von Kaspar Hauser* [The Mythos, Gestalt and Fate of Kaspar Hauser] (Nuremberg and Leipzig, 1931) and also sensitively expressed in some of his essays. Indeed, Kunze even seems to exaggerate this aspect somewhat one-sidedly when he wants to see 'the essence' of Kaspar Hauser 'first and foremost in the mythical phenomenon itself'.[212] In truth it might just come down to this: that Kaspar Hauser's destiny was *at the same time* history in the sense of outer facts, *and* mythos in the sense that significant spiritual impulses for humanity and spiritual laws were expressing themselves.

Hans Wohlbold,[213] for example, rightly felt the similarities to the Parsifal motif in Kaspar Hauser, who was also a 'pure fool' and had to answer all questions about his origins with the words: 'I don't know'. (For the motif of *compassion*, see above, p. 59).

In such contexts many of the outer dates in Kaspar Hauser's life make one pay attention. Only two of these dates will be mentioned *here*. In connection with the whole phenomenon of Kaspar Hauser, one can be particularly touched by the fact that he appeared in Nuremberg, and therefore before the world, at *Whitsuntide* (Whit Monday, 1828).* Similarly, his death occurred at *Advent* at 10 pm, 17 December 1833, seven days before Christmas Eve. (Of course, this way of seeing things, in which certain facts become spiritually symptomatic, has nothing to do with the question of what the external causes of these facts are, and how one, for example, accepts with good reason that Kaspar Hauser was left in Nuremberg on Whit Monday, because on that day the citizens of Nuremberg liked to enjoy themselves outside the city, so that the streets were bound to be empty. Or what motives did those who brought him to Nuremberg have for choosing that city, where—in terms of destiny—Georg Friedrich Daumer, the 'last Rosicrucian' was, as it were, 'waiting' for him.

It is anyway important to be aware that with significant individualities—and we will learn to recognise one such in Kaspar Hauser more and more—there is no 'accident' in such things, but rather, everything is somehow more deeply grounded, so that many outer facts of life show characteristics that are symptomatically revealing. One can also regard as most 'telling', for example, the fact that the gripping confirmation ceremony of Kaspar Hauser, which we noted earlier (p. 39), took place in Ansbach in the *Swan Knights Chapel* of the St Gumbertus Church, a place, therefore, especially connected with an Order which—in whatever sense it may have been—was linked to the ancient, sacred, highly spiritual motif of the swan.

The Order of the Swan, directly indicated here, was founded on 29 September 1440 by the Prince Elector Frederick II of Brandenburg. The

* It has long been felt remarkable that his noble benefactor, Court President Anselm von Feuerbach, fell seriously ill on a Whit Monday (1833) and died in the night of the following day (29 May) (for the dates of Anselm von Feuerbach's life and activities see *Anselm Ritter von Feuerbachs Leben und Wirken* [Vol. 2, Leipzig, 1852, p. 345]) by his son Ludwig Feuerbach. Whether Anselm von Feuerbach died a natural death or, as many have come to believe, was poisoned because of his involvement in Kaspar Hauser's destiny, seems likely never to be clearly established.

Order had its headquarters in a monastery in Old Brandenburg and a filial in Ansbach.[214]

Rudolf Steiner speaks[215] about the ancient meaning of the actual motif of the Swan Knight in a very significant context. He speaks of outstanding men who, after their deaths, were appointed guardians of the Holy Grail. Such 'living dead' were served by certain men incarnated on earth as their 'sheaths', as it were. One said of such a man that he had dedicated himself to the *Order of the Swan*. 'Those who dedicated themselves to the Order of the Swan wanted to be the instrument through whom the Grail Knights would be able to work here in the physical world. And such a man was called a swan through whom such a Grail Knight was active here in the physical world.' In this context, Rudolf Steiner then pointed to the saga of Lohengrin....[216]

★

Certain statements by Rudolf Steiner, which he made in conversation and which should be regarded as absolutely authentic, cast a light on the heart of the riddle of Kaspar Hauser. In view of the very great seriousness of the present time, which can only be helped by truth, more truth and yet more truth, and by an unreserved striving to understand things, something from the core of these statements will now be communicated: in the individuality who was concealed under the name of Kaspar Hauser, we have to do with an individuality whom Rudolf Steiner linked closely with important ancient Mysteries and also intimately with Rosicrucianism. This individuality had a task of the greatest importance for the 19th century, which, if he could have fulfilled it, would have meant that we would be living today in a different, more spiritual world. But that was thwarted.

Only very gradually will we be able to realise something of the powerful dimension of this indication for our understanding of the phenomenon of Kaspar Hauser and of the destiny that enveloped him, and which at the same time has been that of the West since the 19th century.

Rosicrucianism, a word which has been sounded many times in our considerations thus far, here we find named directly and centrally.

'Rosicrucianism means to work with the whole of the evolution of mankind in mind': this and in similar ways was how Rudolf Steiner always characterised it.[217] The 'root symbol of all European spiritual life' was what he called the Rose Cross in a lecture[218] about Goethe's poem 'Die Geheimnisse' [The Mysteries], a poem which itself stemmed from a profound Rosicrucian inspiration.

We should now learn to understand much more concretely than before how the 'Child of Europe' is linked to these impulses.

'Within the Rosicrucian stream there is an old rule that one should not speak publicly to one's contemporaries about someone who is a teacher in the Rosicrucian stream until one hundred years have passed since his death, not before, because only through this rule can the impersonal element be brought into a real spiritual movement.' Does not, perhaps, a clarifying light fall from these and similar words of Rudolf Steiner[219] on the fact that he said comparatively little about Kaspar Hauser, who died on the 17 December 1833?

It is remarkable how the motif of 'a hundred years' , although of course not in the sense meant here, occurs in the Kaspar Hauser literature. *Henriette Feuerbach*, who we have already mentioned (p. 86) wrote to her nephew Anselm Feuerbach, a military doctor, on 2 January 1884: 'When we see each other again, I can tell you much' (about Hauser) 'which is perhaps new to you, for I still know ... more than is in all the books, which always base their statements on other books. Had I the fully valid proof, which is still lacking, I would lock it away in an iron casket and write upon it: to be opened on 17 December 1933.'[220]

It can strike one as similarly remarkable how *Klara Hofer*, in whose book about Kaspar Hauser one can find so much that is as though inspired, and in her deeply felt observations about the death of the mysterious stranger she cites an old phrase,[221] which she calls 'the motto of the Rosicrucians'. And *Sophie Hochstetter*, who also had a certain relation to the figure of Kaspar Hauser that was informed by a finer spiritual understanding, wrote in 1917 a little book with the title *Mein Freund Rosenkreutz, Fränkische Novellen* [My Friend Rosenkreutz, Franconian Novellas] (in which not the content but only this title as such draws one's attention).

What became 'Kaspar Hauser' as a result of the special 'treatment' to which that individuality was subjected was something that did not enable this individuality to be effective in any immediate sense. That treatment produced in the human phenomenon 'Kaspar Hauser' something which to a very great extent had the character of *'Maya'* [illusion] (see above p. 90) in which one could hardly notice the spiritual reality standing behind it. But this human phenomenon powerfully *affected* the souls and the thoughts of countless people, and those effects are only explainable by this spiritual reality. Only this makes it possible to understand that, as Daumer saw so rightly, faced with Kaspar Hauser, the 'faithful' and the 'unfaithful' become separated (before the spiritual world). You can see what kind of person you are by your inner attitude towards the phenomenon of Kaspar Hauser.

It is striking in this context that one can often find people emphasising how Kaspar Hauser was 'anything but a significant person', rather he was someone about whom what was of historical significance was not the man himself but the 'opinions and legends' that formed around him,[222] or one can find someone else who calls Kaspar Hauser merely a person 'devoid of any talents or merits'.[223] This was the view not only of those who, in their inner being, were opponents of Kaspar Hauser but also, for example, of the above-mentioned practising physician Dr Heidenreich, who treated Kaspar Hauser and called him 'insignificant in his personality'.[224] Even Feuerbach,[225] in 1832, could characterise Kaspar Hauser, who had become what had been made of him, with the words: 'in his spirit there was no geniality, not one excellent talent at all....In everything he undertook, he remained a novice or a middling student....'

The 'Prince Theory'. For and Against

We do not claim to be characterising, even sketchily, the whole of the great and truly comprehensive activity of this individuality in the sense of Rudolf Steiner's indication. But we would like to focus on one very important aspect of that activity: namely, how things were predisposed here which, to the extent that they would have been realised in the 19th century, could have been of the very greatest significance for *the history and social life of Middle Europe*, of Europe as a whole and indeed of the entire world, and how the tragic destiny especially of Middle Europe, must be seen in connection with just this fact; elucidation drawn from the depths finds that the individuality of Kaspar Hauser was, in the sense of Steiner's indication, unable to be effective.

Here a question begins to take on a great significance which until now we have considered as secondary: namely, in which outer circumstances of life this individuality was placed by birth, in other words, whether he incarnated as the Crown Prince of Baden, whom many held him to be. For of course, on this depended to a great extent the outer *possibilities for action* of such a personality in the social and political life of Europe.

If this question of origins is raised too early or one-sidedly, it can endanger a proper understanding of the phenomenon of Kaspar Hauser in that it soon distracts from the central and essential matter, namely, that of the real human nature of Kaspar Hauser and from what we have called his 'qualitative' aspect. And thus in fact, in a great part of the Kaspar Hauser literature, all interest turns predominantly, sometimes even exclusively, to the question of whether the 'prince theory' is true or false. People then therefore become interested almost entirely in his origins and in dynastic and political issues, which, do, however, at least serve a *deeper* interest but only to the extent to which one recognises in 'Kaspar Hauser' the special, significant individuality of a highly unique being.

In some cases it was a positive development therefore when a researcher or observer of the Kaspar Hauser phenomenon had no interest in the question of lineage or for whatever reason avoided the 'prince theory' or considered it unverifiable and interested himself all the more in the purely human aspects of the unfortunate foundling. For a long time that was the case with Daumer. In more modern times, something similar has been true for Hans Wohlbold and Wilhelm Kunze and has borne similar positive fruit.

Certainly, in a particularly deep and fundamental sense, the great French Revolution signifies the actual end of the European princely house as an institution appropriate for the present time, but as the past slowly faded away, the culture of princely houses continued to be a real factor for many decades. Someone born in 1812 as heir apparent to a reigning German princely house or kingdom—if his I possessed qualities that corresponded to his rank—had, through that status, possibilities of action which someone else did not have. One should also of course not project back into the past, as it were, anti-monarchical instincts that are widespread today. From a spiritual-scientific perspective, one can point out that the first half of the 19th century was still within the 'Age of Gabriel',[226] which had very much to do with lineage, heredity, blood ties and the like. This age was only replaced in 1879 by the Age of Michael in which blood and heredity become steadily less important and the predominance of those forces is increasingly overcome.

If Kaspar Hauser was born as the Crown Prince of Baden, then one could, as it were, 'deduce' from this fact, in connection with many others, what kind of pre-birth *intentions* he may have brought from the spiritual worlds into this incarnation. But history is all about human intentions. That applies to history that has come to pass, but much more of course to history that has not, and which lies wholly in the sphere of intentions and possibilities, predispositions.

Like an impressive sign of the direction indicated by this individuality, anyone who knows that spiritual connections must be taken seriously would be bound to note the fact that he entered this life on Michaelmas Day, namely on 29 September 1812, a fact that documented, as it were, the spirit in which the individuality sought to work.*

The question also arises as to whether the princely status of Kaspar Hauser belongs to those elements of the 'mythos' of Kaspar Hauser which are at the same time external historical reality. The 'mythical' element appears to be strongly underlined by the fact that this heir apparent to the throne of Baden, born on 29 September, received no Christian name, but came into history without a name because he did not receive a regular baptism[227] with a name-giving. (He is therefore recorded in genealogical tables, if at all, only as 'prince' and as having died already on 16 October 1812, following an emergency baptism. [*Nottaufe*])

In his *Memoir of Kaspar Hauser*[228] *Feuerbach* writes 'not long after the appearance of Kaspar Hauser, the rumour, which came from Baden, went around in Nuremberg that Kaspar was a prince of the House of Baden who had been abandoned and was actually the son of Grand Duchess Stéphanie; this rumour recurred from time to time and was loudest most recently.'

That the facts really were as this rumour suggested became the conviction of the famous criminologist who undertook to prove them to be so in extremely penetrating fashion in his memoir. He showed that Kaspar Hauser was the *eldest son of Grand Duke Karl of Baden (r.1811-1818) and his wife Stéphanie, née de Beauharnais,* and was removed from the succession to the throne in order to do away with the ancient dynasty of the Zähringers and make room for a collateral branch that had resulted from the merely morganatic marriage between Kaspar's great grandfather (the first Grand Duke of Baden, Karl Friedrich, and a woman who was not of equal rank, Luise Geyer von Geyersberg, Imperial Countess from 1796).

In 1832 Feuerbach had sent the *Memoir* to Queen Caroline of Bavaria, a sister to Grand Duke Karl and thus, as the *Memoir* proved, Kaspar Hauser's aunt.

---

* Cf. Rudolf Steiner's indication about the birth of *Raphael* on a *Good Friday:* 'that remarkable personality, ...who was born on Good Friday 1483 and as it were, thereby vividly inserted himself—announcing it already through his birth—into the Mystery of Golgotha.' 'We see him, as he—we can put it this way—had himself born in order to show, as it were, how he places himself into the Mystery of Golgotha.' (Rudolf Steiner lecture of 2 May 1912, Berlin.) In Raphael's case, it was deeply striking, and his contemporaries already felt it to be so, that he also died on a Good Friday (1520).

As early as 1834, the year after the death of Kaspar Hauser, two books—of a low calibre—appeared, in which Kaspar Hauser was presented as the Crown Prince of Baden: 1. anonymous (author *Friedrich Seybold*) in a Romantic and sensationalist form, in which the main protagonists were disguised under false names: *Kaspar Hauser oder der Findling, romantisch dargestellt* [Kaspar Hauser, or the Foundling, Romantically Portrayed], Stuttgart, 1834, and 2. *Joseph Heinrich Garnier, Einige Beiträge zur Geschichte Caspar Hausers, nebst einer dramaturgischen Einleitung*, Strassburg, 1834[229] [Some Contributions to the Story of Caspar Hauser, Together with a Dramaturgical Introduction].

In 1840 *F. Sebastian Seiler* (under a pseudonym) published (in Paris) *Kaspar Hauser der Thronerbe Badens* [Kaspar Hauser, Heir to the Throne of Baden], of which a second edition appeared in Paris in 1845.[230] This was a piece of propaganda against princes and 'clerics', filled with details about the alleged story of Hauser and its antecedents at the royal palace in Karlsruhe. The author borrowed sizeable passages from the above-mentioned 'Romantic' version by Seybold. The tone and content of Seiler's book invited the greatest scepticism; for example, the professor of law and later prominent member of the Frankfurt National Assembly in 1848, *Karl Theodor Welcker*, who had occupied himself a great deal with the Kaspar Hauser affair, responded to a bookseller's question about the book with the words: 'Two thirds truth, one third fiction.'[231]

In evaluating this poor quality literature it should be borne in mind that Feuerbach's *Memoir* was at that time completely unknown to the public. It was first published (see above) in 1852 by Feuerbach's son, Ludwig. It would not have been possible for any reputable historian or politician at that time, even if he had been inclined to do so, to publish anything that would cause difficulties for the House of Baden. Thus, rumours emerged from uncontrollable sources or from people who did not dare to come forward in public or even had no intention to do so, and all these came out in the form of justifiably maligned backstreet literature by dubious authors. These books were written and published partly out of murky personal motives, if they managed not to be immediately suppressed.

Countless controversies were bound up with all these books in the course of the 19th century, and there were energetic researchers on both sides of the debate who exerted a tremendous amount of energy and a high degree of acumen in bolstering their argumentation in support of the opposing views.

In Baden there was a widespread conviction that Kaspar Hauser was the Crown Prince who had been removed. It was precisely from Baden that even the revolution of 1848/49 gained a certain anti-monarchical accent in many respects. Daumer wrote[232] of the much maligned favourite of Grand Duke Ludwig of Baden, Major *von Hennenhofer*, of whom many were deeply suspicious that he had been involved in the darker side of the story of Kaspar Hauser, indeed in his murder, and that during the time of the Revolution, Hennenhofer had been in danger of becoming 'a victim of the people's anger'.

Georg Friedrich Kolb (1808-1884), like Welcker a member of the Frankfurt National Assembly, wrote in his last book about Kaspar Hauser[233] that the interest that the whole of Germany took in the foundling was not in the least based on 'the widespread rumour and belief that the unfortunate one was an heir apparent, because he had been set aside for so long'.

Daumer himself had spoken out *against* the Baden prince theory in a book he wrote in 1859.[234] But later, through new information that he had learned in the interim and which he called 'a whole flood of indications', he turned toward this view that he had at first rejected and that was represented by Feuerbach, Welcker, and the *Frankfurter Zeitung* [Frankfurt News] etc. and declared it 'sufficiently adequately verified'.[235]

We cannot here go into the infinitely complicated details of the arguments for and against—which would lead us far from our subject—but rather, must restrict ourselves here to indicating the existing literature.[236] But we would like to point to one very important methodological point.

Advocates of the view that Kaspar Hauser was heir to the throne of Baden generally argue as follows, albeit with various divergences in detail: the Crown Prince who was born on 29 September 1812 in Karlsruhe and who has been identified with Kaspar Hauser was set aside, that is, abducted with the involvement, in one way or the other, of the following two members of the House of Baden: 1. The above-mentioned Imperial Countess *von Hochberg*, the second (morganatic) wife of the first Grand Duke of Baden, Karl Friedrich, 2. Margrave Ludwig, the youngest son of Karl Friedrich from his first marriage (of equal rank). Both of these, stepmother and stepson, had come to an agreement based on their intimate relations. When the Crown Prince was abducted (allegedly by the Imperial Countess herself), he is said to have been exchanged with another child who was dying, who then died on 16 October and was buried as the Crown Prince. Ludwig's motive would have been that he himself, who had been excluded from the throne by the birth of the Crown Prince, wanted to gain the throne, which he actually did in 1818 after the death of Grand Duke Karl, his nephew. Ludwig reigned from 1818 to 1830. The motive of the Imperial Countess von Hochberg is said to have been that she wanted to help her own children from her marriage to Karl Friedrich; they were eligible to succeed to the throne in the event of the extinction of the senior, Zähringer line (i.e., Karl Friedrich's descendants from his first marriage). And in fact, after the death of Grand Duke Ludwig in 1830, the Imperial Countess' eldest son Leopold became Grand Duke (1830-1852). From him descended the later Grand Dukes who ruled in Baden in the 19th and 20th centuries of Baden: Ludwig II, Friedrich I, Friedrich II (see family tree below, p. 111)

Against this reasoning in the 'prince theory', the objection has been raised as to why the little Crown Prince was not simply *killed* immediately after the exchange of the children or at least after a while, instead of going through with the risky enterprise of keeping him hidden. The advocates of Kaspar Hauser's princely status respond to this: first, that there was the possibility that the perpetrators' conscience kept them from actually murdering the child, but second: the death of the child would have 'satisfied' *Ludwig's* purposes but not those of his ally, the Imperial Countess, for she would then have had to fear that once on the throne, the unmarried Ludwig would marry a woman of equal rank and obtain by her descendants who were legitimate and who would thus be senior in rank to the Countess' own sons, who would then be excluded from the succession. For the Countess, the removal of the Crown Prince would then have been a waste of effort. If he had been allowed to live and somehow kept under control, then the Countess could have played him against Ludwig when she needed to and prevent Ludwig from marrying a woman of equal rank.

Another objection against the argument for the prince theory is the following: the removal of Grand Duke Karl's eldest son born on 29 September 1812 would have had one meaning, if not one fear, for Ludwig and the Imperial Countess, that the marriage of the still young Grand Duke Karl and his equally young wife Stéphanie could have produced more sons, a fear that was very well-founded. In fact, Karl and Stéphanie had three more children, among them a son in 1816, Crown Prince Alexander. Against that objection, it can be pointed out that Prince Alexander in fact died in 1817, and indeed under remarkably suspicious circumstances which contributed very much to deepen or confirm suspicion about the fate of the elder Crown Prince (the later 'Kaspar Hauser' in the 'prince theory'). Soon after the death of Alexander in 1817 came that of Margrave Friedrich, Ludwig's elder brother, who had also had a greater claim to the throne than Ludwig.

One sees that this whole manner of seeing things and this kind of argumentation about Kaspar Hauser's princely origins, in all its pros and contras, comes down to such facts, viewpoints and motives which played out in the sphere of the dynastic and political interests of the personalities in the House of Baden. Within this sphere or in this dimension of facts this way of seeing things is certainly right, both in relation to strong moments of suspicion and in relation to the possible objections raised against them.

But when one reflects on what was presented in Chapter 1 of this book about Kaspar Hauser and his experiences and sufferings, one will be bound to see that a one-sided focus on the dynastic and political 'prince theory', even if one could accept it as accurate in itself, needs to be complemented if one is to come a deeper and more comprehensive understanding. This complementary way of looking at the phenomenon would have to try to look through the direct dynastic and political context in the foreground to a sphere surmised to be behind it. When one does this, then, for example, the above-mentioned objections against the prince theory lose much of their weight. For is it not obvious that someone on whom one wants to carry out certain experiments ('magical educational experiments'—see p. 51) will have to be left *alive*, and must not be killed but only held prisoner and under one's control? Furthermore, if it is a matter of a single, particular person on whom one wishes to work in a particular way for very cogent reasons, then one has to focus on this personality and so it is obviously irrelevant whether it is possible or probable that his parents will have more children or sons! The intentions that were present in this background sphere then would have to work into the dynastic and political sphere, and the motives of the people active in that latter sphere would have to be exploited and influenced. How, for example, can Kaspar Hauser's situation in his imprisonment, which was arranged in such a way that the ego development of the unhappy child was undermined in such a 'professional' manner, be explained from merely dynastic, political motives, as we have seen (see above p. 97f.)? Another hand must have been at work besides whatever dynastic or political motives (e.g. certain suspicions refer to *Bavarian* policy[237]) were involved. With regard to the first question above, only the 'what' can be understood up to a certain point, and from this the explanation of the 'how'—for example, Hauser's incarceration must be sought.*

It may also be mentioned that Kaspar Hauser himself never made the slightest conjecture about his origins, as testified by von Stichaner, the President of the Ansbach local council,[238] with whom he often socialised.

Police chief *Ludwig Wagler,* wrote in his short essay '*Die Bilanz einer hundertjährigen Hauserforschung*' [100 Years of Hauser Research][239] that:

> Entire editions of all the writings that affirm Hauser's princely origin were bought up by the government of Baden and suppressed, while those authors who denied it (Mittelstädt 1876, von der Linde 1887) had official archives opened to them. Hennenhofer's entire literary estate was immediately confiscated by order of the government of Baden after his death (2. January 1850) and his heirs were bought off....

We have already referred to some essentials from von der Linde's book (p. 82). Hennenhofer has also been mentioned. Otto Mittelstädt was a lawyer (Senior State Attorney and Imperial Court Counsellor) who published official documents in his book *Kaspar Hauser und sein badisches Prinzentum* [Kaspar Hauser's Princely Origins in Baden?] in Heidelberg in 1876 that were supposed to prove the actual death of the Crown Prince of Baden who was born on 29 September 1812. The book contains the following threat, which has become well-known:

> Whoever continues, in view of these published documents, to claim that Kaspar Hauser was the Crown Prince of Baden who was falsely imputed to have been set aside by Imperial Countess Hochberg and replaced by a dead or dying child, does so at his own risk. He would be held responsible for this by the Countess' son, who is still alive, and would be convicted and chastised by any judges' bench in the civilised world for libelling the name of the deceased.

* On the assumption of two such layers in the Kaspar Hauser case, is based a significant artistic work by *Paul Michaelis* that deals with the affair out of a deeply human and spiritual identification of the author with the whole story; this is his as yet unpublished work *Kaspar Hauser. Eine Tragödie* [Kaspar Hauser—A Tragedy]. It distinguishes very clearly the Baden dynastic sphere from another sphere of important decision-making that operated behind it. The two relate to one another, one could say, like soul and spirit, or, to use an old expression, like horse and carriage driver.

In the 19th Century

One sees that in the 19th century it was not exactly without danger to assert the princely origins of Kaspar Hauser.

A prominent example of how authors of such books in the 19th century went about it was *Heinrich von Treitschke* and his well-known *Deutsche Geschichte im neunzehnten Jahrhundert*[240] [German History in the Nineteenth Century]. For Treitschke, Hauser is the usual peasant boy of the anti-Hauserians, a fraudster who fatally stabbed himself. Treitschke tells his story in the usual superficial way in the mode of this fraudster hypothesis. Here is his conclusion:

> Only in 1875 did the Baden Court decide to publish the documents about the death of the Crown Prince. Since then, the web of lies (about Kaspar Hauser's princely origins) has finally been torn apart by the writings of O. Mittelstädt and A. von der Linde, and even if some details still remain unclear, the question of where the fraudster actually came from has today lost any historical value.

Of course, none of this has been able to prevent the conviction of Kaspar Hauser's princely origins from remaining widespread. 'The Kaspar Hauser story was also taken very seriously by some in high social circles,' wrote Horst Kohl, the historian who became well-known with his work on the history of Bismarck (in a note to Bismarck's *Gedanken und Erinnerungen* [Thoughts and Reminiscences], where in the 13th chapter 'Dynasties and Noble Houses' Bismarck mentions the 'Caspar Hauser Story' in relation to Baden).[241]

In the enormous literature on Kaspar Hauser[242] the 'Prince Question' was addressed in great detail already in the 19th century, and opinions on it were starkly opposed. Crudely put, they amounted to the alternatives: Kaspar Hauser—fraudster or prince? The fraudster view was 'dominant'.

In the 20th century, a new, very positive stimulus for an interest in Kaspar Hauser was first and foremost given by *Jakob Wassermann* with his novel which appeared in 1907/08 and has been referred to in this book many times already. Wassermann writes from a deeply human empathy for the unfortunate child and has awoken in many thousands of his readers feelings and intuitions that have often lasted for decades.

What really moved him above all, as with Daumer, was the purely human phenomenon of Kaspar Hauser, for whom he felt a deeply-rooted empathic interest. His studies had also evidently convinced him of Hauser's princely origins. In 1921 he was still writing:

> Now I am today as I was before fully persuaded of the view that Caspar Hauser was really the princely boy whom Daumer, Feuerbach and many others who were silenced or slandered, held him to be; I have seen and heard enough documentary proofs and creditable witnesses...; the intrigues speak only too clearly; there are still in high places those in the know; some have given me their trust.... Today as before, I am fully persuaded that the name, the life and the death of Kaspar Hauser amount to a guilt that has yet to be atoned for, which festers like all cases of unexpiated guilt.
>
> All this has only indirectly to do with the writing of the book. In this respect the attacks also missed their target.[243]

For his conviction about Kaspar Hauser's princely origins and his portrayal of them in the novel played no central role for him. And yet for many of his critics this point was the particular focus of their attacks. For various reasons, we would like to cite here one such critique, by the formerly very well-known author *Carl Busse*, who commented on Wassermann's novel very soon after it appeared.[244]

Busse begins by referring to some other mysterious people who have featured in the histories of the nations and who have always occupied and fertilised the fantasy of writers until the present day—such as the figure of the false Demetrius,* but also, for example, the 'false Waldemar' of Brandenburg. Busse therefore finds it conceivable that Kaspar Hauser had lured Jakob Wassermann to interpret his story. He also admits that in the case of Hauser, 'it could have been' as Wassermann describes. But what could not be expected, thinks Busse, was this—and it disturbs him greatly—'that of all the manifold possibilities of a solution' (to the question of who Kaspar Hauser was) Wassermann should subscribe to that which today we find the least pleasing. He warms up once again the old legend of the foundling's princely origin, which 'lost all

---

* The motif of the false Demetrius also appears in the Kaspar Hauser book by *Klara Hofer* (pp. 224, 236) perhaps not without deeper reasons, for this figure, in a deeper sense, may well be seen together with that of Kaspar Hauser.[245]

creditability" through the publication (by Mittelstädt) of official documents from the archives of the House of Baden' in 1875 at the urging of Kaiser Wilhelm I. Wassermann would have benefitted the most, Busse thinks, from today's 'generally accepted view' that Caspar Hauser had been kept hidden in a parsonage in Old Bavaria by his natural father. It is remarkable that Wassermann was not frightened by 'the fabulous backstairs Romanticism' in his novel, which features poison, daggers, masked murderers and similar props.

> In a multi-volume novel by [Marie-Joseph 'Eugène'] Sue—*Le Juif errant** [English title: *The Wandering Jew*—Ed.], I believe,—there is a Jesuit plot of the most secret type and fabulous dimensions. The modern storyteller is not far behind Eugène Sue. One's hair stands on end when reading of the monstrously influential power acting behind the scenes which is constantly held over Caspar Hauser and acts through a chain of paid agents and gives orders for the elimination of the man.... Wassermann... does not hesitate for a moment to make out of Lord Stanhope, who for a time was interested in Caspar Hauser, not only a wild adventurer in the pay of that 'secretive power' but also probably of the throne of Baden and who had the order to get rid of Caspar Hauser and furthermore, he has the noble lord commit suicide....
>
> One sees...that minds such as that of Jakob Wassermann are simply incapable of seeing things objectively....

The stark conflict between supporters and opponents of the 'prince theory' went on.

With the fall of the princely houses in Germany in November 1918, a new political situation arose. The dynasties no longer had any interest in whether Kaspar Hauser was the Crown Prince of Baden or else this interest became politically powerless. Kaspar Hauser research could continue unhindered.

---

* It is also peculiar how *Georg Friedrich Daumer* (though not in relation to Kaspar Hauser) in his 'mysteriological studies'[246] came to speak about this book *Le Juif errant* [The Wandering Jew] by Eugène Sue, of which he evidently thought that although it seemed fantastical, it was also not without truth. Daumer (who in 1858 joined the Catholic Church) took the Jesuits to task and held that 'evil spirits' that he looked to find elsewhere were rather to be found in *their* Order.

In the 20th Century

It received a strong impetus in 1924 (this was also the year of Rudolf Steiner's last powerful activity). In that year was published *Das Schicksal einer Seele. Die Geschichte vom Kaspar Hauser*—[The Fate of a Soul—The Story of Kaspar Hauser], an important book by *Klara Hofer*, to which we have often referred. On the one hand, it made an impact because in it the author revealed (see above p. 70) that she had discovered the cleverly hidden dungeon-like room in which Kaspar Hauser had been incarcerated in Schloss Pilsach (near Neumarkt in the Bavarian Upper Palatinate), which belonged to her and where she was living at the time and from where he had been taken to Nuremberg.* But at the same time, its impact was no less due to the special 'aura' of the book, which affected many souls. The story of the discovery of the cell seemed to speak of a distinctive destiny. Something like a breath from the supersensory world seemed to be felt in some parts of the book. Klara Hofer wrote it from intimate experience of strong heart forces which in essence resonated with those of the unfortunate child which it described. The book speaks strongly to the reader, who therefore does not find it hard to overlook its shortcomings. Also, Klara Hofer's feeling for the deep symbolism of things around Kaspar Hauser touch on deeper realities.

Hermann Pies notes[249] that 'a flood of books, newspaper and magazine articles about Kaspar Hauser followed Hofer's discovery' (of the cell), through which at least one thing was proven: that in the time when Kaspar Hauser was alive, there were still well-concealed rooms similar to the one which Hauser described as his 'prison'.

The books and booklets which appeared from 1924 onwards were like earlier ones of very different quality. They included the writings of very serious researchers such as the Hamburg criminologist *Adolf Bartning* and above all, the work of *Hermann Pies* himself.

---

* Incisive research by Dr Fritz Klee—*Neue Beiträge zur Kaspar Hauser-Forschung* (Nuremberg, 1929)[New Contributions to Kaspar Hauser Research]—speaks for the correctness of this thesis. Until then, many had accepted, along with Feuerbach and Daumer,[247] that Hauser had been held in the Falkenhaus hunting lodge near the village of Triesdorf, not far from Ansbach. (The Comte de St Germain had stayed in Triesdorf (and in Schwabach, also near Ansbach) decades earlier (1774-1776) as a guest of Margrave Alexander von Ansbach and Bayreuth.[248]

We cannot here characterise all this new literature in detail, let alone go into its content, individual results of the research, or individual aspects of its argumentation. But when it is all taken together, what mainly results from this new literature can be summarised under the following two headings:

1. It is absurd to see Kaspar Hauser as a fraud (which, as we have heard, was for decades the official view).
2. It is highly likely that Kaspar Hauser was in fact the heir apparent to the throne of Baden, who was born on 29 September 1812.

This last point is the result of *circumstantial evidence* which has become ever more consolidated over the course of decades as the fruit of endless hard work and acumen by researchers, and indeed to such an extent that for one who allows the entirety of the facts to speak, there can hardly any longer be any possibility of doubt about the external historical facts—however many details remain unclear.

We shall now hear some voices that testify to this:

1. In a review of the book by the French diplomat (ambassador), historian and Kaspar Hauser researcher Edmond Bapst, *À la Conquête du Thrône de Bade* (Paris 1930) [To the Conquest of the Throne of Baden], *Werner Wittich*, former Professor of National Economy at the University of Strasbourg writes in the magazine *Hochland*, Vol. 28, August 1931, pp. 387-401:

   > ...As far as the credibility of this story goes [as Bapst represents it], I hold Kaspar Hauser's identity as the heir apparent of Baden to be certain. His contemporaries, above all Feuerbach, were of this conviction, and systematic Kaspar Hauser research has strengthened the arguments to the point that there is now scarcely any room for doubt....

2. *Friedrich Wencker-Wildberg* writes in the over 100 page-long chapter on Kaspar Hauser, which summarises a great deal, in his book *Rätsel der Weltgeschichte* [Riddles of World History] Berlin 1944 (pp. 90/91):

   > This objective Kaspar Hauser research began only after the [First] World War, when misgivings at various courts fell away and investigation of the

delicate material no longer involved danger for the life and limb of the investigator....

The judgement of this tribunal, which is impartial because it was without personal interest in the matter, was that the thesis that Hauser was a fraud and a swindler was rejected as untenable in any decision about the theory of his having been the heir apparent of Baden. However, ... this verdict applies only under certain preconditions and particular circumstances, for seamlessly detailed evidence was no longer possible, since interested parties had the power and the means to remove all documents that might somehow lead back to them, and to silence fellow conspirators or witnesses through money or poison or to suppress their written testimony. In this way, there were numerous gaps in the evidence which, given the lack of proper direct testimony, had to be bridged by the statements of second-hand witnesses, whose credibility is, however, beyond doubt, or through the aid of logical deductions, in order to reconstruct in accordance with one's best knowledge and conscience the probable course of the whole affair.

3. *Otto Flake*, in his 1950 book, which we have cited several times (pp. 151, 148):

> There is not the slightest doubt that Kaspar Hauser had something to do with the Grand Ducal family.... The probability that Kaspar Hauser was the legitimate heir to the throne is so great that it can be treated as a certainty.

4. In the Swiss journal *Neue Wissenschaft. Zeitschrift für Parapsychologie* [New Science. Journal for Parapsychology] III 7 (April 1953) p. 206 *Dr Ernst Philipp Barthel* (in an essay '*Tatsachen der Überempfindlichkeit bei dem Findling Kaspar Hauser*')[Instances of Hypersensitivity in the Foundling Kaspar Hauser] writes:

> Kaspar Hauser research has remained lively until the present day. All the facts that have been presented ever more clearly over the past decades make it indubitable that Kaspar Hauser, who was born on 29 September 1812, and exchanged with a dying child on 16 October and abducted, was the son of Grand Duke Karl of Baden and his wife Stéphanie Beauharnais and was set aside for reasons of the succession to the throne. A hundred threads all lead to this point. The fraudster thesis is absurd, since such a thing, in the way it

has been reported, cannot be found to be fraudulent and it only proves that there were people who had an interest in placing this absurd hypothesis into the world....'

Of course, despite all this, in modern times there have still been voices raised *against* what some people might continue to call the 'prince legend'. One can probably say today that they mostly stem from people who, through prejudice, preconceived opinions and sometimes will impulses deeply rooted in their character, are not capable of feeling, and above all are *unwilling* to feel the inner certainty of the matter; their own way of thinking makes it impossible for such personalities to *see*. A peculiar 'refutation' of Kaspar Hauser's princely identity was presented by Prince Adalbert of Bavaria as late as 1951.*

---

* In the magazine *Der Ziebelturm* [The Onion Dome] VI 5/6 (May, June 1951) pp. 102-107, 121-128 in his essay '*Königin Caroline von Bayern und Kaspar Hauser*' [Queen Caroline of Bavaria and Kaspar Hauser].

Queen Caroline of Bavaria was, as we have already heard, a sister of Grand Duke Karl of Baden. Their mother, Margravine Amalie, who lived at Court in Karlsruhe, had been present at the birth of the heir apparent on 29 September 1812 and also at the infant's illness and death on 16 October. She had, according to the letters to her daughter Caroline, which were found by Prince Adalbert (and later burnt), no doubt that the child who died was the one who was born on 29 September 1812, her grandson. From this, the author (Prince Adalbert) concludes (op. cit. pp. 107, 128) that both cases actually had to do with the same child. But *how*, if for example, the indication—or suspicion?—of Flake (op. cit., p. 73), was correct, namely, that the sick child who died on 16 October was ridden with fever?[250]

But more peculiarly, Prince Adalbert goes on in his essay to cite many facts from the letters and accounts of his princely relatives which all speak in exactly the opposite sense very much *for* Kaspar Hauser's princely origin. Most impressive in this sense is a note (op. cit., p. 107) from the records of King Ludwig I of Bavaria written on 23 December 1833 (i.e. only six days after the death of Kaspar Hauser), which makes it very clear that the Grand Duchess Stéphanie, the mother of that heir apparent of Baden, had herself expressed the opinion, *already long before the appearance of Kaspar Hauser in Nuremberg*, that 'her eldest son' (i.e. the heir apparent born on 29 September 1812) 'whom she had not seen dead, had not died but had been taken away', as is noted in King Ludwig's records.

(With this, Prince Adalbert of Bavaria provided documentary proof for the correctness of the account which, with regard to Grand Duchess Stéphanie and in the same sense, was made on pp.44/45 of the disreputable little book by Seiler in 1845, mentioned above (p. 98). Seiler's account therefore seems to belong to the

In agreement with the actual results of the latest Kaspar Hauser research, and fully confirming them, was the way in which *Rudolf Steiner* expressed himself in particular conversations. These conversations made it clear that Kaspar Hauser was the heir apparent to the throne of Baden.

Dates in the Life of Kaspar Hauser

In view of what we have learned from our previous observations, we can now extend into the following image what we said earlier about certain external facts in the life of this individuality and the language that those facts speak: it is a fact that he was born on 29 September (Michaelmas Day) 1812. This corresponds to a conception sometime during the 13 Holy Nights of 1811/1812, which reinforces the Christmas motif that surrounds Kaspar Hauser (see above p. 62). In this period (between the birth of—the Nathan—Jesus and the festival of Epiphany/Three Kings Day) also fell the name day of Kaspar Hauser's mother Stéphanie, which she always celebrated: 26 December, the day of St Stephen, venerated in Christendom as the first martyr. The life of the Kaspar Hauser individuality also amounted to martyrdom in the highest degree. The name Kaspar which he was given also appears in the Christian calendar at the time of the 13 Holy Nights, as one of the three Holy Kings: on 3 January.[251] In Nuremberg Kaspar Hauser appeared at Whitsuntide (Whit Monday) 1828. He died in Advent 1833, seven days before Christmas, on 17 December, 21 years and just 3 months old. He had therefore reached the age at which the I awakens (see p. 55 above) whereby, one can surmise, his death in precisely this period is connected.

The Land of Baden. Karl Friedrich von Baden

For centuries, especially in the early Middle Ages, something like the political and cultural focus of the old German Reich was in Southwestern Germany, and particularly in that region something of its politically

'two-thirds truth' which the Baden legal scholar *Welcker* found in Seiler's book. (See above p. 98)

The Crown Prince had already appeared under the name Caspar in 1816 (see Dr Wagler, *Die Enträtselung der oberrheinischen Flaschenpost von 1816*, [The Unravelling of the Mystery of the Message in a Bottle Found in the Upper Rhine in 1816] Nuremberg (1926).

Family Tree

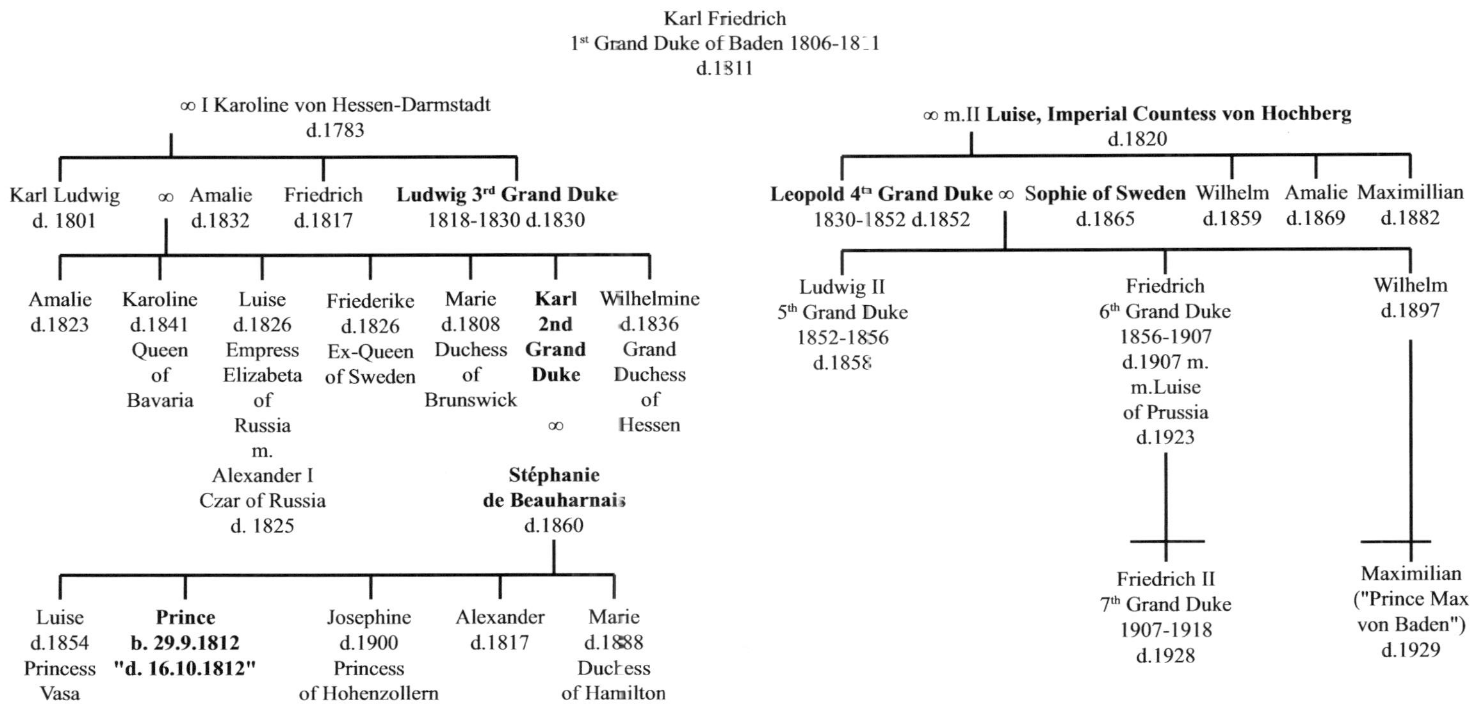
Karl Friedrich
1st Grand Duke of Baden 1806-1811
d.1811
∞ I Karoline von Hessen-Darmstadt
d.1783
Karl Ludwig
d. 1801
∞
Amalie
d.1832
Friedrich
d.1817
Ludwig 3rd Grand Duke
1818-1830 d.1830
Amalie
d.1823
Karoline
d.1841
Queen
of
Bavaria
Luise
d.1826
Empress
Elizabeta
of
Russia
m.
Alexander I
Czar of Russia
d. 1825
Friederike
d.1826
Ex-Queen
of Sweden
Marie
d.1808
Duchess
of
Brunswick
Karl
2nd
Grand
Duke
∞
Wilhelmine
d.1836
Grand
Duchess
of
Hessen
Stéphanie
de Beauharnais
d.1860
Luise
d.1854
Princess
Vasa
Prince
b. 29.9.1812
"d. 16.10.1812"
Josephine
d.1900
Princess
of Hohenzollern
Alexander
d.1817
Marie
d.1888
Duchess
of Hamilton
∞ m.II Luise, Imperial Countess von Hochberg
d.1820
Leopold 4th Grand Duke ∞
1830-1852 d.1852
Sophie of Sweden
d.1865
Wilhelm
d.1859
Amalie
d.1869
Maximillian
d.1882
Ludwig II
5th Grand Duke
1852-1856
d.1858
Friedrich
6th Grand Duke
1856-1907
d.1907 m.
m.Luise
of Prussia
d.1923
Wilhelm
d.1897
Friedrich II
7th Grand Duke
1907-1918
d.1928
Maximilian
("Prince Max
von Baden")
d.1929

individual nature was maintained which was opposed to the centralist territorial concept of the state. Not for nothing did people there, until late in the 18th century, when the old German Empire was on its last legs, use the word 'Reich' as the geographical term for that region of Southwestern Germany. One can also find this usage in Goethe's earlier works.[252]

Probably, we should regard what was alive in the German southwest in its own way as a special cultural atmosphere and as intimately connected with the inner spirituality that did not at all spread outwards but which prevailed there in the 9th century in those regions where, as Emil Bock for example, writes, 'in the forests of southwest Germany, in Switzerland and the Vosges the quiet circle of the guardians of the Grail pursued its sacred ideals'.

> In the 9th century when those events played out which we find described clothed in the imagery of Wolfram von Eschenbach, the region of the Grail must have been there in the general area where the Rhine bends its knee at Basel, where the German, French and Swiss elements encounter each other, where the Vosges, the Black Forest and the Swiss Jura run together radially....[253]

Breisgau in the 10th century was already the home of the *Zähringers,* who later became the Margraves and eventually the Grand Dukes of Baden; in the 19th century they were the oldest, still existing German princely family.[254] It seems important that they were also active as the founders of towns and cities (1120 Freiburg, Villingen, Offenburg; in 1191 a Zähringer founded the city of Bern). One can recall the mediaeval impulse of founding cities and its great significance for the modern development of freedom and think of Elsa of Brabant and Lohengrin, the son of Parsifal.[255]

A key development in the origins of the modern *Land* (province) of Baden was that in 1771 two regions in Baden that belonged to the House of Zähringer were reunited that had been separated for centuries: through the death of the (Catholic) Margrave of Baden-Baden, his margravate passed into the hands of the (Protestant) line of the Margraves of Baden-Durlach (to whose territories Pforzheim, for example, belonged). The small province that resulted from this reunification, ruled by the extremely vigorous Margrave Karl Friedrich of the Durlach line, provided a point of crystallisation to which, especially due to its policy of going along with France, more and more lands in the southwest were added, until finally, by 1806, the Grand Duchy of Baden had finally emerged in its new form, extending from Lake Constance to the River Main. Its capital was Karlsruhe, which had first been the capital of Baden-Durlach. Karlsruhe had grown up around Schloss Karlsruhe, which had first been built as a hunting lodge in 1715, near the town of Durlach. Karl Friedrich, who since 1738 had been the Margrave of Baden-Durlach, the core territory of Baden which came about in 1771 through the reunification of the two margravates of Baden-Durlach and Baden-Baden, was raised to the rank of Elector of Baden in 1803 and finally in 1806 became Grand Duke of the now powerfully enlarged state of Baden. No German state owed as much to the policies of Napoleon for the growth of its lands. Karl Friedrich, who had begun as ruler over 86,000 inhabitants of his state, ended with almost one million more. He died at a ripe old age in 1811, one year before the birth of his great-grandson, that Crown Prince (in the palace at Karlsruhe) who is the focus of our considerations. One can have the feeling that the power of destiny had arranged things here in a very short time to prepare a political vessel with particular qualities that was enabled and made ready to play a role in Middle European and wider European contexts in accordance with the spirit that prevailed within it and for which it could serve as instrument.

At first, this spirit had been very strongly determined by the personality of Margrave *Karl Friedrich*, who had ruled for decades. His main era of activity had been long before the great French Revolution, when the absolutism of princes was still very much alive and which in the person of the prince, a *human being* was still decisive in what occurred in a state.[256] Karl Friedrich was a representative of enlightened absolutism which here in little Baden-Durlach took on a strongly patriarchal form. He was widely appreciated and respected as one of the best German princes of his time. In his *Dichtung und Wahrheit* [Poetry and Truth] Goethe calls him the 'venerable Margrave, praised for the virtues of his reign'.[257] Karl Friedrich's reign was one of the fulfilment of duty in that his ethos was comparable to that of Frederick II (the Great) of Prussia who wanted to be 'the first servant of the state'. Karl Friedrich was evidently less 'the first servant' of an increasingly impersonal state machine and much more the 'father of his country', a ruler in the midst of small, easily surveyable and humanly understandable relationships. He too was concerned in all ways for the welfare of his country. His domestic reforms, in a humane spirit, led to the abolition of torture, the removal of serfdom, the granting of liberties etc. He wanted government to be led by conscience and frugality, promoted agriculture and the beginnings of industry in Baden. He encouraged just as much the country's cultural life, especially its schools. In keeping with the spirit of the times, he promoted religious tolerance, an essential precondition for the growth of a truly modern, multi-confessional state. The country blossomed during his reign and became a model state in miniature. Here were the humanly and morally essential roots of the 'liberal little model' for which Baden was often praised in the 19th century.

As a man, Karl Friedrich had a clear head and a pious heart, well-intentioned and benevolent, without the usual princely pretensions.

After his visit to Karlsruhe on 30 August 1770, *Herder* wrote of him characteristically in a letter to his bride: 'The Margrave...sought me out for conversation, and as he is the first prince I know who doesn't put on princely airs, our conversation mostly fell into matters that have to do with the beginnings and the freedom of the human race about which I was able to express myself so freely as though I were not speaking to a prince.' Repeatedly, Herder declared that Karl Friedrich was the best prince in Germany. Later, at Karl Friedrich's request, he wrote an essay on a programme for an 'idea for the first patriotic institute for the common spirit of Germany'.[258]

To the court of Karl Friedrich, notably in the 1760s and 70s, came, besides Herder, a whole bevy of other significant personalities such as Goethe, the Count Stolberg brothers, Wieland, Klopstock, (who in 1774 Karl Friedrich invited to stay for a long time), Jung-Stilling, Gesner, Pfeffel, Voltaire, Lavater. It was at the Baden court in Karlsruhe that Goethe first met the young Duke Karl August von Sachsen-Weimar.

In old age, Karl Friedrich's pious attitude took more and more of a 'theosophical' turn 'into a mysticism wrapped in Freemasonic and Rosicrucian speculations', as one author put it. This tendency brought him especially into a closer relationship with *Jung-Stilling* (1740-1817), who, summoned by Karl Friedrich, spent the last decade of his life as a Baden Privy Councillor in Karlsruhe.

It may also be of interest to hear that Karl Friedrich of Baden was one of five European princes of whom, as probably need not be doubted, the *Comte de St Germain,* who visited and was active at so many European courts, declared that he admired them and was especially fond of them.[259,260]

Jung-Stilling

We must pause here for a while to consider the significant figure of the above-mentioned *Heinrich Jung-Stilling.* He was a friend of Goethe's youth from the latter's time in Strasbourg. The two were hearty companions. In *Dichtung und Wahrheit* Goethe wrote much about him.[261] It was also Goethe who in 1777 promoted the publication of Jung-Stilling's autobiography.[262] Jung-Stilling was one of the most important personalities in the theosophical and mystical underground or pietistic 'awakening movement' in the second half of the 18th century and the turn of the 18th to the 19th century. Through his novels, his autobiography and a magazine which he published etc., he had a strong influence across the reading public, especially through his four-volume story *Das Heimweh* [Homesickness], written in novel form. In it he wanted to present 'a Christian's journey of suffering to his heavenly home'.[263] It could be called a strongly allegorical account of inner soul development or an initiation process in the Christian sense. Jung-Stilling's motto—'Blessed are they that are homesick, for they shall come home!'—clearly points to the world-denying nature of the book, which also underlies the fact that Jung-Stilling became an opponent of the idea of reincarnation.[264]

Rudolf Steiner writes about *Das Heimweh* in a letter from Weimar at the end of November 1890 to his older friend Friedrich Eckstein in a context in which he emphasises the great meaning for his whole life of his having got to know Eckstein:

> ...Your laconic letter 'Read Jung-Stilling's Heimweh' outweighs many other weighty letters. Such a book teaches us the way to 'die and become!' Do you know that Jung-Stilling also wrote a 'Key to Homesickness'?
>
> Noteworthy is the way in which Goethe opposed Jung[-Stilling]. In his letters he writes remarkable words about this friend of his. And I dare to say of Jung[-Stilling] that for him, Goethe was the most sympathetic person he had ever come across....[265]

In his public lecture 'The History of Spiritualism' given in Berlin on 30 May 1904[266] Rudolf Steiner speaks briefly about Jung-Stilling's detailed account of spirits and spiritual phenomena and how he had tried to understand everything so as to do it justice as a Christian believer etc.

Later, Rudolf Steiner briefly spoke about how Jung-Stillung introduced Goethe to the occult sides of human life.[267] Steiner spoke briefly about this in connection with Saint-Martin[268] and 'the twilight era' of the older theosophical stream, to which such personalities as the Swabians Bengel, Oetinger and others belonged.[269]

In the story of his life, Jung-Stilling also said[270] of his *Heimweh* that it had 'prepared the great, good and pious Elector of Baden'—Karl Friedrich—'so that straightaway at the first opportunity he had determined to place me on my true standpoint', i.e., that by summoning Jung-Stilling to Baden, Karl Friedrich had removed all external concerns about his livelihood and had thereby enabled him to pursue his famous eye treatments and his religious writings. In an epilogue to the story of Jung-Stilling's life, his son-in-law, the theology professor Dr Schwarz wrote that Karl Friedrich and Jung-Stilling, who had been friends for many years, had been friends and Christians of a rare kind; 'whoever saw them, believed he was beholding in them an apostolic dignity'.[271]

For the relationships and circumstances of life in which Jung-Stilling lived, it is indicative, for example, that he was acquainted with the famous Prince Karl of Hessen who, when he came to Kassel on a visit from Denmark, had Jung-Stilling (who was then working in Marburg) come to Kassel in order to converse with him.

'Things of the greatest importance,' writes Jung-Stilling about these conversations,[272] 'relating to the Kingdom of God, were discussed.'

> Prince Karl is a true Christian; he relies to the greatest degree on the love and veneration of the Redeemer, he lives and dies for Him, and thereby has gained rare and extraordinary knowledge and experiences, which, however, are not at all for the ears of everyman and of which no mention can be made here.

This Prince, or Landgrave, Karl of Hessen is none other than the protector and host of the *Comte de St Germain*, who spent the last years of his life with him in Schleswig (until his death in Eckenförde in 1784). Prince Karl was a very significant personality. 'He was', wrote Eduard Vehse[273] of him sometimes effusively, 'at the age of 32 received into the Order of Freemasons in Schleswig and finally became their Grand Master. He was one of the awakened ones of his time and was connected to all the most famous and celebrated of such men, among them Lavater, Jung-Stilling, and with the theosopher, Saint-Martin....'

Jung-Stilling himself was also a friend of Lavater's and likewise with the significant divine, pastor Oberlin in Steintal in Alsace. The well-known Baroness Juliane von Krüdener was closely connected to this whole spiritual stream. In 1808 her path led her to Karlsruhe and Jung-Stilling, of whom we hear that he familiarised her with Swedenborg's ideas. She also visited Oberlin several times, once (1812) for many weeks. This was the same Frau von Krüdener who later exercised a great influence on Czar Alexander I for a time. She, together with another personality, a follower of Mesmer, gave Alexander the impetus to found 'the Holy Alliance' and thus she intervened deeply into the political life of the time, out of her religious, mystical and pietistic ideas and imaginations. She saw Napoleon as the corrupter 'Apollyon' (or Abbadon) of the Apocalypse (Ch. 9:11) and opposed to him Alexander the saviour. Jung-Stilling had a similar view (perhaps Frau von Krüdener had taken her view from him?). He saw in Alexander a kind of divinely-sent holy figure of the End Times, for he (Jung-Stilling) expected (following on from the Swabian theosophist Bengel) the beginning of the 1000-year kingdom in 1836.[274] He too saw in Alexander the great positive counter-pole to Napoleon precisely in a spiritual and religious sense.

Jung-Stilling had a personal connection to Czar Alexander. We find him described as Alexander's 'spiritual friend' and hear how in the period after the Battle of the Nations at Leipzig (1813), when Alexander, 'the Liberator of Europe' passed through Baden, he also met Jung-Stilling. The meeting was in Bruchsal, the location of the court of the Baden Margravine Amalie, the old enemy of Napoleon. Amalie was the daughter-in-law of Grand Duke Karl Friedrich of Baden, the widow of his son Crown Prince Karl Ludwig, who had died in 1801, but Czar Alexander was her son-in-law; his wife was her daughter Luise (known in Russia as Empress Elizaveta), the sister of Grand Duke Karl of Baden (1811-1818) and therefore the aunt of that Crown Prince of Baden who had been born in 1812. Furthermore, Alexander is said to have met Frau von Krüdener who was then resident in Karlsruhe 'and through her, [he encountered] the awakening movement of the quiet ones in the land, a movement which had become modish, with its chiliastic expectations and supra-confessional thoughts of chosenness'. At that time in Bruchsal, decisive changes undoubtedly occurred in Alexander's soul, which became clear after his visit to Amalie's court in Bruchsal and soon expressed themselves politically. In a certain way, a powerful change had evidently already come over Alexander in 1812, but from the same spiritual source.[275]

It is highly significant that the mystical, spiritual, strongly religious tendency indicated here found such a strong response precisely in an *East* European soul such as that of Alexander I. This harmony between spiritual impulses which had emerged in Middle Europe, and the stance of the Russian Czar, and which extended into his policies, can seem like a strongly luciferised prefiguring of what must one day arise for the healing of human development through a bond between central European I-centred spirituality (building on a further developed *Goetheanism*) and Slavic Russian soul forces. Luciferised: for we must of course be very clear that *these* Middle European religious, mystical and pietistic ideas and strivings (they often appeared to be very muddled) which had such an impact on the soul of the Russian Czar did not truly correspond to the deeper historical needs of the time and therefore could not cope with them. This spiritual stream, in which an old spirituality, an old theosophy passed away through its 'twilight' era (see above p. 112) would not have had the power to work into the social reality of that time in any future-oriented sense, even if Alexander I had not been the vacillating, indecisive character that disappointed his friends. The 'Holy Alliance', for example, was not only in a political but also in a spiritual sense a thoroughly 'reactionary' affair, far removed from what the times would really have needed.[276]

However, it is significant in connection with the distinguished figure of Jung-Stilling to be able to touch here on a network of important endeavours and religious and spiritual impulses which just at that time, in the years of distress caused by Napoleon, was actively struggling for the future of humanity and seeking to gain a place for itself within the *new* spiritual impulses that had been most starkly cast into their counter-image by Napoleon himself.[277]

It appears, moreover, highly significant that a personality such as Jung-Stilling had been invited to Baden by Karl Friedrich through the deep relationship of trust that existed between the two men and was living in Karlsruhe at exactly the time when on 29 September 1812 the Crown Prince was born from whom—as we hope to be able to show ever more clearly from many aspects of these decades—the most important impulses for the social and political life of Central Europe should have proceeded. It was as though destiny had, as it were, placed Jung-Stilling in Karlsruhe ready to 'receive' this individuality.

The Mission of Middle Europe

In order to render our observations ever more spiritually concrete, it is important that we become more comprehensively aware of the historical and spiritual situation into which this great individuality incarnated and in which and on which he could have acted or sought to act—if his destiny had not turned out as it did.

We can once again, when we take many factors together, first of all very clearly recognise that the impulse which this individuality was to bring has to be seen in the closest connection with *Middle Europe's unique mission*, rightly understood, and with the activity of the true German folk soul. Earlier, (pp. 71-75) we were able to point to traits in Kaspar Hauser which show that he was closely related to what belongs most deeply to the being of Middle Europe, namely, to the strong *'mercurial'* trait in Kaspar Hauser's being. It is important for the illumination of significant connections here that we recall that another mercurial being was also the great *Buddha*, who in Rudolf Steiner's Christology is shown as so closely linked with the *Jesus in the Gospel of St Luke*, the 'Child of Man', whose nature, we found, with all due respect, to be in a deep sense related to that of the 'Child of Europe'. On the other hand, however, is the fact that the hierarchical being whom we may call the true *Folk Spirit of the German people* had once been 'the Angel of the Buddha', i.e., the angelic being who was connected with the Buddha throughout his earthly incarnations, just as each human being is united with the angel who guides and protects him.[278] From the spiritual body of the Buddha himself there sounded at the birth of the Luke Jesus in the stall in Bethlehem those words of the great message of peace: 'May God's glory be revealed in the heights, and on earth, peace to all men of goodwill'. This motif of peace we find again connected, for a long time, and for deep inner reasons, with the true task and the true nature of the German people. We showed this—amongst much else—in more detail in Volume VIII *Social Impulses of the German Spirit in the Age of Goethe* in the chapter 'How the Goetheanists saw the German People' (p. 175f.). That whole chapter should also be mentioned in the present context. We can add further, that the motif of peace is at the same time the deepest, most intimate *Christmas* motif. We therefore understand that there must certainly be good reasons why for centuries there has been in the inner life of the German people the well-known, especially intimate relationship to Christmas. We also found the aspect of Christmas sounding in and around Kaspar Hauser; peacefulness filled his whole being.*

* Klara Hofer, who out of her spiritual *sensitivity* makes so many fine observations in her book, sensed such a connection when she wrote of Kaspar Hauser: 'There is no activity in him; there is in him as little inclination to fight for his life as there would be in the childlike Asian Buddhas—to whom his soul is so related—to engage in hand-to-hand combat.' (Op. cit., p. 47.)

In that chapter about the way in which the Goetheanists saw the German people there is discussion of the particular link between the Germans as the Mercury people of Europe,[279] between the great task of transforming the earth from Mars to Mercury, and the true *Rosicrucian spirit.*[280] And there again, deeply linked to Rosicrucianism, we always found the being of Kaspar Hauser. We see how this being stands at the centre where genuine Middle European, humanitarian forces are weaving.

'The Age of Romanticism'

The 'anti-Hauserians' have always shown a great inclination to focus on the *Age of Romanticism,*[281] in order to 'explain'—and devalue—the phenomenon and the great reputation of Kaspar Hauser as well as the intense interest in him that he arouses.

Their intention was to claim that an age like the Romantic period, which was so full of wonders and at the same time full of indulgent emotions, had a need for such remarkable occurrences and was inclined to accept everything improbable with an uncritical 'credulity'.* This is of course a very poor, though at the same time a not uninteresting example of the way in which the spirit of denial so often points indirectly but in a positive sense to something essential, which it actually does not understand at all. For certainly, we have to see the appearance of Kaspar Hauser in relation to the spiritual character of these decades. In the period of later Romanticism—and also especially after the turbulent events of the Napoleonic turmoil—many people experienced a strongly emotional urge to deepen their inner life. The individuality of whom we are speaking would most likely have been able to find a reception corresponding to his disposition and a situation in which he could work, and after this had been made impossible, the touchingly pure figure of this unfortunate youngster strongly affected people's feelings, and from this feeling of being intimately connected, in the unconscious depths of their souls there lived more empathic emotional understanding than could be present in the ideas of their superficially rational consciousness.

---

* For example, Meyer's *Grosses Konversationslexikon* [Large Conversational Encyclopaedia] (6th ed.,Vol. 8, Leipzig and Vienna, 1904, p. 886) presents a kind of variation on this theme when it 'explains' the 'strikingly lively interest' which the 'fraudster' evoked in his contemporaries in terms of 'the lack of any other occurrence of other public interest in Germany at that time'.

When we look a little into those decades from such viewpoints, our gaze can fall on some phenomena of the spiritual life, which perhaps seem outwardly to have little to do with one another, but which inwardly may be all the more connected.

It was, for example, the time in which Grimms' Fairy Tales had begun their victorious passage across Germany. In the original version of the Fairy Tales, the Preface by the Brothers Grimm in Volume One bears the date 'Cassel, 18 October 1812'. That was 19 days after the birth of the Crown Prince of Baden on 29 September. In spiritual science it is known that it was the Rosicrucians who had once given fairy tales to the people in this form of a nourishment for the soul that would connect the soul with spiritual worlds to sustain people through the ever greater darkening of soul and spirit due to modern intellectual consciousness. The reappearance of such fairy tales through the work of the Brothers Grimm was a great deed for the soul life of people in the 19th century and beyond. Rudolf Steiner once said[282] that 'the path to the spirit has to be pointed out again through great and meaningful elements in Middle European culture that are really directed towards spirituality. It was really through a higher leadership that the Brothers Grimm were there and had collected German fairy tales once again. When we bring... German fairy tales to our young people, then we are bringing them an inclination towards spirituality.'* Is it not therefore perhaps deeply grounded in spiritual realities that the story of Kaspar Hauser, as we have seen, itself bears in many respects the character of an amazing fairy tale?

In that same period of 'Romanticism' there also sounded out for the first time in the German-speaking world certain *Christmas carols* that have

---

* It also seems noteworthy that the Grimms' Fairy Tales went out into the world from *Kassel*, where Jakob and Wilhelm Grimm were living at the time (though published by a Berlin publishing house), and where, nearby, the well-known fairy storyteller (Dorothea Viehmann) of Niederzwehren was living. The Brothers Grimm owed a large proportion of their Fairy Tales to her. It was also in Kassel that some of the first publications of the Rosicrucian manifestos appeared in the early years of the 17th century (see my book *Historical Impulses of Rosicrucianism*, pp. 26-27.) There must have been an active Rosicrucian centre in the region of Kassel, in Hessen. We can also keep in mind the above-mentioned (pp. 112-116) Landgrave Karl von Hessen at whose estate in Schleswig the Comte de St Germain lived for a long while, and also finally the fact that a son of Wilhelm Grimm was the well-known Hermann Grimm who in the late 19th century was a flag-bearer for the Goethean spirit that is deeply bound to the true German character.

since become very dear to us such as '*O du fröhliche, o du selige …*' [Oh thou happy, oh thou blessed] (1816) and above all, 'Silent Night, Holy Night…' (1818) which with its timeless magic spread from Austria throughout the whole world. If one may rightly say that these carols (and also the older one '*O Tannenbaum*' in the 1824 version that is so well-known today) no longer stem from the spiritual source that older Christmas songs did in many ways, but they nevertheless certainly had a deep and beneficial effect on the feelings of people in ways that were still possible in the 19th century, above all among the German people, who felt especially close to the festival of Christmas with its figure of the child of the Gospel of Luke. It seems to correspond so very much to the soul and spirit of the decades in which the 'Child of Europe' was born and lived out his tragic years of childhood.

Those same decades were also epoch-making for the ingress of a new, highly significant spiritual stream into the cultural life of the West, and not only of this one. Rudolf Steiner compares this ingress with that of the impact of *Arabism* which broke into the, as it were, ongoing stream of world history in which the Christ Impulse was active. Western spiritual and cultural life was enormously fructified and deeply modified by this Arabist 'side stream'.[283] In Arabism a renewed *Moon* influence was at work—one only needs to think of the crescent moon in Islam. In the other side stream which was now beginning to flow into the ongoing mainstream, we have to do with an influence which, as Rudolf Steiner said,[284] we must correctly designate with the symbol of *Mercurius* and in the old manner, in which we think of the order of the planets one after the other as seen from the Earth: Moon, Mercury, Venus, Sun. There was 'nothing present' of this Mercury influence in Goethe's soul; it only appeared after Goethe. But Goethe's pupil Schopenhauer already shows it; his philosophy is permeated with 'oriental wisdom, especially in the form of Buddhism'. Mercury is regarded as the symbol of Buddhism. So after 'the time of Goethe we have the influence of Buddha' and with it, this new side stream. Certain elements from the Buddha stream now also began to enter into Occidental spiritual development, 'such as, for example, the ideas of reincarnation and karma'. This 'side wave' must flow to us 'as a renewed ancient wave' and 'bring understanding of reincarnation and karma'. Rudolf Steiner repeatedly emphasised that knowledge of reincarnation and karma has had to arise in the West in a *new* way, since Lessing.

Rudolf Steiner characterised this same process in the following words elsewhere:[285] 'What occurred during the 19th century was understood by few…, namely, that the Orient, in a very intensive way, penetrated into the culture of the West.' A whole new perspective was added to that which people had had in their souls at the beginning of the 19th century when they occupied themselves with the spiritual life: 'On paths which at first are quite inexplicable for external history, an *inner Orient* entered into the spiritual life of Europe.' It was not only that people got to know ancient Oriental writings such as Vedas and the Bhagavad Gita and through them a whole other nuance of feeling, 'but something appeared which became more and more visible along secret paths in the 19th century': Rudolf Steiner again refers to Schopenhauer here. 'In the course of the 19th century', this new element brought about 'a complete transformation, a kind of metamorphosis of all thinking and feeling' which affected the whole world. Humanity came to reach for very new questions and very new nuances of feeling and perception. As the 19th century passed over into the 20th, 'educated people everywhere on Earth had to begin, through an inner drive, to think in other ways than they had thought before'.

We feel we are not going wrong when we see the incarnation in the year 1812 of the individuality who is the subject of our reflections in connection with all that we have briefly outlined here with the help of Rudolf Steiner's indications. We have repeatedly pointed to Kaspar Hauser's deeply 'mercurial' character;* we found in him very Buddhist elements... the impulses

* When one thinks about what was said (p. 122 above) about the Mercury side stream which was not yet there in *Goethe*, but was very much there in Schopenhauer, then the relationship of both to Kaspar Hauser appears of some sympathetic interest.

Enquiries to two authorities in Weimar and Frankfurt revealed that no comments by Goethe about Kaspar Hauser are known (Hauser lived among people for only four years of Goethe's life). This does not, of course, prove that he never made any such comments, and still less that he knew nothing of the Hauser affair, which, in view of the huge sensation which the affair caused during Goethe's last years, is extremely unlikely.

However, the lack of any comment from Goethe contrasts markedly with those we know of from *Schopenhauer*:

Schopenhauer, of whom it is reported that he himself told a certain person 'a great deal about Kaspar Hauser',[286] brings, for example, in one of his philosophical essays[287] a long quote from an English work of 1834 about the eye, in which the phenomenon (discussed above, p. 53f.) was acknowledged that for Kaspar Hauser, in the first period after his release from his incarceration and before the training of his powers of judgement, the outer world appeared to him at first like a curtain covered with all kinds of colours. In another place,[288] Schopenhauer mentions in a relevant of love and compassion..., and especially the inner relationship with the specific nature of the Nathan Jesus of the Gospel of St Luke. In Rudolf Steiner's christological research, this high being [the Nathan Jesus] had once, in ancient India, overshadowed or inspired Krishna, the great central figure of the Bhagavad Gita, the 'Noble Blood', who in those decades, for example, filled the ageing Wilhelm von Humboldt with deep enthusiasm and emotion. This other feeling, how it lived also in Kaspar Hauser, how it went from him over into other people, who linked themselves to him with loving understanding...!

Napoleon's Egyptian campaign of 1798-99 can certainly be seen as a kind of outer preparation for this new, instreaming 'orientalism'. He had looked purposefully toward the East, and, as is well-known, gave a most important impetus to the blossoming of modern Egyptology. But about the individuality of Kaspar Hauser who, as we shall see more and more, many significant threads linked precisely with Napoleon, Rudolf Steiner gave the important indication that he had been involved in the founding of the highest mysteries of Egypt.[290]

And again: if the 'Angel of the Buddha' is closely related to the German people, as was discussed above (p. 119), that is, if he is (or we could say: wishes to become) the Folk Spirit of this people and who, according to Rudolf Steiner,[291] is intimately linked to Michael and in such a way that both are tasked with bringing the Christ Impulse to expression in our time—then it certainly follows that *Middle Europe* is the appropriate soil for the taking up of impulses of the kind meant here, from the new 'side stream'. One can imagine that from here, that 'inner Orient' in the corresponding metamorphosis appropriate for the times, stemming from a Rosicrucian Christian source and in harmony with it, could have become even more effective throughout *society*.[292] One can sense that the 'Child of Europe' was inwardly very close to such activity.

Finally, in looking at the contemporary background to his life and at the activity for which he was predisposed, we should take note of the powerful

---

context that nothing had convinced him of 'Kaspar Hauser's genuineness' as much as Hauser's statement that he found the so-called natural theology presented to him to be not particularly convincing (see above, p. 40) and that he showed a special veneration for the sun. It is also remarkable that Schopenhauer noted with much pleasure a comparison which a philosopher (Friedrich Dorgruth) made in 1849 between Schopenhauer's own destiny as philosopher and that of Kaspar Hauser, who had been locked away and had been denied fresh air and light. Schopenhauer thus called himself the Kaspar Hauser of German philosophy![286,289]

processes that were playing out at that time in the spiritual worlds from which that individuality had descended: the 'cosmic cultus' under the aegis of Michael from the end of the 18th century and the first half of the 19th, about which Rudolf Steiner spoke.[293]

The Break in German Development

The most incisive event in the tragic development of the destiny of Middle Europe and especially of the German people in the course of the 19th century is the *break* in this development which occurred in the period after Goethe and in which we should see the actual deeper reason for everything that we have to call the tragic *failure* of the development of Middle Europe from that point onwards. It led to German history in the 19th century suffering from a pronounced discontinuity. Its development did not correspond to what had been living in, or had been latent in, German spirituality and culture in the first decades of the century.

It became the destiny of 'Goetheanism' (in the broadest sense) to remain that 'isolated appearance' in the life of Middle Europe about which Rudolf Steiner spoke.[294] There was no continuation or further development of it in the 19th century. Rather, it was overwhelmed by a wave of materialism which broke in from the West from the 1840s onwards and grew to a flood in the 1850s.

How significantly *Herman Grimm*[295] writes first about what was alive in the German people in the time of Schiller and Goethe:

> There developed that wonderful mixture in the people, which was called the educated public, a distinguished people within the people [nation] that consisted of the best elements of the people and which remained until the end of Goethe's life the predominant element that set the tone in Germany....

And then, of Grimm's own time from the end of the 1850s to have to continue:

> ...all those who are still left over from that time speak of the breath of enthusiasm which surrounded them in their youth and they say that the present time does not understand that and that it is impossible to make it comprehend how people looked on life in those days.

From such words we feel how Goetheanism was essentially borne only by a cultivated upper layer of society. It found no reception in the broad masses of the people.[296] This doubtless has to do with the other tragic fact that

Goetheanism and German spiritual culture did not go on to bring forward corresponding impulses for spiritually informed *social ideas and praxis*; these did not become the 'art of the state' [*Staatskunst*] in a positive sense. In itself, a path would have been conceivable which could have led from the task of humanity in tune with the spirit of the age and in harmony with the task of the Germans, as conceived by their true Folk Spirit, to a new shaping of society. That such a path was not taken led to a *gulf* opening up between Goetheanism and the social and political life of Middle Europe. The spirit did not become 'political', and political life remained without ideas, unfructified by the spirit.[297]

We tried to show in Vol. VIII—'Social Impulses of the German Spirit in the Age of Goethe'—that the most important *seeds* or new impulses for social life in Middle Europe were present, especially through what we were able to write about *Schiller's*—in a spiritual sense—'politically' conceived endeavours and further, in relation to *Goethe's* 'Fairy Tale' and *Wilhelm von Humboldt's* book about the limits of the actions of the State. But all this remained only in 'seed-form'; it was not developed further.

From this viewpoint, Schiller's early death (1805) was tragically symptomatic, as was also, 14 years later in 1819, Wilhelm von Humboldt's exclusion from public life in Prussia just when the most significant political opportunities had opened up for him. [298]

The causes of the great turnaround in the times after the deaths of Hegel (1831),* Goethe (1832) and Wilhelm von Humboldt (1835) should be sought of course not in anything superficial but rather, in the depths of events. Only those powerful super-sensory impulses proceeding from the Spirits of Darkness (see p. 11 above), against which Michael's battle began in the 1840s, can account for the huge force with which the materialism of the West, where the predisposition for it existed, was developed and penetrated into Middle Europe, partly as though 'sucked in' through the vacuum that had resulted due to the turning away from true Middle European spiritual culture. At the root of this turning away evidently lay the same dark impulses.

Observers of German cultural history in the 19th century have often been struck by the very different character of the generation which had grown up after the 1830s and which now became the bearer of that 'realism' which ditched the previous strongly idealistic essential impulses. Clearly, it

---

* Here one may recall the later enveloping of Hegelianism by Marxism. See, however, Vol. VIII, pp. 282, 290.

was as though, so to speak, a thrust of very differently oriented souls had incarnated 'in good time' beforehand—souls who were suited to live out these other cultural impulses.

'Just go back ... to the 20s or before the 20s of the 19th century,' says Rudolf Steiner:[299]

> and read what was written scientifically at that time. You will see a quite different tone, there was then none of that completely abstract thinking based on the physical organs of thought [which accounted for the significant men of the mid-19th century] that came later, to say nothing of the things that a Herder, Goethe or Schiller produced. Great perspectives were still alive at that time....

This great turnaround, which above all occurred in the entire human being, was already starkly announced in people's *physiognomies*. Previously there had been many faces in which there was a breath of the ideal and of enthusiasm, testifying to the spirituality of the German soul,—but now everything passed over more into the everyday, the banal and finally into a most decided petit bourgeoisie. It was like a far-reaching exchange had taken place in the same nation, so much so, that in what finally became dominant over the course of all those decades, the earlier characteristics were almost no longer recognisable.

In this connection, what one author[300] noted is symptomatic: Graphologists have noted that from about 1850 handwriting began to change. In the handwriting of men in leading positions in society, traits common in those active in the humanities and the cultural life began to give way before the very different characteristics seen in the handwriting of industrialists and men of facts.

The historian Wilhelm Schüssler[301] writes of the same generational shift:

> The men who were now moving to the fore were different from their fathers and grandfathers. Just as men's and women's clothes were changing, and as the old, colourful and rich clothes ... were put aside in favour of grey and black menswear with long trousers, this generation... had very different experiences and therefore very different desires. It was also about a change in the social classes, an expansion of the educated classes and ultimately about the full embracing of the new technological world by the advancing bourgeoisie....

What all this amounted to was, as Rudolf Steiner characterised it, the crossing of a kind of abyss around the middle of the 19th century so that we can only make sense of the recent past before the mid-19th century with particular methods of understanding.[302]

That humanity has fallen into today's widespread misery, said Rudolf Steiner once again in 1920, is due to the fact:

> that essentially, it has actually made itself...through and through dependent on the particular mode of thinking and feeling of the people of the West. And one can say: if someone in Middle Europe today speaks, for example, about Fichte, Herder or even Goethe, then basically, when he is heard by the general public, he is in most cases much further removed from what was alive as a real spiritual impulse in Fichte, Herder or Goethe than—when he thinks and is active in Berlin or Vienna—he is from what is felt and thought in London, Paris, New York or Chicago. Gradually, things have turned out in such a way that our entire civilisation has been overwhelmed by the impulses of the world view of the peoples of the West....[303]

Could it have been otherwise?

In order not to fall into a one-sided view of all this, we have of course always to bear in mind that the ingress of materialism into the development of mankind was in itself 'necessary'. Without it, we could not have become free. It was a necessary developmental epoch.[304] Rudolf Steiner repeatedly acknowledged its achievements. He emphasised, for example, how especially at the end of the 1850s there was a whole series of achievements in the area of natural science, and in this context he even names the 'first trend-setting work of materialistic historiography', Karl Marx's book about political economy[305] (1859). The reverse side of this coin was that when the centenary of Schiller's birthday was being celebrated in Germany in the same year (1859), that year 'was at the same time in a certain sense precisely the death year of [German] Idealism'.[306]

In general, we can say that the worst was not that materialism came to the West—that was necessary. The real evil is that on the one hand, *no counterweight* that could have prepared the future of a post-materialistic age arose against materialism from the spiritual stream of humanity, and notably from the region in which such a counterweight would have been most present, namely, Middle Europe,—and on the other hand, that people then went on *clinging* to materialism,[307] when its time was actually over and the transition should have been found to something else that could replace it.

For the German people, the surrender of its most essential impulse led to a kind of gradual *abandonment of its own I.* What was approaching in that period around the middle of the 19th century was the development which later threatened the Germans and finally became ever more tragic reality, which in an important essay[308] in 1888 the young Rudolf Steiner called a threatening 'loss of self' and a 'break with the Folk Spirit'. A spiritual vacuum thus gradually developed in Middle Europe in which sinister, demonic *counter-images* were cast into the region in the place of what should actually have prevailed there, until finally, this process led to the appalling break-in of the powers of the abyss around the year 1933.

After this break from their own true folk nature, a particular trait of the Germans—which had long existed—was bound to emerge with a particular fatefulness, as the reverse side or shadow side of something that in itself is very positive, namely, the Germans' predisposition to be open to the world around them. This reverse side is the German tendency to *imitate* others. When this tendency now encountered the 'vacuum' in Middle Europe, which had risen as a result of what was described above as a break, the result could only be that inner 'alienation' of the Germans which had actually been so marked in the decades after Goethe's time.[309] It showed itself in the 19th century in two directions: the adoption from *the British* of the materialistic thinking of modern natural science and the economic life thoroughly informed by it, and also the adoption of socio-political forms and attitudes (to which also belong certain features of 'militarism'[310]) especially from *the French*. In particular, in all political (and economic) Liberalism, the effort was made to imitate *British* models. This had two consequences: the one was that Germany entered into a competitive relationship with the West instead of seeking to complement what lived in the West (and which was justified there to a considerable extent) with what Germany itself would have been called on to represent. The other consequence, which Rudolf Steiner sometimes indicated,[311] was that the French and the British later began to develop a strong antipathy towards, even a hatred of the Germans in that they saw in the German imitation of them much of their own nature reflected back at them as in a mirror; they were thus compelled to a kind of unconscious and continuous self-knowledge. (To this theme of imitation also belongs in a broader sense the contamination of the Germans by the *nationalism* of the peoples of the West.)

Certainly, the discontinuity in German development of which we have spoken here, and the resultant 'holes' and the 'vacuum' were something that had *not been desired* for the progressive development of the world by the *good* spiritual powers. Those powers would have preferred that in the decades when materialism was necessarily prevalent in the West, there would at least *also* have been compensating or counterbalancing factors in Middle Europe that could have worked to fill those 'holes'. Here our gaze is guided again to the great individuality who was hidden behind the 'Maya' of Kaspar Hauser, of whom Rudolf Steiner made the far-reaching statement which we repeated earlier (above, p. 93) that we would be living today in another, more spiritual world if that individuality had been given an opportunity. Apparently, he would have wanted and would have been able to act in the way in which we have postulated would have been necessary in accordance with the great conditions of the age. More concretely, we may imagine that he could have formed a kind of crystallising point around which could have coalesced all the German spirituality in the sense of German Idealism and Goetheanism that was still alive at that time, so as to inaugurate a movement of definite activity. Rudolf Steiner gave an indication in this direction. How this individuality, as a prince in the Southwest of Germany, would have engaged in this activity can only be meaningfully understood in terms of the furtherance of a *social* life that would have been rooted in the sources of genuine Middle European spirituality.

In the light of such perspectives, the following is of great importance. Rudolf Steiner once directly put the question, and answered it in a profound way,[312] as to why the great Middle European movement of the spirit which began in the 13th century (with Walther von der Vogelweide and others) and continued until Goetheanism 'did not bring any transformation of social life, and was not able to conceive of thoughts that would be fruitful for social life' despite 'tendencies for a threefolding of the healthy social organism which were present in people's subconsciousness from the end of the 18th century onwards' (whereby he pointed to the call for liberty, equality, and fraternity, in which these tendencies were alive[313]). His answer was that this entire stream was indeed permeated in a most beautiful way with what is called *soul*, but lacked what is called *spirit* (in the full, real sense, as anthroposophical spiritual science understands this) and that therefore people were unable to perceive the spiritual dimension of the social conditions of life.

This explanation can be understood in its whole tragic reality when one sees how in fact social life can only be adequately grasped and positively shaped through an understanding of real spiritual [*wesenhaft*] impulses and ideas which stem from the supersensory world, that is, ultimately through the process of initiation. We have repeatedly tried to show this in our works about social history. But who came from the highest levels of the ancient Mysteries? Who was deeply linked in a central sense with the progressive stream of the whole of Western culture? It was precisely the individuality with whom we are here concerned [i.e., Kaspar Hauser] and it arose in the most inward region of those sources of objective spiritual experience. It is from those sources, from our time onwards, that a true renewal of social life must flow.

We have clearly seen in the phenomenon of 'Kaspar Hauser' that it was precisely rhythmic impulses from the man of the heart—eminently *social* forces such as compassion and love—which were alive in this individuality. Had they been able to unite themselves with what lived in this individuality as great, deeply rooted impulses which stemmed ultimately from the principle of initiation and had been able to develop appropriately and unhindered, a power that could have renewed social life would have proceeded from them. We saw earlier (p. 68f.) that here we have to do pre-eminently with the stream of the 'shepherds', which seeks to unite with the stream of the 'kings'.

What would such impulses, flowing in a great, wholesome and healing manner, have meant for the dawning age of industrialism? Instead of these impulses, from the 'indolence of the heart' of the bourgeoisie, especially of the bourgeois entrepreneurial class, the modern proletariat was being formed at that time and suffering its well-known tragic destiny in inhuman factories—all those destinies which provided the nourishing grounds for the emergence of *Marxism* with its impulses of hatred, embittered class conflict, its materialistic form of thinking and acting—also produced by Middle Europeans—with the monstrous echo it found all round the world and the equally monstrous effects it had wherever it went!

When we think of the deeply 'mercurial' being of this individuality that was so averse to all the ancient 'martial' qualities and how it appeared to us in a rudimentary, childlike stage in the artificially retarded form of 'Kaspar Hauser', we can sense a tremendous perspective of potential when we think of how from such essential forces a Middle European impulse could have rayed out into the world. Instead, the distorted image of this was given the name 'the Child of Europe'. With such potential that can be felt and more than merely felt—that was present and wished for, one can also think of what *Hölderlin* had once imagined, when those words formed within him as though from a profound intimation, the tragedy of which, in its utter non-fulfilment, can move us so deeply:

> *Germania, wo du Priesterin bist*
> *Und wehrlos Rat gibst rings*
> *Den Königen und den Völkern.*[314]

> Germania, when you are a priestess
> And unarmed, giving counsel to all
> The kings and peoples.

In 1842, the year of the great crisis, when the 'Spirits of Darkness' became powerful on Earth (because they had been cast down out of the spiritual world by the valiant Archangel Michael,[315] he who was born on Michaelmas Day in 1812 would have been 30 years old. When the 1848 Revolution broke out, he would have been 35....

I believe that in view of all these perspectives, we should consider the following words of Rudolf Steiner from 1918:

> The prejudice that what comes later [in history] always develops, or must develop, as smoothly as possible from what comes earlier one can leave to people who have less sense for reality than those who think anthroposophically. ... In reality, what occurs is that the course of events is like a pair of scales in constant movement, where first one beam of the scales sinks and then the other. And therefore, one can characterise the time since the beginning of the 1840s as follows: *There could have been a possibility, if from the year 1840 until 1914*—a period divided in two by 1879 [i.e., the year in which the new Age of Michael began] if from then on, the attempt had been made *in an appropriate manner to prepare that spiritualisation of humanity* which is sought by the Archangel Michael; if the attempt had been made to a greater extent to bring spiritual concepts, spiritual ideas to mankind.* When such a thing is *not done*

---

* Rudolf Steiner's comments in his lecture of 23 September 1916 in Dornach are an important addition here:

'For those... who know how human history advances, it is clear that actually, from the middle of the 19th century onwards, the human race was rife gradually to develop other capacities' (than mere intellect). From the middle of the 19th century onwards, there arose 'through a kind of intimate process a certain yearning to know something of the spiritual worlds.' (The peculiar thing, evidently, was that this yearning manifested itself in a form which was itself 'suited to the materialistic attitudes of the time': namely, in the form of spiritualism.)

> by the free human will—since in the modern age humanity must be free to act—then the scales sink down to the other side. Then what could have been achieved on spiritual paths is discharged through *blood*.[316]

We can add to this what Rudolf Steiner said in the same year 1918 on 25 October, thus shortly before the collapse of Middle Europe in November 1918:

> That was an important point in time, those years of the forties! For the powers that impel world evolution had foreseen a kind of significant crisis for that time. This crisis expressed itself in outer social life essentially in that the so-called liberal ideas of the modern age developed precisely in these years. In the forties it seemed as though the impulse of the Age of Consciousness could also break through into the outer political world in the form of political views....[317]

The 1840s and the Impulse of Liberalism

The years of the 1840s and Liberalism were further characterised by Rudolf Steiner, and for the sake of the larger contexts in which our considerations have to be integrated, his comments have to be repeated at least briefly:

Proletarian consciousness was not yet there in the 1840s. Political civilisation was essentially borne by the *bourgeoisie*. The peculiarity of the ideas that could have become political in the 1840s was their 'very intense abstraction'. But this abstraction 'was not harmful, for in the age of the Consciousness Soul, humanity has had to pass through abstraction. Humanity's leading ideas had to be grasped through such abstraction.' Until the end of the 1870s, humanity had time to find itself in the reality of the ideas of the 1840s and to actualise these ideas. It is extraordinarily important to comprehend these decades. In them liberal ideas in an abstract form began to flow into human evolution. When in the 1840s some outstanding people (there were some in the civilised world) in the middle class heard others speaking about what needed to happen in all areas of human life, 'something like an approaching Peoples' Spring' occurred in the forties and on into the beginning of the fifties. But the opportunity was missed. By the end of the 1870s, the middle classes had not grasped the liberal ideas. They *slept through* this period. (People should realize that, Steiner goes on, in order to 'wake up' in the right sense in the present.)

> When the bourgeosie had not grasped the impulse of liberal ideas in politics by the time of the appearance of the Archangel Michael as the Time Spirit

> at the end of the 1870s, then it showed that those powers which I have also characterised [Rudolf Steiner here alludes to the beings he has characterised as the 'Spirits of Darkness'—see above, p. 11, 126] first spread darkness over those ideas. How differently people thought then about the shaping of political life from what had come about by the end of the 19th century over the whole civilised world! There is no greater contrast....*

So, 'the most productive and fruitful period of time', from the forties until the end of the seventies, was for the bourgeoisie a time when they were in 'a kind of state of sleep.... Later, it was, as it were, too late, for later, nothing more was to be achieved on the path on which it could have been achieved in the period mentioned. Later, something could be achieved only by a full awakening in spiritual scientific experience.'[318]

Through such indications we gain an insight into the deeper developmental dynamics of the 19th century: into what could have been possible, 'desired' and was actually latent but was 'slept through' and not achieved, and as a result of which, development in the later course of the 19th and 20th centuries took a very different path that was most harmful to humanity—one that served the interests of the retarding cosmic powers. Apparently, much should have happened, and precisely from Middle Europe, which could have prepared in a positive way for the new Michael Age beginning in 1879. Does it not seem evident that the activity of that great individuality [Kaspar Hauser] was (apparently therefore) excluded who could and should have contributed in a decisive way to precisely such a positive course of events? I believe that, taking everything together, we can see things in the following way: Liberalism, which for profound reasons appeared with great human enthusiasm but was conceived at first only with the power of abstract thinking, would have needed just that spiritualisation [through Kaspar Hauser] to complement, deepen and facilitate the transition into a way of life that was more humane and full of vitality. To Liberalism, which corresponded to

* We find the consequences of the activities of the 'Spirits of Darkness' characterised elsewhere in an indication as to 'how it must look in an age which does not want to apply itself to understand the idea of freedom to the fullest extent. The second half of the 19th century, and the early 20th century until our own time—this epoch set itself the task to dull down more and more the idea of freedom in all areas of life and actually to exclude it from practical life. People did not want to understand freedom, it was not wanted....' (lecture by Rudolf Steiner, 17 December 1917, Dornach).

and sprang from the impulses of the 'kings', the thinking of the 'kingly heads'—which leads to the grasping of freedom—should have streamed together with, united itself with that Liberalism, complementing it, something from the impulses of equality and brotherhood for the sake of human social life—something from the stream of the 'shepherds', from the warmth of the 'poor shepherds' hearts'. But we found a being deeply united with *this* element in the unfortunate foundling who was yet, in the form he appeared in the world, actually a deeply hidden, great individuality. But this being was excluded. Instead of genuinely human social impulses arose the shadow power of Marxism, and likewise, instead of a genuine spiritualisation, arose its counter-image in Spiritualism. Thus, even in Middle Europe, no development occurred that could have created the balance and the counterweight to the materialistic stream throughout the world and that could have led the Gabriel Age which was coming to an end over into the approaching Age of Michael, and therefore also to the social forms appropriate to the new age.

Baden, Liberalism and the French Element

The Southwest of Germany, with its strong individualism, was a region which was especially favourable for progressive impulses, both 'liberal' and 'democratic'. Various nuances have developed there. In recent times, people said, for example, that the people of Baden were more liberal, the Württembergers more democratic. In Baden Liberalism appeared deeply connected to the character of the people. We find much evidence of this, for example, in Karl Friedrich (see above, p. 112f.), the first Grand Duke of Baden, who was so important for the state. A very great role in Baden's development towards Liberalism was especially played by its great western neighbour France, from where the impulses for freedom and democracy from the French Revolution were taken up very strongly in Baden in connection with the German policy of the Revolution's 'executor', Napoleon.

That Napoleon destroyed much in Germany was only the well-known negative side. 'The positive will of history' was expressed by a Baden historian[319] in his own way, albeit not so profoundly but nevertheless perceptively, when he wrote that that positive will:

> aimed at creating a German democracy from a merging of French will with German methods. Baden was the natural starting point for the march of the new ideas: the roots of democratic attitudes in the 19th and 20th centuries in Baden and elsewhere in southern Germany lie here. It was a reflection of that

> pioneering time when Baden became the first German state to give itself a constitution with popular representation,* when it later became a kernel of the German Revolution of 1848, when in the liberal period it was given the name 'Model country', when from 1918 to 1933 in its Weimar form it preserved its stability in contrast to all the other German states. Baden never went along wholeheartedly with the dangerous development of Prussian Germany: it was as if this grounding by Napoleon somehow inwardly protected Baden against a shift in its popular democratic, Alemannic-Frankish nature that was inclined to the West.

Symptomatic of this French impact is, for example, the significant figure of *Karl von Rotteck* (1775-1840), even in his outer physiognomy: he was the son of a German father and a French mother and was strongly influenced by the French Revolution. He became one of the most important and most respected leaders of Baden's Liberalism, a Baden campaigner for freedom. He was a cultural force in his time and had the greatest influence on his contemporaries; it was mainly through him that liberal ideas were brought to the educated middle class (in Germany). Rotteck also became known as a historian. (Rudolf Steiner often referred to his *Allgemeine Weltgeschichte* [General History of the World]. Representative of southern and western German Liberalism was his *State Lexikon,* which he published with another significant Baden Liberal, the previously mentioned important politician of the Frankfurt National Assembly in 1848, *Karl Theodor Welcker.* In addition, Welcker—characteristically, we may say—played a not insignificant role in Kaspar Hauser research in that he published materials which served to support Kaspar Hauser's descent from the princely house of Baden (on this, see also p. 98 above).

Something that bore the greatest potential, and which could have followed from a productive connection between the Germans and the French, between the tasks of the German and French peoples in the sense of truly future-oriented impulses and indeed could and should, in a profound sense, have emerged from Baden, appeared in the person who concealed himself or else was concealed under the name 'Kaspar Hauser' but was unable to become effective.

---

* In 1818, at the instigation of Baron von Stein (see Haebler op. cit., p. 251). Bavaria had adopted a Basic Law [*Grundgesetz*] (Constitutional Charter) a few months earlier, but the Baden Constitution was, one is often assured, praised as the most excellent and liberal constitution in Germany.

Karl von Baden and Stéphanie Beauharnais

Born on 29 September 1812 as the heir apparent to the throne of Baden (see above pp. 97-101), he was (see above p. 111) the eldest son of Karl, the second Grand Duke of Baden—who was reigning at the time (1811-1818) and who was the grandson of Karl Friedrich—and his French wife Stéphanie de Beauharnais (1789-1860). Stéphanie was a (distant) niece of the French General Alexandre de Beauharnais, who was guillotined in 1794 in the French Revolution and whose widow Josephine later married Napoleon in her second marriage. Stéphanie was also a niece by marriage of the Empress Josephine.[320]

The marriage between Karl and Stéphanie was arranged by none other than Napoleon himself, who wanted it to bind Baden more closely to France. In order to make Stéphanie, who was only a simple noblewoman, eligible for marriage with a member of a princely family, Napoleon adopted Stéphanie, who from then on bore the name 'Stéphanie Napoleon' and became a 'daughter of France', an imperial princess with the title 'Imperial Highness'. The wedding between Karl and Stéphanie took place under glittering pomp and circumstance in Paris on 8 April 1806.[321]*

The course of this marriage[322] was one of the most bizarre affairs known to history. For a long time, Stéphanie stubbornly refused to allow her husband his conjugal rights. She must have harboured a deep aversion to him. She also had good reason to complain about his extremely undignified lifestyle. The marriage remained unconsummated for years. Napoleon himself, who on account of his French-Baden policy, required descendants from the marriage, saw himself obliged to intervene forcefully. But only in the summer of 1810, and apparently it was a surprise, did the young couple become close and in June 1811 the first child of the marriage was born, a Princess Luise, whose godfather was Napoleon. The second child was then the heir apparent who was born on 29 September. Three other children followed.

We do not regard it as our task to describe the story of the unusual marriage between Karl and Stéphanie in detail or to analyse it psychologically or even to go into the dangerous consequences of the years of its non-consummation for the state of Baden,[323] and even less to occupy ourselves with

---

* Understandably, many (e.g. Klara Hofer op. cit., p. 70) held Stéphanie to be Napoleon's natural daughter. Hans Wohlbold too, in his essay 'Kaspar Hauser' (op. cit. p. 159), allowed himself to see this perspective as a possibility. But all concrete points of support for Napoleon's paternity of Stéphanie appear to be lacking, and many known facts contradict it.

the details of Karl's shameful and scandalous lifestyle which, although they were not so very bad in themselves nevertheless prematurely weakened him and eventually led to his ruin.

When, however, we take more of a bird's-eye view and look at the larger context in which the marriage went on, two things appear to us as very significant.

The first is that a particularly bright light would be cast on the peculiar and mysterious story of the years of unhappy relations in the 'marriage' between Karl and Stéphanie were one to assume that there could have been influences—of whatever kind, from whatever sphere they may have worked and however the methods of their activity or 'intervention' may have been—which had a conscious interest that no descendants would result from the marriage between Karl and Stéphanie. Certainly, this 'hypothesis' from a more external kind of observation must seem less illuminating in a conventional sense, and perhaps even arbitrarily conceived. But in the whole, many-sided and mysterious complex of factors around 'Kaspar Hauser', we have to realise that what may seem unusual in the conventional sense, is actually the principle of the whole phenomenon.

The other thing is the corrupt nature of Karl. In the Kaspar Hauser literature this shameful fact is always said to have resulted from Karl having been systematically and deliberately ruined.[324] His mother, the ambitious Margravine Amalie is supposed to 'have encouraged rather than opposed the heir apparent's first adventures'—since corrupted young people are more easily influenced.[325] Much is also traced back to the influence of the immoral Margrave Ludwig (Karl's uncle and later successor as Grand Duke). We therefore find Karl described as having fallen into evil ways; he was known for his indolence, indifference, lack of interest in governing etc.[326] K. A. Ense von Varnhagen[327] who, as Prussian Legation Councillor, experienced Karl at the Baden court, wrote of him that he had a good heart, and was a man of fairness etc., but also thought he had to place him among the worst of the reigning princes [in Germany] and among the most incapable. Karl succumbed early on to debauchery. He himself was firmly convinced that he had been poisoned when he had attended the Congress of Vienna (and certain circumstances do indeed point in this direction) just as his sons' lives had been taken from them (the eldest, the heir apparent, born in 1812 and his brother Alexander, who was born in 1816 but soon died in 1817).[328] Karl died in 1818, aged only 32. His eldest son would then have been a child of six years old, or rather, he *was* the six-year-old Kaspar Hauser.

Is Karl's ruination and destiny a part of the story of Kaspar Hauser?

Napoleon's Adopted Grandson and His Mother

When the heir apparent was born to the grand ducal couple on 29 September 1812, he was also the adopted *grandson of Napoleon*, entitled by birth to rule the state of Baden, which had become what it then was because of Napoleon. But Napoleon's star at that time had already begun its marked descent.

The Emperor was then engaged in his campaign in Russia, which turned out so unfortunately for him; 29 September fell between the famous burning of Moscow (15-20 September) and the beginning of the retreat of the '*Grande Armée*' from Russia (19 October 1812). On 2 October an envoy from the court of Baden left Karlsruhe for the East in order to inform the Emperor personally of the birth of the heir to the throne of Baden, his adopted grandson. Accompanying him, like a sinister presence foreshadowing events that would soon take place was that Hennenhofer,[329] who (see above, p. 99) was later held by very many in Baden to have been the murderer of Kaspar Hauser or at least to have been very involved in the murder. (Decades after Hennenhofer's death, new inscriptions by an unknown hand kept appearing on his gravestone in Freiburg-im-Breisgau, branding him as the murderer of Kaspar Hauser.)

Now the remarkable thing is that when Kaspar Hauser had later appeared in Nuremberg, some people, as we have heard (see above, p. 72) believed him to be a *son of Napoleon*;[330] some thought they detected a physical resemblance between him and the Emperor. But such people at that time did not likely assume that Grand Duchess Stéphanie was Kaspar Hauser's mother, and therefore also were probably very far from accusing her from having had [sexual] relations with her adoptive father Napoleon.

This last assertion we find in an obscure text (that every scientific mind would regard as a mockery[331]) published in 1953, which sought to claim that Kaspar Hauser was a son of Napoleon and Stéphanie, without being able to present any evidence for this thesis or even to render it plausible.[332]

In Stéphanie's life, that summer of 1810, in which she finally reconciled with Karl after four years of marriage, seems to have been a very significant time in her development. Whereas she was previously described as endearing but rather superficial, now emerged[333] 'all those good and fine qualities which had been slumbering within her'; she became a loving and caring wife to her husband and soon a good mother to her children. One has the impression that at this time—Stéphanie, born on 28 August 1789, became 21 in the summer of 1810—the great soul which had prepared its incarnation from the spiritual world and which had sought for profound reasons to be born to these particular parents, by succeeding in its incarnation after all the years of difficulties between Karl and Stéphanie, achieved something like a victory over the opposing powers which were evidently present and which had seemed, as it were, set on thwarting the possibility of the incarnation and took every opportunity to obstruct it .... The phenomenon of Kaspar Hauser is especially little suited to being understood only through physical relationships and the motives of the people who live in the physical world.

Of how Stéphanie had now become after 1810, Varnhagen von Ense[334] writes from his time in Karlsruhe about 'the depth of her thinking', 'the purity of her soul', 'her judgements of literature were surprisingly assured and effortless...; she comprehended worldly affairs with acuity and a serene clarity.... When one returned from this peaceful visit (of Stéphanie to Scheibenhard) that had been enlivened by spirit and sense, to Karlsruhe, it was as though one were transferred from pure uplifting mountain air to the stagnant vapours of oppressive lower regions.'

Varnhagen's wife, the famous Rachel Varnhagen, also praised Stéphanie highly. 'The one metaphysical mind,' she said,[335] 'which I ever got to know among women was that of Grand Duchess Stéphanie von Baden. Open and capable of thinking under any circumstances; spontaneously engaged in every conversation, not always, due to outer disturbances, engaged in the highest, most serene regions of the mind, but ready to apply herself there at any moment.'

In such ways, the 'daughter of France' was a noble representative of her people.

Napoleon was the decisive experience in her life, the great destiny of her existence, as one historian accurately wrote; she herself calls him the 'hero of my youthful dreams'.[336] She was obviously someone who belonged very strongly to his circle of destiny.

She brought her personal destiny into a prototypically effective position between France and Germany, 'between a passionate love for her native land and an earnest sense of duty towards her second homeland'. Later, 'in her advanced age, she felt herself two-sided and called on to bring France and Germany into a more mutually trusting relationship and to build new bridges between the two peoples'.[337]

By such outer and inner facts is revealed something of the mission which her eldest son, who was later called 'the Child of Europe', would have taken on.

Stéphanie died in 1860 and so was spared from having to live through the tragic development of relations between Germany and France that led to the Franco-German War of 1870/71, which would have been for her a terrible disappointment and a dreadful blow.

It was noteworthy again how one of her grandsons was involved in the events leading up to this war: Crown Prince Leopold von Hohenzollern-Sigmaringen, the son of her daughter Josephine (1813-1900) from her marriage to Prince Karl Anton von Hohenzollern-Sigmaringen. Crown Prince Leopold was the Hohenzollern candidate for the Spanish throne. His candidacy, which was advocated by Bismarck, played a significant role on the eve of the Franco-German War, as is well-known. It was later renounced by Karl Anton in the name of his son.

Even the *name* which the destiny of Napoleon's adopted daughter and Kaspar Hauser's mother bore can be transparent to one who has a sense for such things. The family name *Beauharnais*, 'beautiful armour' seems to point to the 'martial' life in which Napoleon figured so powerfully and which was supposed to be led over and transformed into something new. But 'Stéphanie' reminds us, as we noted earlier (p. 110) of St Stephen, the first Christian martyr.

The fact that the day of her eldest son's birth—that Michaelmas Day in 1812—fell on a *Tuesday*, the Mars Day of the week, is also telling: to the old sense of Mars her son stood essentially opposed. There lived in him, as we saw earlier (p. 71) something 'mercurial' that seemed called to heal and transform the old martial spirit.

Kaspar Hauser and Napoleon

It is precisely from this trait in his nature that light is cast with such astonishing clarity on his destiny relationship to his martial opposite, *Napoleon*. If he had become effective, he would, as we have already indicated (p. 72) and will find increasingly borne out, have become the bearer of a mercurial impulse that would have been the spiritual balance to Napoleonism, i.e., a healing impulse which could work against the destructive, untransformed but outworn martial spirit that worked through Napoleon with a fateful effectiveness to retard development in Europe in many ways.

But that is not by any means the deepest aspect of his inner relationship to Napoleon. One can approach this deeper aspect when one takes into consideration what Rudolf Steiner said about Napoleon's 'actual' original mission and what we brought in some detail in our Vol. VII, p. 329f., within a broader historical context. Here we can only briefly recapitulate it. In his pre-birth existence Napoleon had taken up a particular impulse when he was passing through the Mars sphere after the beginning of the 17th century, that is, at the time when in the declining world of Mars a decisive transformation had begun through a spiritual deed performed by Buddha, who was working on in the spiritual world; it was a deed that had for Mars a significance similar to that of the Mystery of Golgotha on Earth.[338] Only in view of the power of these—mercurial—forces of transformation can we understand the task which Napoleon, who was approaching his period of activity on Earth, was given. This 'task' was that in his coming incarnation he was to make an essential contribution to the *peaceful* unification of Europe out of the renewed, spiritualised forces of Mars.

In the moment of his incarnation, however, Napoleon had *forgotten* this 'task'. Nevertheless, it worked on in him in a dull, instinctive way and tragically caused him to fall back into the old methods of Mars. It therefore became his endeavour to unify Europe by warlike, military means of coercion....

But let us assume—in the sense of that 'history that did not come about'—that Napoleon had *not* forgotten his mission but had worked at it in the true sense in which it had been intended, then he would have brought about a unification of Europe through *spiritual* impulses. He, who himself represented something more all-embracing than just France, would have placed the special politically formative and socially visionary capacities and forces that live in French culture in the service of a great future-oriented mission that was appropriate to the times, and thus he would have prepared the way for the Age of Michael and with it, the form of social impact suitable for that Age (i.e., the Threefolding of the social organism). We can perhaps say that Napoleon would have become a real '*Father of Europe*'. With *this* kind of activity by Napoleon, the great individuality who incarnated in 1812 as the Crown Prince of Baden, and who was so close in destiny to Napoleon, would have been able to *connect* and work together within the most complete harmony, and augment out of the power of the true Middle European spirit, out of the power especially of the German *spiritual life*. Then a strong spiritual content would have been added to the more political formative element and the whole thing would have taken a turn towards what is genuinely social, in the sense of a transition to the approaching age, which was to begin in 1879. But Napoleon 'forgot'. He did not become a true 'Father of Europe' but rather, the multi-faceted inaugurator of the opposite or the counter-image of what had been his true 'mission', an inaugurator, namely, of materialism, militarism, nationalism, and a mighty promoter of the unitary state in the functional sense (see our Vol.VII for more on this). The Crown Prince of Baden was shut out; he was made into 'Kaspar Hauser', he became the '*Child of Europe*' in that tragic and touching sense in which we have come to know him.*

The 'Child of Europe' came from the Rosicrucian stream. But it was the great figure of Christian Rosenkreutz himself who inaugurated the transformative mission of Buddha.[339]

There were, as can be understood from what we brought forward in our Vol.VII, powers who were well acquainted with the task that Napoleon had 'forgotten'. Since their own intentions were radically opposed to that task, they sought in the course of time to prevent Napoleon from remembering anything of what he had forgotten, and to this end, operations were conducted on a grand scale. After the fall of Napoleon, they must have feared that such a remembering could always come upon him (or perhaps now more than ever?). 'Care was then taken to isolate Napoleon permanently.' That is the background to the way in which he was kept captive on St Helena. Much that is instructive here about this captivity and its history can be found in the book *Sainte-Hélène* (2 vols., 1935) by the French historian Octave Aubry. Especially interesting in this context is how Napoleon in his conversations on St Helena expressed certain political thoughts, for example, about a European system he had wanted to found, about which he said that it had been on his mind during the years of his political activity.[340] During his activity in those years there is little of such plans or intentions

* Something of Napoleon's real task seems to have been *sensed* by some personalities at the time as well as later. That may well have been the case with Goethe, for example (see Vol. VII, p. 334). Some others imagined something similar, thinking of a possible collaboration of Napoleon and Goethe, after the memorable meeting between the two in 1808 in Erfurt. The composer Richard Strauss also seems to have been another such person; it is said of him how shortly before his death (1949) he had said in a conversation: 'Think of it, 140 years ago Goethe and Napoleon shook hands in Erfurt! What a development that would have been: Napoleon as the conqueror of a united Europe and Goethe his first Minister of Culture—and the others there, Friedrich Wilhelm [of Prussia], Alexander [Czar of Russia], Franz [Emperor of Austria] could have quietly disappeared, the world would have been spared a great deal' (*Stuttgarter Zeitung* newspaper No. 81, 8.4.1953 'The Departure of Richard Strauss'). Here something was felt that could have become reality, even if things had gone differently, only if Napoleon had not 'forgotten'. The meeting in Erfurt was therefore an encounter between two *alien* worlds.

to be found, so those statements have often been dismissed as mere lies, hypocritical phrases and the like. But in some of them that very 'forgotten mission' actually seems to sound forth again strongly, albeit mixed with illusionary notions.

Aubry[341] characterises the statements as follows: Napoleon puts himself in them, in the way he imagines himself.

> In front of the people who he knows are almost all writing books about what he is saying, he brews the theory of his reign and unites his deeds and ideas in a doctrine which is certainly capricious but which serves to present something which has in it inner conviction, simplicity and greatness. He is like a sower who sows around himself the elements of his story—the story that he wants written, the story that could put his son on the throne.... And this mythos is a thousand times finer, more resounding, more effective than his life was able to be. From what he dreamed and from what he regretted not having accomplished, he shapes his great message for the world.... He casts himself as the apostle of a policy of reconciliation and liberation....

From this 'mythos' a legend was later born which his nephew, Louis Napoleon, wrote in 1839, namely, the 'Napoleonic Ideas', which helped Louis Napoleon on his way to the throne and to the re-establishment of the Empire.[342]

In the chapter, for example, about the goal at which the Emperor had aimed: 'When the destiny of arms had made Napoleon the master of most of the Continent, he wanted to put his conquests to serve the creation of a European Confederation.' 'The Emperor's policy was to found a solid European Association in that he wanted to build up his system on whole nationalities and on satisfied general interests.'[343] One sees in addition how here in the phrase 'whole nationalities' already something of the later Woodrow Wilson programme of the 20th century lights up, or 'is fore*shadowed*': unity (here that of Europe; in the case of Wilson, that of the world) built up on its opposite: nations organised as political bodies. Here it becomes clear how the unity of Europe that was Napoleon's original spiritual mission is turned into its opposite, which *appears* (as 'counter-image') to be similar to it.

Napoleon's Son

Napoleon's son, the Duke of Reichstadt (who was earlier made 'King of Rome' and who was for the later Bonapartists 'Napoleon II') from his marriage with Marie Luise, the daughter of the Austrian Emperor was also—as was discussed in our volume VII—an object of concern and precaution for the opponents of a European formation which could have corresponded to his father's 'forgotten' mission. They therefore did not neglect to 'ensure that even the slightest *possibility* that the Duke of Reichstadt might *eventually* revive his father's original task remained excluded by keeping him captive [in a gilded cage] in (Habsburg) Vienna'.[344] This again is the deeply significant background to the special treatment which his son received after Napoleon's fall. The story of this unfortunate child and youngster is also described in detail by Octave Aubry and in a way that speaks to the hearts of his readers.[345] The background to what he writes becomes transparent in many places.

He describes how Napoleon's son, for whom his father had a boundless love, was brought up in Vienna in such a way that every memory of his short life in France would be erased, how the effort was made 'gradually, to remove from him his true, original soul and to replace it with another which would be dedicated entirely to the traditions of Austria', and how, for example, he was not allowed to receive anything of the legacies determined for him by his father. Finally, thanks to Metternich's 'educational' methods, 'the spirit of the Napoleonid was duped and caught in a web of custom and habit' (though evidently, as Aubry shows, not with lasting success). 'Through his mere existence, the Duke of Reichstadt threatened the peace of the Europe of the *ancien regime,* which therefore prevented him from having a life.' '[Friedrich von] Gentz said later: "One had to have attended a Ministerial Council in order to understand the extent to which the Ministers of the Empire were troubled by the existence and the future of the Duke of Reichstadt."'

Sentences such as the following especially make one's ears prick up:

> Metternich was far from wanting to influence the Duke's mind through sympathy or persuasion. He could not abide the Duke's gaze or the sound of his voice. When the Duke celebrated his eighteenth birthday, he [Metternich] spoke a few words of congratulation to him at a court banquet but then immediately left his side with a particular haste. Afterwards, he seemed to those who spoke with him unusually distracted, and as soon as he could take his leave, he departed from the palace without attracting attention.

Of his father, whom he held in the highest regard, the Duke of Reichstadt said things in which something of Napoleon's 'forgotten' task actually seemed to sound:

> No one understood my father. It is a wretched lie to ascribe to his actions no other motive than ambition; his whole life and work was governed by a great, wholesome plan for Europe....

He also said:

> the Emperor, in dying, had forbidden him from taking revenge. But there at least remained for him the duty to restore his reputation and, if it would be possible one day, to take up again his work for European regeneration, that he had not been able to bring to a conclusion. Sooner or later, he believed, France would call him back ....

But the hopelessness of his situation caused him to waste away. People spoke of a drive to self-destruction, which gradually possessed him. In his final severe illness—he died aged 21 of tuberculosis—he faced death with great courage and—an unspeakable bitterness. His last words have become famous: 'I have to give up this useless and inglorious life so young! My birth and my death have been my entire history....'[346]

How much these final words of Napoleon's unhappy son remind one of the destiny of that unfortunate one, Kaspar Hauser, Napoleon's adopted grandson! Some people felt this and noted especially strongly the remarkable similarities in the destinies of the two young men, despite the—even polar—differences that *also* existed between them. It is as though everything together makes visible the secret bond that linked both of them and that ultimately we will have to look into what played itself out around Napoleon, both in his 'forgetting' and also in his historical reality.[347]

Both young men were born from Franco-German marriages. Kaspar Hauser had a German father and a French mother; the Duke of Reichstadt a French father and an Austrian mother. The Duke was born in 1811 and died in 1832; Kaspar was born in 1812 and died in 1833. Both, notably, were a little over 21 years old (the Duke of Reichstadt 21 years and 4 months. 2 days; Kaspar Hauser 21 years, 2 months and 19 days). The many years of captivity for Kaspar Hauser which were of central significance in his life had their counterpart in the life of the Duke of Reichstadt in his being kept for the rest of his life at the palace of Schönbrunn in Vienna after the fall of Napoleon. Aubry writes strikingly how Metternich 'made a prison for him' in Austria, which was only supposed to have been a land of refuge for him, and characterises his existence at Schönbrunn as 'his moral prison'.[348]

The similarities go further, however, into what appear to be quite external things. What we heard earlier about Kaspar Hauser's special, loving relationship to horses and his excellent riding skills we also find in the Duke of Reichstadt: 'For horses he had a really rapturous fondness; from a very young age he sat flawlessly on the saddle.' He 'was an excellent rider and mastered the most difficult horses,' writes Aubry.[349]

In the development of their intelligence, there was obviously the greatest polarity between them: whereas Kaspar Hauser was artificially held back at the level of a small child, the Duke of Reichstadt's intelligence was highly developed; he had a strong and free spirit, far beyond his years, and was extremely articulate in his conversation, which was full of ideas.[350] While we saw the greatest aversion in Kaspar Hauser to all that was 'Mars-like', Napoleon's son showed by contrast an instinctive joy in all things military: 'everything of a military nature pleased him'; everything that had to do with war 'drew him irresistibly'.[351]

A Threefold Europe

With all this in mind, it is of great importance to heed what Rudolf Steiner once said in a lecture in 1920[352] about 'a *European threefolding* which exists *between Middle and West Europe*. This does not have to do, as is otherwise so often the case[353] with the threefold relationship in the most wide-ranging sense between East, Middle and West, but with the special character and tasks of three European peoples: the *French*, the *Germans* and the *British*. The Germans have a disposition for the life of the spirit, the French for the life of law, politics and the State (which the Germans greatly lack),* the British for the life of the economy.† Rudolf Steiner once said that for them to work together internationally, social threefolding would have to be extended to all three cultures. Then the talents of one culture could pass over to the others. 'That is the historical impetus.' He added: 'The history especially of the 19th century should actually be studied in this way.' 'The history of the 19th century', he says earlier, would only result from going into the significant difference between Middle Europe and western Europe.

* 'The most important thing in the spread of the French element,' said Rudolf Steiner in his lecture of 17 January 1917 in Dornach 'is not the conquests but the permeation of the world with a political spirit, with political and diplomatic thinking and feeling.'

† '*The British folk soul* is especially called—one-sidedly called—to unfold and develop the Consciousness Soul; and one can scarcely imagine, when one goes into all the details of it, that anything could have been more intentionally carried out than the guiding of the British folk soul to this material task in life. This was fully foreordained in the development of humanity.' (Rudolf Steiner, in a lecture of 17 January 1915 in Berlin)

This book began (p. 11) with the statement by Rudolf Steiner that the true history of the 19th century has yet to be written. Here we have a significant indication of an important complex that would enable such a true history to be written. The history of the 19th century therefore appears as the history of what happened or did not happen—what was 'striven for', as it were, by European development—in relation to this necessary 'threefold' life together and the collaboration of the three above-mentioned European peoples, but was in reality counteracted.

Very much in line with such a working together and a safeguarding of the peoples of Europe would have been what we meant above (p. 142), in relation to Napoleon, about a collaboration of the political formative element of French culture and the spiritual (or spiritual and social!) element of Middle Europe.* With this, as the third element, the economic mission of the British would have been integrated, which was foreordained to extend over the whole world as a service to the world, as it were. One can sense profoundly how such a truly contemporary and productive harmonious working together of the peoples and of the areas of social life in Europe could have prepared the beginning of the Age of Michael in 1879 appropriately and could then, by bringing healing here, have streamed out into the larger global context. In just such a shaping of events, those impulses which had sought to proceed from the great spiritual individuality we have been concerned with would have taken the greatest conceivable share. Here, pre-eminently, would have been his sphere of activity.

But Napoleon 'forgot'. His forgetting followed the failed development of the French Revolution, the inheritor of which he became. His forgetting and this failed development belong closely together; they created those distorted counter-images of what should have been inaugurated from the great positive inspiration of the age and became its opponents which, because of their egoistic drive for power, did not want to see such a new world and soon called forth a very justified conflict against the Revolution and Napoleon which was ultimately fought to a victorious conclusion.

* We can here also recall what we wrote in our Vol. VIII (p.21f.) about a certain relation between what lived in personalities such as Schiller, and even Goethe, and in what fired the impulses of the leaders of the French Revolution, such as Mirabeau, Danton, 'or even Robespierre'. This latter trio allowed the relevant impulses to flow out into their *political* tendencies; in Schiller, Goethe and so many other great Germans, they worked themselves out on the basis, and with the means, of the *spiritual* life.

What then appeared instead of that European 'Threefolding' was this:

France did not move beyond its '*Étatism*' and became the greatest instigator of nationalism. Instead of carrying out a great European political mission, it fell into routine party politicking.

Germany did not find a spiritual path from German Idealism and from Goetheanism into the political and social world (cf. above p. 126f). The impulses of the great individuality which had incarnated there remained unrealised and without consequence. The results of this affected all areas of society.

Britain's economic mission—in itself eminently contemporary—was increasingly placed in the service of the one-sided power drives of global imperialism and fell ever more under the spell of materialistic economic impulses which, as it were, 'overwhelmed' the world.

The Child of Europe and His Relations

In the destiny of Kaspar Hauser, the son of a Franco-German marriage, Napoleon's adopted grandson, the 'Child of Europe', this Britain is also symbolically represented through the shady figure of Lord Stanhope, his 'foster father'....

Highly symbolic—and more than only symbolic—is that through his birth the 'Child of Europe' was involved in a complex of dynastic European relationships through his royal relations and in-laws. It was not only his father's belonging to the age-old House of Zähringer which wove him into some very important dynastic and political ties or his mother being the adopted daughter of Napoleon, or even because of Napoleon himself, but beyond these connections, it was also due to the illustrious marriages of his father's sisters in various directions across Europe.

The Crown Prince's paternal grandmother, Margavine Amalie (1754-1832) had succeeded in securing excellent marriages for five of her daughters:[354] *Caroline* (1776-1841) married the later King Max Joseph of Bavaria; *Luise* (1779-1826) under the name *Elisabeth* married the later Czar Alexander I of Russia in 1793; *Friederike* (1781-1826) married King Gustav Adolf IV of Sweden in 1797. Amalie's daughter *Marie* (1782-1808) became the Duchess of Brunswick and her youngest daughter, *Wilhelmine* (1788-1836) became the Grand Duchess of Hesse. Her only son, *Karl*, was born in 1786 between Marie and Wilhelmine, and his marriage with Stéphanie de Beauharnais produced the Crown Prince [Kaspar Hauser], the centre of our focus in this book. Genealogically speaking, the 'Child of

Europe' had truly placed himself most intensively within a European network! The grandmother of the 'Child of Europe was known in court circles for her extraordinarily successful matrimonial dynastic politics by the sarcastic title of '*the mother-in-law of Europe*'![355]—independently, of course, of her grandson's later 'title', 'Child of Europe'. It is sometimes the case that history itself seems to have a higher, objective sense of *humour*....

Beyond the symbolism of these relationships of the Crown Prince of Baden, they are especially significant in that if he had become the ruling prince of the small state of Baden, they would have given him countless possibilities for activities and making connections—an instrument, as it were, on which he could have played at a time when it was valid in the Age of Gabriel, which had not yet come to a close, to create the transition from the old, the given, to new social and political configurations. In so doing, it would have been important that these configurations which, in terms of historical continuity seen from a social perspective, would have come 'from above down', could also have been guided on their way by new spiritual impulses—a fundamental principle of spiritual work, which reminds us of the endeavours of the Comte de St Germain in the 18th century in the period before the French Revolution to awaken understanding at European courts for what was needed then and which should have been inaugurated by the princes themselves at the appropriate time.[356]

In the extensive Kaspar Hauser literature, we have only found one author who has considered the question of what kind of prince Kaspar Hauser would probably have been if he had come to the throne of Baden. This is *Klara Hofer* in her book about Kaspar Hauser.[357] Understandably, however, she only takes up the question in terms of what kind of prince he could have been when he had mounted the throne after all the suffering he had been through. Klara Hofer assesses his character traits: his human understanding which was healthy at its core, his pure goodwill for all human beings, his good moral character, his sure instincts about people etc. and concludes he would have been a most loved and popular prince; the people would doubtless have welcomed him from the first with open arms, rejoicing and happy. He would also have been well capable of fulfilling the more 'decorative requirements' of his office.... Understandably, from her particular standpoint, this sensitive, empathic author cannot go much further. To avoid ending in mere groundless speculation would only be possible within the framework of anthroposophically oriented considerations, which would then obviously immediately extend the question of how the individuality hidden under the mask of Kaspar Hauser could have acted as prince if he had been spared the destiny that made him 'Kaspar Hauser'. Then, this question of a history which did not come about and which seems so hypothetical would even take on a central significance.

For such a view (and precisely for such a view!) it would seem hardly realistic to want to imagine all the possible details of how the impulse with which this great individuality was born could have worked out if its way forward had not been cut off. But it can yet be very instructive in a large context to set before oneself in a few essential strokes the *qualitative possibilities*, as it were, of what might have been.

No 'Nibelung' Prince

First, it is important to state most emphatically something *negative*! This German prince would never have been what, following on from very significant remarks by Rudolf Steiner[358] about the destiny of Middle Europe, we can call a '*Nibelung prince*'. That means he would not at all have been a bearer of that 'Nibelung wildness' which lived on as a surviving outmoded attitude of soul, an atavistic element in the blood of many members of the German princely class and their hangers-on from the time in Middle Europe before 1200. The people of those classes stood fundamentally opposed to that element of German culture which had been developing since the 13th century and which was borne essentially by the bourgeoisie of Middle Europe, that other great stream in the German people (which we referred to above p. 130), which began with figures such as Walther von der Vogelweide and culminated in the 18th/19th centuries in Goethe and his great German contemporaries. We have discussed the 'Nibelung' aspect in some depth especially in relation to Frederick II of Prussia, who Rudolf Steiner described as a typical representative of this decadent kind of 'Nibelung'—and we must here particularly emphasise Rudolf Steiner's indication that it was the peculiar destiny of Middle Europe that the people whose soul development had remained behind were those with political power who *ruled over* the others who were the bearers of the advancing cultural stream.[359]

This situation is to be understood as a special case of the much more widespread general phenomenon that has obtained in modern times: that the relatively 'worse' sort of people have come to rule over the 'better' sort. We have repeatedly spoken of this 'selection of the lower'.[360] Mainly, those exercising such rulership have been those belonging to the type '*homo economicus*', which in modern times has increasingly become dominant.[361] In Germany in the late 19th century both types, the 'Nibelung' princes, together with their aristocratic element and the '*homines economici*' in the rising Big Business world, united in a kind of luciferic-ahrimanic 'marriage' which has had the most unhealthy consequences for Middle Europe, as characterised[362] by Rudolf Steiner and as the older people among us have had to experience.

To all such forces Kaspar Hauser was the complete opposite pole. That there was nothing of the 'Nibelung wildness' in him but rather its opposite needs no further explanation after all we have learned about him! We have heard that he—unlike the representatives of the Nibelung stream, who were alien, indeed in many respects directly hostile to the true German spirit, was predisposed and called to unite himself with the bearers of this spirit for large-scale activity for the sake of spiritual impulses of humanity. Rudolf Steiner has informed us that the people of the 'economic type' who have been dominant in recent centuries mostly only have a short life in the spiritual world before incarnating and therefore bring little spirituality with them with the result that they are one-sidedly oriented towards the world of the senses in their life on earth. Kaspar Hauser, however, we learned, was a very particular radical case of someone who must have spent a very long time in the spiritual world before his incarnation.

He would have worked on Earth in the service of the good powers who promote spiritualisation. It would therefore have been a rulership and activity '*from above down*', and not only in the outer social sense referred to above (p. 150). Both would have combined to inaugurate something new.

This of course was not allowed to be, and it seems very telling that we find arrayed against him something from the 'wild Nibelung' forces, in that his destiny was to fall victim to ambitious, unscrupulous machinations by certain dynastic personalities at the court in Baden.

A 'Transformation of the Concept of the Prince'

From what we have been able therefore to place before our souls, a direct path now leads to our understanding of a further statement by Rudolf Steiner that has very great ramifications: through this individuality *a new priest-kingship* was to have been founded. Objectively, that can of course only be understood when one starts from the right concept of the *old* priest-kingship. In those ancient times, through initiation in the Mysteries, people (who were of the right bloodline) were made instruments of hierarchical spiritual powers so as to lead and shape social life. This was the case to the greatest extent throughout the third post-Atlantean Epoch. We described this in Vol. I of this series. But we were able to show later (in what we said in Vol. IV in relation to Louis XIV) that the 'repetition' of aspects of the third post-Atlantean Epoch that happens in the fifth post-Atlantean Epoch also includes that Age of royal Absolutism which occurred in the first centuries of this fifth post-Atlantean Epoch as something like a reflection of *the period of decay* of the third post-Atlantean Epoch, or seen another way, that in this social phenomenon something that is ahrimanically *anticipated* confronts us, i.e., in a distorted form, something which in a spiritually justified sense will seek and be able to arise only in the further course of the fifth post-Atlantean Epoch as the contemporary *metamorphosis* at that future time of certain social phenomena of the third Cultural Epoch: personalities will emerge who, having become ripe through a renewed principle of initiation, will seek to intervene in social life in a spiritual way. This can of course only happen in the future on the basis, to the fullest extent, of the awakened Consciousness Soul, that is, in a way that reckons with the freedom of each individual (as is the case above all in terms of the impulse of the Threefolding of the social organism).

It must have been intended by the spiritual world to inaugurate this through that individuality who we heard (p. 93) was already deeply connected with important Mysteries in ancient times and later in a spiritually (inspirational) connection with Rosicrucianism. In order that everything possible could happen in terms of real continuity, that is, by linking on to what exists and has occurred historically, the individuality [Kaspar Hauser] incarnated in a Middle European dynasty, as we saw (above p. 111), in the oldest surviving German dynasty so as to reveal that what was at stake was a fundamental transformation of the most ancient human institutions out of the spirit of a new inspiration, in order to lead the institution of monarchy over into something new.

In the name 'Kaspar', which we have referred to several times, there still sounds what was wanted *and* what was prevented: the name of one of the three, who were also 'priest-kings', of whom the Gospel of Matthew says that they came to worship the Jesus of the Solomon line of the House of David.

'A new priest-kingship'! In this context certain ideas of *Saint-Martin* (1743-1803), the 'unknown philosopher', are important, and what Rudolf Steiner said about them in connection with those ideas which still stood so strongly in the old spiritual traditions, the old occult wisdom, in all that was ancient. Saint-Martin also developed particular social and political ideas.[363]

Rudolf Steiner said[364] of Saint-Martin's political concepts, for example, that he had specifically urged that every ruler should be a kind of Melchizedek, a kind of *priest-ruler*. Rudolf Steiner then said:

> And think how if this demand, which was put forward in a relatively small circle before the French Revolution broke out, had *not been of the nature of a sunset but of a dawning*, if something of the fundamental character of a Melchizedek had entered into the consciousness of the time and with its ideas and forces had been able to permeate human destinies, how everything would have had to be different in the 19th century from what it actually became! For the 19th century was in fact as far as possible from the idea I have just now characterised. Naturally, the demand that politicians should go through a school of Melchizedek would only have been dismissed with a smile.
>
> One has to point to Saint-Martin because in him there was something like a last glimmer of the wisdom that had developed since Antiquity. And it had to be a last glimmer because in the future, humanity must rise to spiritual life in *other* ways ... [not the merely traditional reproduction of ancient ideas...].

What emerges here is therefore the perspective that what in Saint-Martin was passing towards its end as a twilight of the past and as such cannot be continued, calls forth something new in the sense of a 'dawning'.

It is in *this* sense, apparently, that the astonishing remark is to be grasped that 'a new priest-kingship' was to be founded through the individuality of Kaspar Hauser.

This is then about a deeply significant perspective for social development into the far future emerging from the largest developmental and historical context, with a new stage on the path of the '*transformation of the concept of monarchical rule*'. We ourselves have tried to throw light on the past stages of this process: in broad outlines for the times of the ancient theocracies and in more detail for the centuries since the Renaissance....[365]

What spiritual and social impulses could have proceeded from a great individuality in terms of the above remarks can be characterised as follows: it was neither 'revolutionary' in the usual outer sense nor 'reactionary' and 'restorationist'.

The sequence of revolution and restoration was striking in the decades after 1789: at first, the revolutionary and chaotic flaring up of what were, in a deeper sense, 'misunderstood' impulses of the times and the way in which they burst out, seemingly leading to absurdities, and then the reaction against these absurdities, when people sought to return 'restoratively' to the outdated conditions which had led to the revolutionary outrages in the first place. This swaying of the pendulum would only have been avoided if the true progressive impulses of the age in the spiritual sense could have been grasped in their essence as something new in the historical process that was breaking in, and could have been brought to bear and implanted into the times in transitional ways that corresponded to reality. This would have been action out of the spirit of the 'middle' against the fury of anticipated and retarding social forces bound up with the past. It is in this way that, to put it very generally at first, we can imagine the 'qualitative' nature of the task of that great individuality who had entered through his birth into the right external circumstances for just such a purpose.

1848

A new hour in history had evidently struck with the unforgettable year *1848,* 33 years after the downfall of Napoleon, when the age of Restoration and Legitimism had set in. 1848 began the turnaround with the February Revolution in Paris, which brought about the overthrow of King Louis Philippe and the proclamation of the Republic. These events set in train a movement which went through several European countries: Germany, Austria, Hungary, Italy. Hopes for a period of new life, freedom and national unity filled people with an elementary strength in many lands. The 'Peoples' Spring' seemed to have arrived. A wonderful atmosphere must have prevailed, especially in Germany, beginning with those splendid spring days in March 1848. A breath of liberation passed throughout society, emanations of the strongest feelings, borne by a tremendous enthusiasm, of the will to sacrifice and devote oneself to an ideal of life, permeated by rapturous feelings, and the hope, indeed, the subjective conviction: now everything must get better!

'My heart feels warm whenever I recall those days', wrote *Carl Schurz* (1829-1906) later in his memories, who had taken part in the events of the year of revolution, then went to America, where he became a significant American statesman. He especially emphasised the willingness for sacrifice which had then gripped countless people of all kinds.

Friedrich Payer, born in 1847, who still strongly felt the afterglow of the year of '48 in his youth, thought in his old age that the expression 'the Peoples' Spring' most resembled what the German people were experiencing at the time, namely, that it was like a proliferation of the feeling which young people felt awaken in themselves when the oppression and night of winter gives way to the bright, warm spring sunshine. 'There must have been something glad and victorious in the air', a feeling that in a miraculous way renewed itself for months on end....

All of this was described many times over.[366]

It is also well-known how the German national Assembly of 1848/49 in the Paulskirche [St Paul's Church] in Frankfurt, with its high level of discussion and debate, was incomparably the best parliament that Germany has ever had.

'Never again,' wrote Wilhelm Mommsen, for example, 'in a German parliament, and seldom in any foreign parliamentary body were fundamental political issues struggled over with such earnestness and such depth, with such honesty and such inner maturity. What seems immature about it is mostly to be traced to the fact that any political experience was lacking and necessarily had to be lacking ....'[367]

What was later rather scornfully referred to as the 'professors' parliament' contained in itself the spiritual aristocracy of the German people—from the higher levels of the bourgeoisie, who felt themselves called to shape the political life of Middle Europe. Friedrich Naumann once made the perceptive remark about the Paulskirche that in it, *Schiller*'s pathos and sentiment had sounded once more through German politics, they had really sounded forth.[368] It was the best spiritual substance of the German people from the time of German Idealism, from which political problems were now once again being discussed.

From the Speaker's podium of the Frankfurt Parliament, recounts the congenial and noble Malwida von Meysenburg in her well-known *Memoiren einer Idealistin* [Memoirs of an Idealist], 'sounded splendid speeches in which the most noble views about the highest questions of humanity were elaborated. One really saw on this occasion what a people of thinkers the German people were and how quickly words and brilliant oratory were put at the disposal of the thoughts that preceded them...'.[369]

What expressed itself in Germany from 1848 as the striving for unity 'came from the finest qualities of the German people,' said Rudolf Steiner in 1921.[370] 'It was indeed *precious metal in the cultural development of humanity.*'

And he added that 'it had a particular quality to it ..., that is despised and hated by no nation on earth; on the contrary, it is accepted by all...'.

These words seek to express something essential. They point to what valuable human substance—for a short time leading the way and of great moral authority—was available in Middle Europe at that time, a substance, we could add, with which in the right circumstances great things could have been achieved.

We might perhaps indicate here, as a symptom of what we called 'qualititative possibilities', a particular personality who was a member of the Paulskirche Assembly for a time. This was the Austrian *Count Anton Alexander von Auersberg* (1806-1876) who is known as a poet under the name *Anastasius Grün*. Owing to the 'liberal sentiments' of his poetry, he was regarded as one of the leaders of the Liberal party in Austria and in April 1848—at the age of 42—was elected to the German pre-Parliament and soon afterwards to the Frankfurt National Assembly, which he left already at the end of September. Rudolf Steiner, in an important lecture, (5.5.1912 in Düsseldorf) speaks about one of his poems : '*Die Tatsache des durch den Tod gegangenen Gottes-Impulses. Fünf Ostern*' [The Fact of the God-Impulse that has Passed through Death. Five Easters.] In this lecture the motif of *Rosicrucianism* sounds very strongly and Steiner refers to a very significant spiritual poem of a peculiar magic intimately connected with Rosicrucianism by this very Anastasius Grun which includes a vision of the distant future—about how he feels about the power of peace which will reign on earth from a non-denominational, Rosicrucian Christianity.

But when we think of what was said earlier (p. 134), we want Auersberg's 'Liberalism' and this deep spiritual poem of his, inspired by Rosicrucian impulses, *to sound together*. This, however, would have needed a strong ingredient that would bind that Liberalism and the power of the Rosicrucian impulse that creates this peace in the world....

The two goals and ideals of the movement of 1848, as they lived in the consciousness of those who bore them, are contained in the words 'Freedom and Unity': the 'liberal' and the 'national' motifs. From these demands for liberty, insofar as they were supposed to benefit *every* citizen, there arose with an intrinsic necessity also the demands for equality and justice. All these together were intended to prevail as constitutional factors in the political unity or unification of the German people that was supposed to be secured in 1848. That yearning had already been living among the Germans since the Wars of Liberation against Napoleon.

'In the liberal citizenry,' wrote Wilhelm Mommsen,[371] 'the aristocratic ideal of personality was politicised. That applied in the best sense to the Frankfurt professors.' The impulse of liberty originated in the sphere of *thinking*. This impulse becomes 'political' when one seeks to protect each individual's scope for freedom and thereby gives to the individual the possibility of free political activity and with it, a share in the government through a constitutional arrangement. The struggle to set aside class privileges and abolish the nobility as a class etc. goes back to the same impulse of the growing Consciousness Soul, which seeks to base everything on the capacities and abilities of the individual, without regard for the context in which he is placed by his blood (which was the bearer of all social life in former times).

When the last point is taken into consideration, then the whole issue of the 'national' element arises, and the striving for unity that was based on it, which played such a great role in the movement of 1848. It was itself, directly, in natural terms, a matter of the blood. But it also had its *spiritual pole*, and it was precisely this which was living most strongly in the deeply idealistic German movement of the year 1848. The deeper concern of the national striving for unity was that the whole German people should give itself political forms which could provide the body appropriate to the nature of the German people that could serve the spirituality and the great cultural task that so many people strongly felt.

That people wanted to move in the direction of the political state from a basis of German culture and spirituality which until then had been completely separate from politics, was the actual 'revolutionary' step, because it meant confronting the particularistic self-serving will of the monarchical rulers of the various German states. Until 1848 they had taken care to ensure that it was held to be a crime—except in the purely cultural, i.e., politically 'safe', space—to wish to be 'German', and not merely a Prussian, a Saxon, a Mecklenburger, a Bavarian, or a Württemberger etc.[372] That the will-to-power of the ('Nibelung') rulers should seek to uphold and maintain this particularistic fragmentation, together with what were in many respects the lamentable circumstances and the fusty atmosphere that was common in the individual German states—albeit in different degrees of course; Prussia, for example, was relatively progressive—had long been rightly felt by many people (and much more of course went on subconsciously) to be deeply offensive to the true nature and destiny of the German people. For this destiny, at that time, an exalted sense of the remaining German idealism of the Goethe-Schiller period was felt by the German bourgeoisie. *That* was what gave the burgeoning national sensibility that was so strong in those days its colouring. Certainly, it had also been sparked by Napoleon and the resistance against him. But in the sentiments of many of the best people of the period, it had for a long time ultimately signified something spiritual. It was of an *idealistic* nature.

This national feeling did not perceive itself as something opposed to other peoples. One regarded one's endeavours more in the sense of brotherly collaboration with various liberated peoples. This was an essential element of what lived in the overwhelming feelings of that 'Peoples' Spring'.* Of course, there were many ideas that were very unclear and shot through with illusions of various kinds, but people did not yet sense anything of the *demonic* nature which would later so often take possession of nationalistically agitated and whipped-up masses of the people.

Causes of the Failure

How did this German sense of exaltation in 1848 shatter and fail? Basically, it was due to the same factors that had not allowed the Congress of Vienna (1813-1815) to arrive at a solution to 'the German Question', in other words—the power of the old 'Legitimist' forces. The National Assembly in St Paul's Church, which was widely expected to fulfil all the high-flying hopes of so many, did indeed possess great moral authority. But what it and the newly-formed Reich Cabinet of Ministers lacked was—as has been repeated so often—real political *power*. The central figures in the new Reich had no civil service substructure which could have served them as executive organs, no finances of which they could dispose. The only ones who had such things were the historically existing German states and their princes, their territorial rulers on whose goodwill the central authority depended. The longer the 'revolutionary' situation went on, however, the less the traditional rulers were minded to submit or to give up their power voluntarily. (Württemberg was the only larger state which formally accepted the legal validity of the Frankfurt Assembly's work.[374]) To carry out a bloody, violent actual revolution against the landed nobility was far from the style, the will and the external possibilities of those who were the bearers of the will for freedom and unity. Moreover, the Germans as a whole did not want a radical abolition of the individual states or the overthrow of the monarchies, and for

---

* In view of such feelings, one can even understand how such a prominent Frenchman as the historian *Jules Michelet* could welcome German unity: 'May God give us a great [united] Germany!... The European council remains incomplete and disharmonious, subject to cruel plans [and the] godless wars of kings as long as the high spirits of the nations do not in their majesty participate in this council and add to the brotherly balance of the world a new element of wisdom and peace.'[373] (In 1871 Michelet was to experience great disappointment through the way in which German unity then came about.)

a deeply justified reason, namely, that abstract political unity was something that would not at all have been suitable for the being of Germany and its tasks.

The 'particularism' of the German states in fact corresponded to deeply rooted traits in the German character. It was therefore highly significant that the German movement of 1848 held back from attacking the thrones. The 'Revolution' was actually already over in the moment when liberal representatives were accepted in the Cabinets of the individual states, where they should have been able to act in line with those in the freedom movement. Also in line with these very German character traits was the fact that the constitutional assemblies, which sprang up in all the German states, soon showed themselves as particularist opponents of the National Assembly in Frankfurt,[375] that is, they became representatives of the separate political wills of the individual states, albeit of the progressive elements in the parliaments of those states that were seeking freer arrangements within their own particular states.

The German movement of 1848, in the way it was actually formed and progressed—and this has often been emphasised—, was bound to remain without success in its striving for national unity in freedom because of the existing *external political* situation around Middle Europe. The European Powers around Germany could not tolerate such a strong political Power in Middle Europe of the kind that would have arisen if the movement for political unity in Germany had succeeded. Especially, speaking completely hypothetically, in the case of a decisive (and in practical terms, not even possible) outer victory over the landed nobility, a German unity that would have arisen on that basis would have fallen into the arms of the Legitimist Powers. If the Prussian king Friedrich Wilhelm IV had in early 1849 accepted the German imperial crown that the Frankfurt National Assembly offered him in line with the so-called 'small German' solution of the German Question, Wilhelm Mommsen, for example, writes[376] that on the king's acceptance of the imperial crown, war would have broken out, which Russia and Austria would probably have won 'and then, quite apart from all the consequences in foreign affairs, reactionary forces would have been victorious in a very different way, [and] the principle of constitutionalism would have been completely eliminated...'.

When one looks at all this taken as a whole, then in these events and circumstances, the great 'void' that had opened up through the removal of the individuality who was concealed under the name of Kaspar Hauser becomes vividly clear. The great movement of the times required, as it were, the participation of that individuality. All depended on an understanding between—on the one hand—the progressive forces within the German people, with their impulses for liberty and their will to shape things in Middle Europe in accordance with the nature of the German spirit,—and on the other hand—those who historically possessed actual power, the German landed nobility, the princes and kings.* Only in this way could meaningful, organic further development that included the necessary transitions in terms of historical continuity have been achieved.†

In this situation it would have been tremendously important if on the throne of Baden, admittedly one of the smaller German states but one in which very special conditions prevailed, there had been a personality from one of the oldest Middle European princely families, someone who also in his individuality was linked with the most ancient impulses of leadership in the ongoing development of mankind. In 1848 this Grand Duke of Baden, as already stated above would have been from 35 to 36 years old. External [hereditary] legitimation and the highest inner, personal authority would have been united in his person and would have enabled him, in the crucial events of the time and into European conditions, to take the initiative and speak decisive words out of great impulses of humanity and out of the genuine Middle European spirit. For one who knows something of the true, future-oriented impulses and goals of the age, it is not difficult to see how in such a way developments could have taken another course: through the collaboration between an enlightened prince and the bearers of the most elevated German impulses of the time.‡ Since this very thing did *not*

---

* A profound sense for this historical necessity is evident in a call which today is mostly regarded as almost naïve and which was voiced in 1849 in Saxony by none other than *Richard Wagner,* then the 36-year-old Court conductor in Dresden. Wagner, who felt himself so deeply bound to the German people and their cultural and historical task, urged that *the king should himself declare his country a free state and place himself at its head* (see Mommsen op. cit., p. 131) (As is well-known, Richard Wagner, 'compromised' by his participation in the revolutionary movement, had to leave Dresden. Threatened by a 'wanted poster', he escaped via Weimar and Paris and eventually got to Zurich.)

† '... In Germany it was completely impossible,' wrote W. Mommsen, for example, (op. cit., p. 122) 'for a people to jump straight "from police oppression" into a republic and, "having been without their own will for centuries", then to be able to gain complete freedom in months...'.

‡ One can think of particular men who were apparently bound by destiny to Kaspar Hauser and who, if the course of events had gone differently, would very likely

happen, the actual course of events proceeded under the sign of a hopeless abyss—between the National Assembly, so rich in ideas and filled with high idealism but powerless and politically inexperienced, and the German 'Nibelung' princes and monarchs, who were devoid of ideas and stood so very far from the true German spirit but who possessed and routinely exercised political power.

'Against democrats, only soldiers are of use': with regard to this slogan which appeared in a reactionary pamphlet in the autumn of 1848, the Grand Duke of Mecklenburg notably wrote to King Friedrich Wilhelm IV of Prussia: 'Goethe did not write anything I would have liked.'

Friedrich Wilhelm IV, who refused the German imperial crown offered him by the Frankfurt National Assembly is a special case in himself. His opposition to the spirit of 1848 was rooted in the old impulses of rulership, notions of 'divine right' and the like, which were very strong in him. Jürgen von Grone discussed this in a significant essay, which relates very specifically to the subject of this book: '*Vom Zusammenstoss bewegender und beharrender Mächte in der Deutschen Erhebung von 1848*' [On the clash of progressive and conservative forces in the German uprising of 1848] (in *Die Drei* XVIII 2/3, April/June 1948, p. 135f). Friedrich Wilhelm IV brought these outdated impulses into effect in line with those of the 'Nibelung' princes, of which he himself, although a Hohenzollern, was by no means a typical representative.

One can very well imagine how, in which sense and in which direction a great source of individual strength such as the one which was shut out, could have been effective. One can perhaps best gain an idea of this direction by considering the inefficiencies, errors and absences that characterised the movement of 1848 and what has often been described (with regard, in a broad sense, to what would have had to have been corrected, clarified and pioneered), namely the many examples of vagueness and confusion in

---

have served him as capable helpers in his cultural mission. We are thinking here—as examples—especially of the two politicians and members of the Frankfurt National Assembly who we have already mentioned several times: *Karl Theodor Welcker* (1790-1869), who became one of the leading personalities at the St Paul's Church and the founder of the so-called Great German party, and *Georg Friedrich Kolb* (1808-1884). Both had friendly relations with one another. As late as 1857, Welcker told Kolb that he was 'deeply convinced' that Kaspar Hauser was really the eldest son of Grand Duke Karl and Stéphanie (Kolb, op. cit., p. 35) and from Welcker's letters to Kolb, we know that Kolb published important arguments in favour of Hauser's princely origins (see p. 99 above).

the discussions at the St Paul's Church and the many obstacles, not only to actions but also to feeling and thinking. These showed themselves in the fundamentally idealistic tone of national feelings, to which we referred earlier, but also in early examples of the more disastrous kind of nationalism that would emerge later on. The striving, which was quite justified in a deeper sense, for Germany's 'standing in the world' became mixed up in various ways with the idea that this would have to be achieved forcefully, 'at the point of a sword'. There was a more profound contradiction between the idea of a broader, federal Middle Europe, the borders of which were conceived as extending as far as the Black Sea, and a national, German unitary state, which could only have been much smaller (and later actually became so) and which basically did not correspond at all with the German way and mission: it could only be conceived of as a power block in the heart of Europe, a bone of contention over which opposing powers would necessarily come to blows. W. Mommsen, for example, characterised the process as follows:

> It was understandable that the St Paul's Church [assembly] would strive for the German people's position in the world. The democrat List had been the first to argue for this most decisively and impressively. It might have been possible to maintain the influence of German culture and German business in the Balkans—which was in itself quite natural—if one had restricted oneself to those two areas and had not fallen for dreams of political domination, which were already clearly sounding in the St Paul's Church. The German tendency to pursue everything through to the last consequence was also evident here ....[377]

This above all was the problem—that things were pushed, in thought, to the last consequences by thinking in terms of the *unitary state* [*Einheitsstaat*]. It is so clear how at that time people could actually have begun to distinguish the three parts of the threefold social organism in accordance with their their inherent tendencies and thus could have arrived at a federal form of a broader Middle Europe which would at the same time also have functioned in foreign policy terms, because it would not have presented any threat to its neighbouring states in East and West.

Dreams of political dominance! They were dreamed by a movement and a national assembly which never had any real power in Germany and which was therefore not at all taken seriously abroad. Quite rightly, such dreams were seen in connection with 'the German tendency to pursue foreign policy on the basis of their own dreams'.[378] This is the opposite of an objective grasp of reality. It is one of the cliff-edges for Middle Europe. We should see it in connection with what Rudolf Steiner[379] said about the rulership of the 'silver king' (in Goethe's 'Fairy Tale') in the middle countries. This 'silver king' is indeed the king of feeling, of 'semblance' or of 'the phenomenal', of 'beautiful semblance', as exists especially in all the arts. As the representative of the middle soul force it also has to do with law and 'the State'.[380] But when it works, one could say, in the political sphere in such a way that it loses contact with 'the golden king' of wisdom-filled knowledge and with the 'brass king' of a spiritual will, then there arises the tendency to illusionary dreaming, which must shatter on the rocks of reality. From illusions, things develop further, into lies (as the balance swings over from the luciferic to the ahrimanic).

Rudolf Steiner[381] said that if one wants to set the soul force of semblance, of the phenomenal, which corresponds to what is symbolised in the 'silver king' e.g. the aesthetic penetration of thinking and the like:

> on the basis of solid reality, if one even wishes to become a politician in this way, one can easily become unreal, easily fall into so-called dreamy idealism, where one wants to found empires of unity, where one fantasises for decades about empires of unity—and then actually founds empires of force, falling from the one into the other. There has never been in political life a greater contrast than that between the German dreams of unity in 1848 and what was then founded in 1871. There you see the swaying out of balance of something which actually strives to shape things aesthetically—and which can become unreal, can become a semblance, a dream picture, when it wants to set itself up on the ground of politics....

Were we to speak in pictures, we could say: 'The 'silver king' stood there 'alone' in Middle Europe in 1848. It lacked the wise light of the 'golden king' who knows how to grasp social life (who, if he had been able to set to work, would also have called on the forces of the 'brass king').*

---

*We can find this inner situation also in comments made by Rudolf Steiner in 1899 in a commemorative essay he wrote in the *Magazin für Literatur* [Magazine for Literature] on the occasion of the 70th birthday of Henrik Ibsen:

> The Revolution [of 1848] which the twenty-year-old [Ibsen] experienced was the forerunner and symptom of something greater, the revolutionising of the spirits. The political revolution could not achieve what the spirits had promised for it. Movements for the transformation of the social order are only victorious when they are the expression of newly born worldviews. Christianity was able to found a new order in human relations because it proceeded from a revolutionising of the whole life of feeling.... The Revolution of 1848 was purely political. It was borne by no new worldview.[382]

What was lacking was precisely that which had been provided and was wanted—and which powerful forces of opposition had prevented.

Baden – Prussia – Hohenzollern

For the same inner reasons Southwestern Germany (see above pp. 110f., 112, 135) was the region from which the activity of the great individuality, of whom we have been speaking here, to inaugurate a social future should have proceeded and from which, after the exclusion of that individuality, the German uprising of 1848/49 actually began. For one who looks more deeply, the spiritual 'vacuum' which resulted from that exclusion was clearly and closely related to the fact that it was *in Baden* that the movement of 1848/49 was especially fierce and that it was there and in the neighbouring Palatinate that in early 1849 there was a real republican uprising, in which the army was involved. The process of events is deeply symptomatic: how the Bavarian government could not cope with the uprising in the Palatinate, and then Grand Duke Leopold von Baden (the first Grand Duke of Baden from the Hochberg line) had to flee his country and then appealed to *Prussia* for military assistance.[383] The Prussian troops were under the command of Prince Wilhelm of Prussia, the younger brother of King Friedrich Wilhelm IV. They bloodily suppressed the uprising (which had been a hopeless case from the beginning, in military terms) with great violence. On 25 June 1849 the Prussians entered Karlsruhe and then occupied the whole of Baden down to the Swiss border. The 'Cartridge-Prince', as he was widely known for his role in these years became Prince Regent in 1858 because of the illness of Friedrich Wilhelm IV, and King of Prussia after his brother's death in 1861. In 1871—through Bismarck's founding of the Empire, Wilhelm then became German Emperor! In 1856 he had already had his daughter Luise married to Grand Duke Friedrich I of Baden (the younger son of Grand Duke Leopold). Baden and Prussia were thus brought closely together. It was as though the 'vacuum' that had developed in Baden sucked in the Prussian-Hohenzollern element.

Everywhere in these events, the karma of Kaspar Hauser played in. Sometimes it is as though the darkly concealed figure of Hauser appears only to a more penetrating gaze in the deeper background of events. In other places it appears much more clearly.

It is almost tangible how the shadow of Kaspar Hauser falls most heavily on the *House of Baden*. That must already have been the case with Grand Duke Leopold, and still more with his mentally ill elder son and successor

(1852-1856) Ludwig II, who was deeply oppressed by this shadow which he believed he could see during attacks of his illness. 'One should remove the story of Kaspar Hauser from his head, then he would become healthy again', the sick man once explained to his cousin Marie of Hamilton (daughter of Stéphanie and therefore Kaspar Hauser's sister).[384] After Ludwig, his younger brother headed the government as Grand Duke Friedrich I (from 1856-1907). He was himself a healthy, virtuous man of goodwill, but one hears of him that a nervous tremor came over him[385] whenever Kaspar Hauser was clearly mentioned to any degree.

Wencker-Wildberg writes in his book, which brings together a great deal from the Kaspar Hauser research literature[386], that when Grand Duke Friedrich married Princess Luise of Prussia, Queen Victoria of the United Kingdom expressed her concern to King Wilhelm (Luise's father) 'that he is uniting his daughter with a family widely accused of murder' (that of Kaspar Hauser). Wencker-Wildberg here brings in the activities of the energetic Grand Duchess Luise, known in the Kaspar Hauser literature for the great role she played in seeking, everywhere her influence could reach, in archives, and in other documents and writings, to have all mention of Kaspar Hauser destroyed. Even Napoleon III was successfully influenced by her with regard to the French archives. The works of the anti-Hauserians Otto Mittelstädt, a jurist,[387] and the archivist Antonius von der Linde, Wencker-Wildberg believes, can be traced back to orders that both had received in connection with the document-destroying activities of Grand Duchess Luise—about which Wencker-Wildberg provides many details[388]—in order finally to destroy Hauser's 'imaginary princely status'.*

Baden and Prussia! The inauguration of a spiritual formation of Middle European affairs by the one who was born on 29 September and would have been Grand Duke of Baden, from Southwestern Germany, did not come about. Its place was taken in a fundamentally different way, filling the

---

* Many of the efforts of Grand Duchess Luise characterised here should be seen in relation to *Henriette Feuerbach*, the daughter-in-law of Anselm von Feuerbach, Kaspar Hauser's protector. For example, Thomas Stettner[389] writes of her that she had long had relations with the Baden Court and possessed many letters from ladies at Court in which Kaspar Hauser was mentioned as having been the Crown Prince of Baden. During the war of 1870 a friendly relationship developed between her and Grand Duchess Luise. 'Since she [Henriette] now knew that the burden of suspicion on the House of Baden was a source of great worry for the grand ducal couple, she did not want her friend to become ill by her feeding the suspicion with further nourishment and she therefore burned those letters before her death (1892).'[390]

vacuum that had arisen, by what came in one-sided fashion from north German Prussia as the 'solution' to the German Question through the genial statesmanship of Bismarck in collaboration with Wilhelm I. There arose the political structure of the 'German Empire' of 1871, completely dominated by Prussia, and with the former 'cartridge-prince' from the House of Hohenzollern at its head as German Kaiser, continually and selflessly supported and promoted by Baden under Grand Duke Friedrich, the son-in-law of the Prussian king and the 'the most distinguished princely protagonist of German unity'.[391] After the German victory in the German-French war of 1870/71, which manifested German unity and so powerfully strengthened it, the solemn imperial proclamation of the Emperor took place on 18 January 1871, as is well-known, in the Palace of Versailles, in the Hall of Mirrors where once Louis XIV, the 'Sun King' of the mighty French national unitary state, and his court nobles had seen themselves reflected. Who was it on that solemn and splendid State occasion, sealing all that had been accomplished, as it were, who called out to raise the cheers of all those assembled to celebrate the Emperor Wilhelm I? It was none other than Grand Duke Friedrich of Baden, his son-in-law, the grandson of that Imperial Countess von Hochberg; he who—personally unimpeachable as he was—only held the throne of Baden because that other, great one had been shut out and who at that time, if he had lived, would have been 58 years old.

One can see as a kind of preparatory, intermediate step in this whole process towards the Prussian Hohenzollern Empire those events of the year 1849 which we (see above, p. 160) mentioned, namely, how the Frankfurt National Assembly offered the position of German Kaiser to Friedrich Wilhelm IV, a man who not only seemed called to the role as the monarch of the largest German state in terms of the 'small Germany solution' (i.e., without Austria) but also through many of his personal and spiritual qualities. It seems symptomatic that Karl Theodor Welcker, who we have mentioned several times in this book in connection with Kaspar Hauser, had a considerable share in the activities of the National Assembly, because Welcker, as we have heard (p. 136 above), was the founder of the 'big Germany' party, but then, after this goal proved to be unattainable, he turned to supporting Friedrich Wilhelm IV as German Emperor. At that time, people evidently did not think of a Germany dominated by Prussia but actually of a Prussia subsumed by Germany. As we have already mentioned, Friedrich Wilhelm IV rejected the German imperial crown for his own deep motives: he did not want to receive it from the hands of those who were offering it to him; his ideas of 'divine grace' were firmly against this.

His younger, much more sober brother, Wilhelm I, was also very loath to accept the imperial title in 1871: he felt himself fully to be king of Prussia and he wanted to remain as such. But he nevertheless accepted the imperial dignity in a completely different situation: from the hands of his fellow princes, for whom the Grand Duke of Baden spoke, and also under heavy pressure from Bismarck. Now began the short history of that second 'German Reich', which we have to learn to understand as a counter-image of what was 'actually' wanted and provided for.

This German Reich, as was immediately recognised by everyone, was in reality a 'Great Prussia', with all the traits associated with that.

For millions it was an object of patriotic enthusiasm; for others who were looking more closely, this whole development was the greatest disappointment and concern. One of these was *Georg Friedrich Daumer*, the former teacher and fatherly friend of Kaspar Hauser. Already at the end of 1866 he was writing in a letter to his niece words which in all their sharpness and bitterness at the same time can seem archetypal for what (by just some at first and by many later) was thought and painfully felt in the world and in Germany itself:

'We are going for unity ... or at least heading towards it, but not towards freedom, moral greatness, national and human excellence; we are becoming the slaves of the Prussian, dynastic, military despotism. From merely outer gestures comes no healing and no new blossoming of humanity and nations.'[392]

Bismarck

We must now include the figure of *Bismarck* in our considerations, the great statesman who dominated the destiny of Middle Europe in the [second half of the] 19th century with a real I, one of the great expressions of the many-sided German nature. One can certainly feel that in his way, he was intimately related to the German Folk Spirit and was called to serve it as an instrument in his own fashion. From an absolutely credible report, we know that Rudolf Steiner said that in Bismarck something like the last shadow of the German Folk Spirit descended.*

A remarkable light also falls on him when we see him from the viewpoint of the 'history that did not come about', when we try to distinguish the task of his destiny from what became history through him and how it

---

* *Herman Grimm* may have felt something of this when he wrote of Bismarck: '... his writings and speeches were a part of the voice of the people. He was no single individual, he was a piece of the nation, like Napoleon was an army.'[393]

did so to such an overwhelming degree, powerfully deflecting away from that other possible historical reality through the tragic and unwholesome actions of destiny which we have been speaking about in this book.

Soon after Bismarck's death (he died on 30 July 1898) Rudolf Steiner published a very insightful article in the *Magazin für Literatur*[394] with the striking title 'Bismarck, the Man of Political Success' which was, typically, ignored by the academic world. In 1919,[395] Steiner referred to this essay as one of those which can show how at that time (before the catastrophe of the world war) the attempt had to be made 'to get some truths across through the cracks'. In 1921 he gave further weight to this essay when he said that he himself had had it reprinted in particular circumstances in the weekly *Dreigliederung des sozialen Organismus* [Threefolding of the Social Organism] and provided the essay with an additional section that re-emphasised the essay's main idea.[396]

In the essay we do not find Bismarck described as following leading political ideas, but as acting out of specific political situations.

Steiner writes:

> To avoid running the risk of being regarded as someone who denigrates Bismarck by those who only know how to recognise a great man through the superlative praise he receives, I will say clearly that Bismarck owed his success to the fact that he was never more than a few years ahead of his time....
>
> He was far from feeling that one can have an ideal and seek to realise it.... He had a fine sense for the actual way things were, for the real demands of his time; and he had the relentless will to realise what the times, the moment, demanded ....
>
> I shall say without reservation: Bismarck was the greatest politician because he understood, in the very best sense of the word, to turn his coat to the wind. But I'm only echoing Bismarck's words. In the sitting of the Prussian Parliament on 2 June 1865, Bismarck replied to the member of parliament, Virchow, who had accused him of having no principles and of making his political decisions first this way and then that way, each one blown by the wind: 'Virchow has accused us of turning the rudder whichever way the wind changes. *Well, I ask what else should one do when one travels by ship other than turn the rudder according to the wind, if you don't want to make wind yourself?*'*

* Bismarck said something similar on his 80th birthday on 1 April 1895 in an address to German students: 'Politics is something which can only be compared to a voyage by ship across an unknown sea. One does not know what the weather and the currents will be, or what storms one will experience. Also, in politics one is essentially

> Bismarck never thought how the world should be. He regarded such thinking as pointless. He allowed events to tell him what should be:* his task he saw as responding *powerfully* to the demands of events.†
>
> But his power had a very particular direction to it. No one else gave it this direction. Bismarck was born on 1 April 1815 in a Prussian Junker family.‡ His upbringing and education led him to become the personality that would have to place on his gravestone the single striking phrase: *A true German servant of Wilhelm I.*[402]§
>
> One will search world history in vain if one wants to find two men more destined for each other than Bismarck and Wilhelm I....

Later in Rudolf Steiner's essay, Bismarck is described as always having been the greatest enemy of the liberal bourgeoisie, in which he saw incorporated the republican spirit. But the proletariat, he believed, would extend its hand to a social monarchy against the republican inclinations of the bourgeoisie.

> I believe that there would have been a possibility for Bismarck to have realised his social monarchy. This would have come about if Lassalle had not lost his life to Rakowitza's pistol shot in a frivolous duel in 1864[403]. Bismarck could

---

dependent on decisions made by others.... Man cannot create and guide the current of the age, but can only travel and steer with it with more or less experience and skill, he can be shipwrecked or stranded—and can also reach safe habours.'[397] Finally, a more religiously expressed variation of the same thinking from Bismarck's belief in providence are his often-cited words: 'One cannot create something oneself; one can only wait until one hears God's steps resounding through events; then leap forward and grasp hold of His coat-tails—that is all.'[398]

* 'In 1848, he spoke of the "German swindle" and in the '50s fought against Austria in the Frankfurt Parliament, but not for a German Reich. In the end, he identified himself with the desire for German unity only when a keen observation of the facts had taught him that Prussia had to realise this desire for national unity or else go under. His spirit was so constituted that a necessity, once perceived, ...became a force within his soul...' (Bernhard Guttmann in his essay '*Bismarck: das letzte Stück des Weges*' [Bismarck: The Last Stretch of the Path].[399]

† Compare this with the comment by the Bismarck scholar Erich Marcks: Bismarck was the man who 'did not think for the whole but acted for it'.[400]

‡ 'The best part of me and of my actions in life was always the Prussian officer,' said Bismarck on 26 March 1898 in an address to Kaiser Wilhelm II.[401]

§ In Bismarck's whole world of traditional ideas, a great role in his life was played by his feeling himself to be a Brandenburg 'vassal' of his liege lord Wilhelm I, before whom he stood with a 'vassal's loyalty' as his ancestors had done for centuries.

> do nothing with principles and ideas. They lay outside the confines of his world view. He could only deal with human beings, who confronted him as real facts. Had Lassalle remained alive, he would probably have brought the workers to that point where Bismarck was ready for social reform plans so that, together with Bismarck, the workers could have found a solution to the social question. But to solve the social question at the right time, in Bismarck's sense, Lassalle was missing. Bismarck could do nothing with the socialist parties which asserted themselves after Lassalle's death and which were led by abstract Marxist theory as a political factor and not by a living human being. With Lassalle as a power factor and with the power of the workers led by Lassalle, Bismarck could have founded a social state with the king at its head, but with party doctrines, Bismarck did not know how to proceed.
>
> He knew how to deal with factors of power.* To theories and principles he was indifferent....

We shall return later to this extremely important relationship with Lassalle. Here, we need above all to see and to emphasise what could have resulted from everything we have heard so far: if, to express it in Bismarck's own images, in the time when he was active, another 'wind' had been blowing in Germany and other currents had been flowing, then the work that he accomplished with his genial political acumen, would have turned out very differently.

He himself was aware that without the liberal movement for national unity and without the Frankfurt [National Assemby in] St Paul's Church, his own founding of the Reich in 1871 would have been unthinkable.[405] That movement, despite all the antipathy he had shown towards it in its time was nevertheless a political reality. It had created a strong 'wind' with which he then 'sailed' (along with the other 'winds' that were also blowing). If there had been in Germany, above the abstract liberal movement for national unity, corresponding spiritual streams strong enough to assert themselves as politically active forces and social realities, then the great statesman who held the destiny of Middle Europe in his hands could have taken the wind from those streams into his sails and turned the rudder in their direction to shape something politically. The 'Reich' would have been made in other ways and much better: it would probably have come about very differently, namely, with such a dynamic and with such forms of the inner life in Germany and its relations to the world around

* 'I have,' said Bismarck himself, 'an inborn respect for all real powers and forces.'[404]

it that would have corresponded to what had truly been sought since the French Revolution, that is, it would have corresponded to the demands of the coming spirit of the age and in Middle European ways which would have been appropriate for the true German Folk Spirit. In the light of everything we have said so far in this book, this 'wind' could have blown in Germany if the mighty impulses of the great individuality of whom we have been speaking had become effective. This enables us to think that Bismarck, who was certainly incarnated not by chance at precisely this time (1 April 1815, he was therefore 2½ years younger than the true Crown Prince of Baden), would have collaborated in a very significant way with *this* German prince and with the Middle European movement that would have been linked with and led by him—just as, in lacking all of this, Bismarck collaborated only with Wilhelm I, with whose destiny he must have been deeply connected.

We have just said that this enables us to '*think*'.... It now seems, with a high degree of probability which is not far short of full assurance, that we can state* that such extremely important perspectives were *actually given by Rudolf Steiner* in very concrete ways through indications in some of his conversations, the sense of which was that: Bismarck's political deeds in the 19th century were only able to lead to the kind of shaping of Middle European events (the foundation of the German Empire in 1871 etc.) that they did because the 'partner' who was predestined for him (or for whom he was predestined) was not there: namely, Kaspar Hauser. Only because of this did it happen that Bismarck then worked with *Wilhelm I* as his partner in the way known to history....

★

From all that has been presented (and by no means only from the last points) it is clear that one cannot do justice to Bismarck and the political development of Germany in the 19th century when one only considers them 'one-sidedly'. Rather, one has to differentiate between two levels of events and consider them in terms of two different niveaus.

---

* This view is the result of a careful examination which we have made but the individual elements of which would be of no significance for readers unfamiliar with the personalities involved. It will only be mentioned here that what we have repeated here stems from a *different* source from the other comments by Rudolf Steiner about Kaspar Hauser that we have cited thus far, which it complements and with which it is in complete agreement.

In one of these, one is dealing with what is immediately given, with processes as they actually played out more on the surface and which were moved by those given relationships.[406] Into these relationships, however, there came a (negative) constituent factor, namely, that around the middle of the century Middle Europe did *not* receive a great impulse from the truly progressive activity of the Spirit of the Age and from the Folk Spirit.

This factor led to the founding of the German Reich in 1871 as a political and military structure (on a Western model) that Germany needed for its external security in view of its geographical situation—Germany, which for centuries, and notably since the Thirty Years War, had been without protection and open to devastating incursions from its surroundings, and which in the 19th century found itself in a dangerous middle position between two extremely powerful military powers, France and Russia.

This same factor also led to the *method* of German unification by means of political and military power and much violence i.e., with the same methods that had been applied everywhere else in the world and with which national states had earlier arrived at unity—with 'practical' means, after the failure to achieve unity in the idealistic efforts of 1848/49.

This was the much mentioned 'martial' method of '*Blood and Iron*', which all had resorted to since time immemorial but which Bismarck also very publicly *stated,* and in typically martial terminology, in the 19th century, when war was still fundamentally regarded by politicians as a justified means of effecting decisions.

Bismarck made this (in)famous statement, after similar phrases in letters by him (notably in a letter of 12 May 1859 to the Prussian Foreign Minister), as newly appointed Prussian Prime Minister on 30 September 1862 in an evening sitting of the Budget Commission of the Prussian Parliament: 'Germany doesn't look to Prussia's liberalism but to its power; ...Prussia's post-Vienna Congress borders are not favourable for the healthy life of the State; the great issues of the day will not be decided by speeches and majority decisions—that was the great error of 1848 and 1849—but by iron and blood.'[407]

Realpolitik?

All this belonged to *realpolitik*—policies in line with the power interests of one's own state: 'The only healthy foundation of a great State ... is the egoism of the State and not Romanticism' (Bismarck[408]). As long as states are organised as power blocks in unitary fashion, confronting each other as rivals, they can do nothing other than make their own interests the guide for their actions and as long as this is the case, the statesman who did not wish to do this would be failing in his duty.

Bismarck differed from other statesmen mainly in two things: as a statesman of titanic genius, he practised his 'realpolitik' with much greater *success* than the other statesmen of his time, and furthermore, he expressed the viewpoint of 'realpolitik' openly whereas others were wont to disguise it or make false appeals to 'morality'.

When in 1866, after Prussia's victory over Austria, Wilhelm I wanted to see Austria punished by annexations of territory, Bismarck (who looked forward to positive possibilities for future collaboration with Austria) opposed him by arguing that Austria had only done the same as Prussia, namely fight for its position of leadership.

Rudolf Steiner said to the author on 4 December 1914 (4 months after the outbreak of the First World War) that if Bismarck had been an English statesman he would have acted just as the English statesmen had done but he would not have used the moralising excuses that they had used (by which he meant that they had said that England must go to war against Germany because Germany had infringed Belgian neutrality, and the like).

The important motif of *truthfulness* is everywhere evident here; it was a trait of Bismarck's nature. Arnold Oskar Meyer, in his major work on Bismarck,[409] writes that already in his time as an envoy, Bismarck expressed his 'contempt for conventional, untruthful diplomatic phrases'. Diplomats often felt that his way of saying what he thought was even uncanny. 'Take care of that man!' [i.e., be careful of him, pay attention—*Ed.*] Disraeli, the significant British statesman, said about him: 'He means what he says!'[410]

That obviously does not mean that as a politician, Bismarck was not a master of the 'Machiavellian' arts of cunning, cleverness, and violence[411] or did not apply them successfully. Indeed, in a certain sense, he recognised this in himself: 'In a speech of 1 May, 1872 he himself said that hypocrisy would always have to be regarded as perfectly permissible: "You see, I do not exclude myself. I also make use of it under certain circumstances"'[412]—which was again a very frank, 'unmachiavellian' declaration.*

---

* It is very much in line with the paradoxical self-annulment of the Machiavellian 'system' at that time which we characterised thus: whoever wants to go along with this system has to disavow it (if he wants to remain morally creditworthy) and whoever does go along with it has a hard time following it (because he thereby undermines his own creditworthiness!).[413]

Despite all his 'Machiavellianism', the fundamental trait of truthfulness in Bismarck's character should be contrasted with what in later political life became ever more common and led to the important motif of the 'karma of untruthfulness' to which Rudolf Steiner repeatedly referred throughout his lectures.

It was precisely Bismarck's frank statements such as that the solution to the German Question would be through 'blood and iron', which he then put into practice, that sparked such strong disapproval of and opposition to him throughout the world and in Germany as well. One has to ask why people took such strong offence at what was actually traditional and commonplace (offence which in Germany itself, through capitulation to the external successes of Bismarck's 'realpolitik', soon yielded in most circles to a mood of patriotic enthusiasm)? Why were people offended by what was normal? Because since 1848, people felt—even if more unconsciously in many ways—that a new age was coming about, which was striving, in living together with other people and nations, towards very different methods from the outdated 'martial' habits of the past, that Germany was particularly called to pave the way to this new age, and that it was a denial of Germany's better self when it held fast to the old ways in order to achieve the goal of the creation of a functional unitary nation state, which in truth did not correspond to the German character.

Was it actually, one must ask, a policy of 'realism' that Bismarck carried out (with Wilhelm I), a policy which took little heed of the true nature of the people and of their task?

With this question, we are now clearly right in the midst of *the other* of the two ways of seeing things mentioned above (p. 173), which sees things less from the surface but rather, from a higher level. From the viewpoint of *this* way of seeing things, it is very clear that it was anything but a realistic policy to ignore the true task and calling of the German people, which is what should have been the focus, and to act instead 'as if' Germany in the second half of the 19th century could, without challenge, behave as 'people' had usually behaved 'until then'.

But this realisation remained hidden from most people; only a few voices calling in the wilderness such as Karl Christian Planck or Constantin Frantz were well aware of it. Most admired Bismarck's 'realpolitik' and its practical success. Rudolf Steiner even said of Herman Grimm in 1919[414] that he had seen Bismarck as a 'tower' of practicality. In saying this, Steiner demonstrated how it is so necessary to revise one's judgements in important matters: until the catastrophe of the world war of 1914-1918, it might have seemed outwardly and apparently right to call Bismarck a practical man. But 'the catastrophe of the world war', Steiner went on in the sharpest tones, 'showed that he was a fantasist..., for the creation of the Reich was of course a fantasy', that is, wanting to solve the German Question in *this* way, by these means and with these methods. Reality soon rejected them through the catastrophe of the world war.

In the spiritual sense, a truly realist policy would above all have reckoned with the realities of the Folk Spirits. Their powers and their impulses are not to be grasped through moralising points of view or in legal, juridical categories such as are held valid in relations between individual persons. Nations act 'like forces of nature', Rudolf Steiner said, for example, in the above-mentioned conversation (p. 174) with the author on 4 December 1914 (in Munich), and he said it cannot be otherwise (namely, in relation to the way in which these impulses express themselves in the policies of statesmen) until a new world view [*Weltanschauung*] takes hold, namely, theosophy (the name which Steiner at that time still often used for anthroposophy), through which human beings must (or can or will) 'penetrate into the consciousness of the folk souls'.

That is an indication of fundamental significance especially in relation to the often-mentioned subject of 'policy and morality'. In ancient times, initiated priests and kings acted out of an awareness of Folk Spirits (and of other hierarchical beings). There was no conflict for them between policy and morality. People regarded it as their highest moral duty to carry out the will of the Folk Spirit. This relationship, which had to be lost like all the ancient bonds with the spirit, now has to be regained in freedom through a renewed principle of initiation in a modern, transformed fashion.

A first step or precondition for this is to orient one's political judgements and, insofar as it is possible, also one's political actions, to that psychology of peoples which results from an anthroposophically-based study of the human being. Any other political judgements and actions will remain pure dilettantism.

The next step will have to be the 'penetration of the consciousness of folk souls'. At the present time that is still—alongside other things that have to be achieved—a prime need, indeed a high *demand*.

It would be fulfilled through a new 'priest-kingship', as should have been inaugurated in the 19th century (see above, p. 152f.). If what was already predisposed to occur at that time had indeed occurred and had become effective, that strong and powerful 'wind' would have been created in Middle Europe which a Bismarck could *then* have taken into his sails.

He brought moral qualities with him which would have been necessary to sail with *this* wind: his truthfulness, his true attitude of service, his religiosity.

The perspective opens up (in the sense of 'the history that did not come about') that what should have happened to bring about a shaping of Middle Europe that was in accord with the spirit of the age, instead of through a one-sided northern German element which could *not* bring it about, would have occurred through collaboration between the northern and southern German elements: the northern and eastern German way of being, in which Bismarck had placed himself through his birth, with its particular capacities and virtues which were so well incorporated in him, would then have been able to find a way to serve what would have been inaugurated out of high inspiration from southern Germany. Such a collaboration would have been bound to have a transformative effect on all those involved, on Bismarck himself and on Prussia.[415] Prussia would then really have been able to 'merge itself' in a spirit of service in a true Germany, as the best minds in 1848 imagined.

Something else can come from such a viewpoint, for example: Bismarck was from his youth an enemy of state 'bureaucracy'; by nature, he felt himself to be a man of *rank* in the old sense. The functional, bureaucratic unitary state was not at all in line with his character. He therefore failed because the other option was not available to him,—and following the motto 'standing still is retreat', he became the great promoter of precisely what should have been overcome....

In 1862 Bismarck entered into was called the historical 'bond' between himself and King Wilhelm of Prussia. As the king's vassal, he wished to stand by him in unconditional loyalty, to get through the conflict between the government and the Parliament that had arisen over the question of the reorganisation of the Prussian *army*: the government wanted this i.e., the strengthening of the army as a necessary instrument of Prussia's Great Power policy;* the liberal majority in parliament opposed it and refused to approve the necessary expenditure. King Wilhelm had already decided to abdicate, because he believed he would not be able to endure the conflict, when Bismarck then stood strongly by him and was able to bring the conflict to a victorious conclusion for the sake of a strong monarchy and a militarily strong Prussia.

---

* The Swiss historian L. von Muralt (loc. cit., p. 23) agreed with the army reform as objectively necessary in this sense.

Roman Boos, where he writes in his book *Reichsgeist und Schweizergeist* [Imperial Spirit and Swiss Spirit] about this process between Bismarck and King Wilhelm,[416] impressively conjures up images from the ancient time of the *Nibelungs*: how in 1862 with colossal atavism Bismarck as a Nibelung warrior with the power and greatness of a Hagen stood before a king who had the indecisiveness of a Gunther; how this new Hagen swore faithful service, unconditional and without reservation, to the new Gunther....

This was at Michaelmas 1862: the fateful conversation between King Wilhelm and Bismarck occurred on 22 September at Schloss Babelsberg near Potsdam, the next day Bismarck was appointed Prime Minister, and on 30 September he gave that speech to the Budget Commission of the Prussian Parliament, in which, as we heard, the words 'iron and blood' sounded out, like a fanfare.

Historians confirm that with this, a new era had begun for Germany. It was exactly half a century after the birth of the Crown Prince of Baden on 29 September 1812.

Through his three wars (1864 against Denmark, 1866 against Austria and its German allies, 1870/71 against France) Bismarck solved the German Question in the Prussian sense and achieved the greatest success of his life. The German Reich had been created, which was a Greater Prussia. From then on, Bismarck unstintingly served the cause of peace.

If we see all this in the light of, and as the consequences of, Bismarck's not having found the 'right partner' and his therefore having had to depend on King Wilhelm with whom he was deeply connected, and only being able to work with him, then Bismarck, with all his powerful 'successes', seems like an eminently *tragic* figure.

'Blood and Iron'

Bismarck and Wilhelm I stand there with their successes as the complete opposite of that Prince of Baden who so soon after his birth was torn from his path, from whom all action was denied, and for whom an early death was arranged. The Nibelung spirit which dominated* events from 1862 appears as the complete opposite of the one who would have been no Nibelung prince, and the 'Mars' methods of 'blood and iron' as the complete opposite of the 'mercurial' power of his being.

---

* It had virtually been called for: 'A man is needed, a scion of the Nibelungs', the poet and playwright *Emanuel Geibel* had written in 1844.[417]

When Bismarck was raised to the rank of Count by King Wilhelm in 1865 in recognition of his great services, a motto was added to his family's coat of arms with the words *In trinitate robur* (In the Trinity—or should one say: in threefoldness?—strength). This motto relates directly to the threefold structure of the Bismarck coat of arms—some readers will know it from numerous illustrations—on a blue shield, a golden three-leaved cloverleaf with three silver oak leaves in the corners.[418] When one looks at the great issues at stake here, such facts too can seem very special; like an indication of a mission placed before the great statesman who came from this family: socio-political activity out of trinitarian forces. But in the reality of the 19th century, he became—again, on the contrary—one of the great promoters of the 'praxis' and the ethos of the anti-trinitarian, functional unitary state in a Middle Europe that had been called to realise something so very different.

And when he died in the evening hours of 30 July 1898, as we know from witnesses of his final hours, the last, understandable word that came from Bismarck's lips was the word '*Staatsraison*' (*raison d'état*). Erich Eyck, who records this in his great book on Bismarck,[419] is not wrong to say that if such was the case, then that last word symbolises the core of Bismarck's life just as *Mehr Licht* [More light] (the last words ascribed to Goethe) symbolise the core of Goethe's works.

Bismarck and Lassalle

A highly significant piece of the history of Middle Europe in the 19th century that 'was not to be' is distinguished by the name of *Ferdinand Lassalle.*

We heard earlier (p. 170) how Rudolf Steiner wrote in 1898 about the 'social kingdom' that could have arisen out of a collaboration between Bismarck and Lassalle if Lassalle had not been prematurely torn from life (at the age of 39; he was born on 11 April 1825).

In the history of socialism, Lassalle is known as the man with whom the workers' movement in Germany began. His 'Workers' Programme' of 1862 was the starting point of the German social democratic movement.[420] He was a genial personality, a Jew by heritage, deeply rooted in the German cultural life of the great classical period, especially the idealist philosophy of Hegel and Fichte. 'The ideas of the French Revolution and of German Idealism,' wrote his biographer Hermann Oncken,[421] 'brought his store of ideas and the powers of his will into movement in the fiery fundament of his being: both tendencies in and with one another!' That truly says a great deal when we recall what was said about the relationship that should have developed between the French Revolution and German cultural life (especially in Vol. VIII of this series). From a German spirit, Lassalle, a man of great political gifts, sought in the second half of the 19th century to find the way to shape external social and political circumstances, which was exactly what would have been needed.

'From its whole development and in the greatest conformity with its inner and outer history,' said Lassalle in his speech titled 'The Philosophy of Fichte and the Meaning of the German Folk Spirit' (18 May 1862)[422] 'there falls to the metaphysical nation, the German nation, this highest metaphysical lot, this highest world-historical honour: to create out of the merely spiritual concept of the nation a national ground, a *territorium*, and to create out of thinking an existence for itself. A metaphysical task for the metaphysical nation!...'

From the most spiritual and human viewpoint, Lassalle conceived of the task of the future-oriented fourth estate, which for him stood for the whole of mankind.

We cannot enter into all the details of this here but would like, for example, to point to the fine essay 'Ferdinand Lassalle'[423] by Wilhelm Salewski about this 'last knight of the spirit', as one who was close to Lassalle called him. In a most enlightening way, Salewski shows how close Lassalle came to anthroposophy in the way that was possible at that time.

Incalculable consequences could have resulted if Lassalle could have worked on longer: a non-Marxist socialist movement[424] could have developed which could have drawn the best forces from the genuine German spirit, a 'national' socialism in this sense (in the Age of Gabriel that was drawing to a close) from which an organic development in human forces could have led over to the Age of Michael that was about to begin. In 1913, a German historian[425] referred to Lassalle as having been a 'national socialist agitator'. Ten or twenty years later, in the womb of a darker future, seventy years after Lassalle, that same notion 'national socialist' would give birth, from the evil *counter*force of the true German folk soul, to the dreadful counter-image of what Lassalle had striven for, because, like so much else, Lassalle's impulse did not come to fruition.

In May 1863 there took place the first meetings between *Lassalle* and *Bismarck*. They came about from a more tactical viewpoint through their common opposition to the liberal Progressive Party. But in a positive sense, there was also much that related Lassalle's view of the state, which was strongly influenced by Hegel, to that which lived in Bismarck. We cannot go into these subjects in detail as this would take us far beyond the scope of our considerations here, but the essential point is that the known historical facts support the perspective of Rudolf Steiner in 1898 in relation to the 'social monarchy' that could have developed in Prussia if Lassalle had lived longer and Bismarck had collaborated with him. (see above, p. 170f.)

Lassalle himself said on 24 February 1864: '... I have been a republican since my early childhood. And yet, or perhaps because of it, I have come to the conviction that nothing could have a greater future and play a more beneficial role than *monarchy* if it could only decide to become a social monarchy. I would then take up its banner with enthusiasm....'[426]

Of real human significance is the way in which Bismarck and Lassalle, despite all the great differences that existed between them, came to know each other, and how they felt drawn to one another. Lassalle had for Bismarck, as has been said,[427] the understanding of a genius for another genius. In Bismarck, 'he found the greatest energy, a contempt for mere words, a political nerve. As different as their personalities were, the common bedrock in their natures brought them closer to one another on a human level.'[428] Bismarck himself praised Lassalle highly: 'I saw him and from that time when I spoke with him for an hour, I have not regretted it.... What he had was something extraordinarily attractive to me as a private individual; he was one of the most spirited and the most agreeable men I have ever met, a man who was greatly aspirational.... Our conversations lasted for hours, and I always regretted it when they were ended.'[429] [I.e. by Lassalle's death—*Ed.*]

In 1878, 14 years after Lassalle's death, Bismarck was still speaking about him in the German Reichstag in the debate over the anti-socialist law (directed against Marxist Social Democracy) in a way dubbed by an important member of the Reichstag as 'a posthumous declaration of love'.[430]

From everything we can learn about the relationship of these two personalities, one can gain the impression that they were actually meant to do something together and that something great in a positive sense could have resulted from their collaboration,* that historical development in Prussian and Germany could have taken another course.

---

* With regard to such a possible, though unrealised train of events, one can recall the way in which the unification of *Italy* came about in the 19th century through the collaboration of personalities as different as Garibaldi, Victor Emmanuel, Cavour and Mazzini and what Rudolf Steiner said about their karmic connections in his lecture of 23 March 1924 in Dornach.

Such conclusions were drawn from a bold overview of many things by *Roman Boos* in his important book *Rudolf Steiner und die Politik*[431] [Rudolf Steiner and Politics] in which he wrote:

> Let us look at the *world war.* One who takes account of the realism in what Steiner says about Bismarck's relation to the proletariat could be tempted to pronounce the paradox: if Lassalle had not been murdered [He actually died after a duel—*transl.*], Bismarck would have brought about his 'social monarchy' with a workers' movement led by Lassalle; in such a social monarchy he [Bismarck] would have created a front against the republican tendencies of the liberal bourgeosisie, which he overestimated, and thereby would have prevented the forces of this bourgeoisie from directing the German people towards *economic* development, which... would then have forestalled the global tensions that resulted in the explosion of 1914. To present such a paradox—that it was Racowitza's pistol and not Princip's[432] revolver that unleashed the world war—may be futile in itself [but] as a pointer to the underlying reality it has its own profound justification.

Boos here speaks, evidently in a figurative sense, of the 'murder' of Lassalle. Rudolf Steiner wrote (see above, p. 171) of Racowitza's 'frivolous pistol shot' which killed Lassalle in the duel. That duel was about a woman, Helene von Dönniges, only 19 years old at the time, who was the daughter of the Bavarian historian (a pupil of Ranke) and diplomat, Wilhelm von Dönniges. We cannot go into the detail of this affair here[433], but the following is of importance: Helene von Dönniges later lived as Frau von Schewitsch in Munich, where she was the centre of a circle which concerned itself with knowledge of anthroposophy (then called theosophy) as a spiritual stream among others at that time. In his book *Mein Lebensgang*[434] [The Course of My Life], Rudolf Steiner writes the following about her:

> For me—and also for many other participants in the circle—Helene von Schewitsch was a significant piece of history. She was the lady on account of whom Ferdinand Lassalle's life came to a premature end in a duel with a Romanian [this was that Herr von Rakowitza] [Iancu Racoviță—*Ed.*]. She later had a career as an actress and in America had become friendly with H.P. Blavatsky and Olcott. She was a woman of the world, whose interests appeared to be very spiritual at the time when my lectures took place at her home. The strong experiences that she had had gave an extraordinary weight to her presence and also to what she brought. Through her, I would like to say,

> I was able to see the work of Lassalle and his era, and also through her, much that was characteristic in the life of H. P. Blavatsky. What she related was subjectively coloured and formed by her imagination in many ways arbitrarily, but when one took that into account, one could see what was true under various covers, and an unusual personality was revealed.

When we learn that Helene von Schewitsch gave Rudolf Steiner the possibility to see, through her, the work of Ferdinand Lassalle and his era, then what has been reported that Rudolf Steiner said to trusted pupils and friends in Munich (1910 or 1911) about Lassalle right after a visit to Frau von Schewitsch can become all the more meaningful to us. His remarks, namely, again culminated—we only want to repeat the main point of them here—(and this is comparable with Rudolf Steiner's 1898 essay about Bismarck) in his underlining of the great, positive significance which the further activities of a genius such as Lassalle, in collaboration with Bismarck, would have had for developments in Germany in a truly progressive spirit. In Lassalle's endeavours, Steiner remarked, there were impulses 'from above' ...; something tremendous would have arisen ..., a spiritual socialism (not one 'from below')....

Helene von Schewitsch, weighed down by a heavy karma, committed suicide at the beginning of October 1911.

However, do Lassalle's impulses 'from above' not seem like a reflection of that much mightier impulse 'from above' which would have lived in the 'new priest-kingship' that was turned into 'Kaspar Hauser'?

The exclusion of Kaspar Hauser seems like the first act of a powerful drama. The second act of the same drama, although of much lesser significance than the first—is the fate, the exclusion, of Lassalle.

The third act of the same drama—obviously on a still further diminished scale—can perhaps be seen in the blows of destiny that caused Wilhelm I to be followed in 1888 for only three months by his severely ill son, Emperor Friedrich III, and then his grandson Wilhelm II.

The German Empire of 1871

'If the German spirit,' wrote the leading Swiss historian *Jakob Burckhardt* in a letter of 3 July 1870, 'reacts once again from its own most inward and unique forces against this great violation (overestimation of money etc), when it is able to put against it a new art, poetry and religion, then we shall be saved, and if not, then we shall not. I say: religion, for without a supramundane will which outweighs the whole power and money racket, we are lost.'[435]

A religious reform, namely, 'the resumption and completion of the German Reformation, the actual goals of which were interrupted and impeded', was seen by Immanuel Hermann Fichte, the philosopher, as the main task to be accomplished by German culture, and he wrote to this effect in the introduction—dated: 'in the first month of the new German Reich, 18 January 1871'—to his new edition of the 'Addresses to the German Nation' by his great father, Johann Gottlieb Fichte.[436]

Another voice, very different, from the same period: that of the German *Crown Prince Friedrich Wilhelm*, the later German Kaiser Friedrich III, who wrote in his war diary on 23 February 1871: 'Our next job, in peace at home, will be to solve the social question; for this lofty purpose all the treasures of German education and the German spirit must be used.' (France, he felt, could not do it, for the lack of a spiritual foundation, and nor could England, due to the excessive gap between rich and poor which prevailed there.[437])

Countless other such voices could be cited. Only someone who measures the reality of the Germany of the last third of the 19th century and the Bismarck Empire against the objectives, expectations and hopes expressed by such voices out of a feeling for Middle Europe's true tasks, can fully foresee Germany's tragic, failed development.

A key perspective for understanding this failed development of the German Reich of 1871 can be found in a lecture by Rudolf Steiner,[438] which we shall cite here. He begins by speaking about the great threefold streams or dispositions in the world in East, Middle and West: in the East from ancient times there has been the spiritual life but in our time it has come to its end; in the Middle are jurisprudence and the State (which decisively began with Rome), which are now glimmering like fading coals about to end; in the West is the new 'contemporary' nature of the economy in a very external sense.* What was founded in the last third of the 19th century as the German Reich, as characterised by Rudolf Steiner here:

> took up into itself this fading, glimmering element of ancient Rome and went down with it, already in the way it built itself up, but especially in the way it then shaped itself. Basically, within this German Reich there

---

*We are concerned here therefore not with the small, existing threefolding between Middle Europe and western Europe, which was the subject of a different discussion above on p. 147f, but with the more well-known, more all-embracing threefolding of East, Middle and West. Both of these two forms of threefolding of course have a particular, living relationship with one another.

> was only a continuation of the juridical, political element of the State that organised everything and had great genius in organisation; but it wanted to assimilate the economy without having any economic thinking. For everything that drove the economy into this sphere, wanted more and more to crawl under the State system.... So this Middle Europe could neither adapt to real economic life nor to a spiritual/cultural life that was living from its own roots.

But it was the economy that greatly, even excessively flourished in the 1870s in Germany (these years were known as the 'years of the founders'), and the economy was to play an ever greater role as the basis of the growing political and military might of the Reich. Notable in this economic aspect of the Reich is the fact that the real core of the German Reich was in the German Zollverein [customs union], founded in 1834, itself an economic and financial structure, as has often been emphasised.[439] Germany became one of the great 'industrial nations', but the political State framework for the Reich 'carried the imprint of Bismarck', as Rudolf Steiner characterised it,[440] that is, 'the imprint of a man for whom modern industry had never been a concern, who never knew anything of it, who never reckoned with it, who constructed a framework without including the growth of major industries. Within that framework there then developed the whole Americanism of big business, which went for beyond the framework....'

Looked at from the more human side, from this very inorganic industrial nature that ran wild in Germany (notably very different from what happened in England) came the kind of men who—as big industrialists of a certain type—entered into that unwholesome 'marriage' of a luciferic-ahrimanic kind with the 'Nibelung' nobility, as we mentioned earlier (p. 152), who were such a socially and politically powerful factor in the Bismarck Reich.

As the 'shadow' of this whole economic, industrial development, so to speak, there arose powerfully within the Reich, and completing the tragic destiny of Lassalle, the Marxist form of social democracy, the great movement of the masses in the socialist sense, 'from below'. Bismarck tried in vain to combat it through his anti-socialist laws.

Intended as a defence against the social democratic movement was also Bismarck's great, positive social legislation which, announced in the Imperial Proclamation of 17 November 1881, led to a new era in this field: the great social insurance laws which were much admired and copied abroad represented a significant beginning for which, however, there would be no corresponding further development.[441]

Just as social democracy had a strongly ideological basis in the materialistic theory and thought forms of Marxism and in modern materialistic science, so too did the other great counter-movement against Bismarck, the political mass movement of the party known as the 'Centre' have its own ideological basis in Roman Catholicism. The ever-growing spiritual vacuum in Germany, like social democracy, enabled political Catholicism to grow substantially. Misjudging its grounding in the spiritual and religious sphere, Bismarck also sought to combat this Catholic 'enemy of the Reich' through the methods of political power. Behind his '*Kulturkampf*' against the Catholic Church stood the idea of the power of the State,[442] the ethos of the bureaucratic, unitary State. Bismarck also lost this false battle against Rome.

From the spirit of the bureaucratic unitary State and its economic and political statism, Bismarck went over to protectionist tariff policies: the State protects industry and agriculture (the latter especially in the interests of self-sufficiency in time of war) against competition from 'abroad'—in opposition to the liberal tendency (in which the universal Michael impulse of the age declared itself and was prepared) to let the economy develop beyond national and state borders in the direction of a world economy. Bismarck made this incisive, historically most inappropriate turn towards protectionism precisely in the year 1879, a few months before the beginning of the Age of Michael in November of that year....

Thus, in this connection, the 'German Reich' of 1871, despite its federal and in *this* sense, non-centralised, non-unitary state nature, was, in the *functional* sense—and that above all is what matters—very much a unitary state: only one which was made up of a larger number of states.

At the same time, it was a *nation* state on the western European model, despite the number of 'national minorities' which, as foreign bodies, were part of it (Poles, Danes, French). This meant that this political entity was no real 'Reich', when one understands by 'Reich' (empire) a more universal, supranational structure such as the mediaeval 'Holy Roman Reich of the German Nation' had once been. The new 'Reich' wrongly sought to link itself with that earlier Reich. Bismarck adopted the word 'Reich' from the Frankfurt National Assembly for reasons of expediency and understood under Reich nothing other than a larger state.[443] However, what lived in this state as a national ethos—given the extent that the spiritual substance of German national striving in 1848 had dissipated in the years of 'realism'—more and more turned into an external nationalism such as obviously existed among other peoples but which very little befitted the German people in particular.

That the nature and dynamic of the Reich corresponded so little with the real needs of the times and with the conditions of the European peoples is also related to the often stated artificial character of the system of Bismarck's foreign policy in which he sought to ensure the existence of the Reich and to maintain peace in the world and which he knew how to manage with masterly virtuosity, as long as he himself was in charge of the Reich.

Deeply impressive words about the essential points of Germany's failed development are those which Rudolf Steiner wrote in his book *Die Kernpunkte der sozialen Frage* [The Core Points of the Social Question, today titled *Towards Social Renewal*] in 1919 after the collapse of the Bismarck Reich.[444] One feels one is listening to the language of destiny itself:

> And the German Reich? It was founded at a time in which people were striving to realise modern demands for a healthy social organism. If these demands had become reality, they could have given the Reich the world-historical justification for its existence. Social impulses came together in this Middle European Reich and in the region that could have seemed predestined for their historic realisation. Social thinking appeared in many places; in the German Empire it took on a particular form, from which one could see in which direction it was tending. It should have led to concrete actions for the Reich to work on which should have been put before the Reich's public servants. The justification for the Reich could have shown itself in the modern, collaborative life of various peoples. ... Instead of turning to the big picture with this task, people remained stuck on 'social reforms' which resulted from the demands of the day and were happy when foreigners admired the validity of *these* reforms. Along with this, people came ever closer to wanting to ground the Reich's external position of power in the world in line with forms that had been shaped out of the most outworn ideas about the power and grandeur of states. A Reich was shaped that... contradicted what was emerging historically in the forces of the life of nations in the modern era. The governors of the Reich saw nothing in these forces. The structure of the State that *they* had in mind could only be based on military power....

One sees that what is being discussed here is not at all the difficult errors associated with the birth of the German Reich through the way in which it came about; rather, here the Reich founded in 1871 is taken as a fact and what is indicated is what should have happened with it once it was founded. In his lectures to an audience from Britain about the history and overcoming of imperialism with regard to the Anglo-American world and the possibilities of its further development, Rudolf Steiner once uttered the radical words: 'It's not about how something has arisen, but about what one does to take further what has arisen.'[445]

His published *Call* to the public in January/February 1919 was titled 'To the German People and the World of Culture!':[446]

> ...The Reich was founded. In the first years of its existence, the effort was made to arrange its inner possibilities of life in accordance with the demands that showed themselves through old traditions and new requirements from year to year. Later, people began to consolidate and enlarge the Reich's external position of power, which was grounded in material forces.... The Reich was thus placed into the world without essential aims that justified its existence. This was revealed in a sad way through the course of the catastrophe of the [world] war. Until the outbreak of the war, the outside world had not seen anything in the behaviour of the Reich that could prompt the view that: the rulers of this Reich are fulfilling a world-historical mission which ought not to be swept away. That the Reich's rulers did not find such a mission inevitably created the view in the non-German world which for those with insight is the deeper reason for Germany's downfall... [i.e., the view that the Reich ought not to exist—*Ed.*].

But all these failures after 1871 were in the end nothing other than the continuation of the German developments that had been going on in the previous decades, the causes of which were deeply spiritual.

Nietzsche characterised the danger of the Bismarck Reich right after its victory in 1871 with his well-known words (often cited by Rudolf Steiner[447]): *'The extirpation of the German spirit in favour of the "German Reich."'*[448] As time went by, these words took on a tragic notoriety for many Germans.

But now, after all that we have considered, it can seem that Nietzsche's words must be taken far more concretely than we suspected, and that we can point to a specific act that was carried out decades before the founding of the Bismarck Reich—when, with the exclusion of a great individuality who had been called to leadership in Middle Europe, that 'extirpation' was already most decidedly accomplished.

Wilhelm II

Amidst all that was sucked into the spiritual vacuum that arose in Middle Europe belongs a human phenomenon that is qualitatively revealing of a great deal, namely, *Wilhelm II.* It is not that Wilhelm II had a particularly great influence on German politics and policy—he did not; in this he was greatly overestimated, especially abroad. Rudolf Steiner once said that the fact that foreigners thought him so hugely important was a wrong done to the German people.[449] It was precisely foreign opinion of Wilhelm II that succeeded, in its way, in placing him in the foreground, paying attention to him and seeing him as an exponent of the whole of Germany—much more, as Germany itself. That a person of his type was so *present* that he could take on this position and fill a certain circle with his being is nevertheless a symptomatic fact. Rudolf Steiner once spoke about what it shows in the following words:

> You see, if the Germans had always had the great talent for monarchy that the French have preserved so brilliantly until the present day, they would never have fallen for 'Wilhelminianism'; they would never have allowed this peculiar caricature of a monarch to be there, never would have needed to put him there....[450]

This caricature of a monarch, with his 'amateur dramatics' in the worst sense, fits the dynamics of the *counter-image* in a place [Germany] from which, by rights, completely different social impulses should have emanated.

Rudolf Steiner occasionally remarked on some notable comments by Bismarck about Wilhelm II.[451] When, for example, Bismarck once:

> expressed his thoughts about what would happen to Germany because of this emperor, he said: 'This man will live as though every day was his birthday; the likes of us are happy when we have our birthday again...; but he wants to have his birthday every day!' Those are words full of concern once spoken by Bismarck by way of characterisation at the beginning of the 1890s. Well, birthdays bring human egoism out very strongly....

Countless times traits of Wilhelm II were witnessed such as those—to give only one example here—which Queen Maria of Romania wrote in her memoirs:

> The Kaiser had placed great weight on honouring this... family event with his high presence. He came with an enormous retinue of huge men in

> brilliant uniforms. Everything that surrounded the German Kaiser was big and loud. The monarch lost no opportunity to show that he was the First. He changed his uniform several times a day like an elegant lady changes her attire....[452]

What was the phenomenon of Wilhelm II? Rudolf Steiner expressed it in 1919 (even if he did not mention Wilhelm II by name): at a particular point in time the soul of this personality had left him. That goes back to a karmic guilt from an earlier earth life, in which he engaged in unjustified occult activity.... But his body, abandoned by its soul lived on outwardly. 'Think what an opportunity that was for all kinds of ahrimanic spirits and individualities' to live on in such a person....[453] Much that in his outer appearance seemed to indicate a very strong I was based in fact on the lack of one. It was a shattering event in the karma of the people of the I, the Germans, to have had such a human husk at the helm of the Reich....

Prince Max of Baden

To the general observer it can appear striking, but it is entirely related to our theme, that at the end of the 'Kaiserreich' of the Hohenzollerns a man stepped onto the stage of history for a short time, a German prince and the heir apparent to one of the federal German states, who played a uniquely significant role which in various respects, through his intellectual and human bearing, stands apart in a beneficial sense from what had become the leading tone in the German Reich and its leadership circles. This was *Prince Max von Baden*, a significant, distinguished and cultured personality of humane and progressive ethos, not at all a 'Nibelung' prince, but the 'democratic prince' from southwestern Germany. He made the ears of many in the public prick up when, for example, in a public session of the First Chamber of the Baden parliament on 14 December 1917, he spoke out against the 'Moratorium on the Sermon on the Mount', that is, against the fact of its exclusion from political life, and emphasised that power alone could never ensure for Germans a position in the world. In the autumn of 1918, as is well-known, Prince Max became Chancellor of the German Reich for a few weeks before the collapse of the Central Powers. He was the seventh Chancellor after Bismarck and the last Chancellor of the '*Kaiserreich*'. All in all, he was 'a man on whom many in German-speaking lands placed something like their last hopes', as Rudolf Steiner put it in his 'Core Points of the Social Question'.[454]

Rudolf Steiner must also have expected something from Prince Max for a time and trusted that he would have understanding for larger perspectives.[455] Steiner was ready—as, basically, he was with everyone who wanted his advice—to have a conversation with Prince Max, which took place in January 1918 (in the prince's palace in Karlsruhe).

A few years later, Rudolf Steiner himself spoke about this conversation in a lecture in Kristiania (Oslo), and for a specific reason. He related that his counterpart in the conversation had noted:

> how necessary it actually was to have a psychology, a study, of the European peoples; for the great chaos which people were sailing into would demand that those who wished to lead in some way would be well-informed about the activities of the nations and the forces that lived within the souls of the various peoples. This personality regretted that actually there was no possibility in public affairs of being able to establish something like a study of the folk souls.

'I replied,' Rudolf Steiner went on:

> that I had held a lecture cycle on the study of the European folk souls here in Kristiania and I then sent a written copy of the lecture cycle to this person together with an introduction relating to the then present situation—January 1918.[456] ... It came to nothing, despite the introduction that related to the situation at the time, because the maturity that would have been necessary actually to see how strong the forces of decline were, the maturity which already a large number of souls could have had, these very souls did not consciously wish to strive for.

Rudolf Steiner said further that for him, 'this setting aside of my course on the psychology of the Nordic peoples by one of the leading personalities at such a senseless time' was 'deeply symbolic'....[457]*

There was therefore the highly meaningful fact that this personal meeting took place between Rudolf Steiner and Prince Max, who nine months later was to play such an important political role. Destiny seems to have offered something like a last chance for this German statesman to take up the impulse of ideas from the great bearer of human progress in the West, an impulse that corresponded to what the times required, if that statesman had been awake and open enough for it. Like many before him, he was not. In this historic moment, he too failed.

---

* On the important role that Rudolf Steiner's lecture cycle on the Folk Souls played here, see above, pp. 168/176.

But we need no great capacity for historical divination in order to grasp that this contact between Rudolf Steiner and Prince Max was a latter-day piece of the karma of Kaspar Hauser that had turned up in the 20th century. Prince Max was the prince of Baden from the Hochberg line of the Zähringer dynasty, the line that had taken the throne through the removal of Kaspar Hauser, but also someone whose whole personal ethos made him a man of goodwill who strove for appropriate forces of renewal in modern times; what he could have taken up from Rudolf Steiner would have corresponded to what he himself was deeply seeking and it would have been entirely in line with the impulses which, 70 years earlier, would have sought to proceed for the healing of the world from that individuality who had been 'extirpated'. As though linking onto that old historical destiny connection, something could have happened once again that turned Germany's direction back to that line.

It is remarkable how even in small traits of Prince Max, one can see the line of destiny which was, as it were, laid out before him and on which he lived. During the war, he served the Red Cross, a 'mercurial' deed, which, tellingly, sometimes earned him the sneering term of abuse: 'Baden's General of Health'.[458] Another area of his activities to which he turned soon after the outbreak of the war (on leaving the staff of the general headquarters of the XIV Army Corps, to which he belonged) was the care of prisoners of war and the international exchange of prisoners of war, where he worked against what he called 'war's brutalisation of feelings'.[459] Can one not feel destiny working here—how as if this prince of Baden wanted to make up somehow for what a noble prisoner from the House of Baden had suffered?

The line is clear. But the strength was insufficient. And so, when Prince Max, appointed by Wilhelm II in a catastrophic situation—became the Imperial Chancellor of Germany on 3 October 1918, his first important act as head of the German government was to propose an armistice to the American President Wilson on the basis of the 14 Points (5 October), whereby in the name of the German people he brought about what Rudolf Steiner called 'the dreadful spiritual capitulation' which, as 'a mere submission to Wilson's 14 Points', accompanied the collapse of the military,[460]—capitulation to that against which Middle Europe itself should have found an active, spiritually powerful answer. It was in this sense that Rudolf Steiner had written his '*Memoranda*' in 1917, which had presented social threefolding as the way out of the war through a positive and meaningful reshaping of conditions in

Europe. And yet Prince Max had been one of those who had read the '*Memoranda*'.[461]

His other act as Reich Chancellor was that he brought about Wilhelm II's necessary abdication. Indeed, the extremely dire situation in a certain sense required Prince Max to dismiss the Kaiser in that he announced, had to announce, the abdication of Wilhelm II, which had not yet taken place. Without wanting to, indeed against his will—he had hoped to preserve the succession for Wilhelm II's eldest grandson—he ended the rulership of the Hohenzollern dynasty in Germany. Here karma spoke a clear language: what Baden had once—in deviating, we can say, from its actual line of destiny—so strongly co-founded was now annulled by Baden's last heir apparent as Imperial Chancellor: the Hohenzollern Empire. To the 'Hurrah for the Emperor!' which the Grand Duke of Baden, Friedrich I, led on 18 January 1871 in the Palace of Versailles, the 'dismissal' of Kaiser Wilhelm II by the nephew of that Grand Duke Friedrich I, Prince Max of Baden—and precisely by him!—stood as an act of karmic compensation on 9 November 1918.

A prince of the same House with which that profound 'transformation of the concept of the monarch' (which we discussed on p. 153 above) had sought to link itself, now made a decisive contribution to putting a radical end to all monarchy in Germany.

Another man from Baden, Friedrich Ebert, the chairman of the Social Democratic Party, became the first President of the 'Weimar' Republic and thus successor to Wilhelm II as head of state.

Prince Max's significant political and historical role only lasted for a little over five weeks. Afterwards, he left the political scene but still made a name for himself occasionally;[462] on the whole, however, he was politically inactive. In 1920 he founded the well-known private boarding school of Schloss Salem, one of his properties (an old Cistercian abbey near Lake Constance)—a deed that can remind one again (like his work for POWs in the First World War) of the Kaspar Hauser karma.

In his book *Á la Conquête du Trône de Bade*[463] (1930)[The Conquest of the Throne of Baden] the French diplomat, historian and Kaspar Hauser researcher *Edmond Bapst* wrote of another link (mentioned already on p. 192 above) between Prince Max and Kaspar Hauser:

> In 1913 Prince Max von Baden, the future German Imperial Chancellor, who was at that time the presumptive heir to the throne of Baden, promised his cousin, the Russian Grand Duke Nicholas Mikhailovich, that he

would '*have the remains of Kaspar Hauser moved to Pforzheim*'[464] [i.e., to the vault of the House of Baden] immediately after his accession to the throne. Prince Max von Baden did not become the Grand Duke of Baden! Grand Duke Nicholas Mikhailovich had gone to great pains and much expense to put together a respectable dossier which made it clear (he explained it to me personally) that Kaspar Hauser really was the son of Grand Duchess Stéphanie; was the dossier destroyed by the Soviets, like the Grand Duke who had made it?*

* This Grand Duke Nicholas Mikhailovich was, on his father's side, a grandson of Czar Nicholas I (and therefore a nephew of Czar Alexander I) and through his mother, a princess of Baden, he was a grandson of Grand Duke Leopold von Baden. Prince Max too was (through his father) a grandson of Leopold and therefore a cousin of Grand Duke Nicholas, who was a scholar and a member of various scholarly bodies. Grand Duke Nicholas mostly occupied himself with historical studies and memoirs. He was an admirer of Napoleon, paintings and images of whom he collected. This we know from Baroness Louise von Reibnitz-Maltzan, a lady-in-waiting to his sister, Grand Duchess Anastasia von Mecklenburg-Schwerin, in her book *Gestalten vom letzten Zarenhof...* [Figures from the Last Russian Court], Dresden, 1928.[465] She knew him well. At the end of the 1890s, she writes, Nicholas Mikhailovich was mostly interested in the story of *Kaspar Hauser* and in a detailed but unfortunately unpublished draft manuscript proved that he had been the Baden heir apparent, the son of Grand Duchess Stéphanie. She herself [Louise von Reibnitz-Maltzan] had known the manuscript. The draft was to have been published only after the death of Grand Duke Nicholas. It was probably lost during the Russian Revolution.

It should also be mentioned that Otto Flake writes of Grand Duke Nicholas (whom he confuses with his father Michael Nikolaevich) that he had associated with Kaspar Hauser researchers because he had been prompted by the studies he had made to write a biography of Czar Alexander I's wife [Princess Luise, known in Russia as Elizabeth Alexeyevna], who was of the House of Baden.[466] This Czarina Elizabeth was an aunt of the Baden Crown Prince who had been born in 1812, and as the wife of Czar Alexander I, was the great-aunt of Nicholas Mikhailovich. She also interested the Grand Duke in view of his work on Alexander I. We find Grand Duke Nicholas referred to, what is more, as the 'most significant historian' of this Czar.[467]

Conclusion

Homeless Souls

In an observation about certain historical spiritual antecedents of the anthroposophical movement, Rudolf Steiner[468] spoke about the '*homeless souls*' who were becoming relatively more numerous from the last decades of the 19th century onwards. These were souls who, affected by the nature of their pre-birth existence in the spiritual world, were less inclined in their earthly life to place themselves into a normal existence, in the life of 'the common man' in the way it impinges on people externally; their souls were much rather filled with a longing for deeper spiritual experience. This made them homeless souls in the style of life which had become superficially dominant in the 19th century because of the materialism of the age. Rudolf Steiner described how many such souls especially were drawn to Richard Wagner and 'Wagnerism', seeing this not only as a musical element but as a cultural phenomenon. There they found something of what they were seeking: 'a door into a spiritual world'.... Later, many such homeless souls turned to the theosophy of H.P. Blavatsky and related personalities.

It is not difficult to imagine that such souls could have found a certain ground on which to stand precisely in the Middle Europe in the 19th century if the impulses of the great individuality who was called to leadership and whom we have been considering in this book had been there to encounter—indeed, that they had actually been waiting for these impulses in order to unite themselves with them in a stream which, in the midst of the materialistic civilisation of the 19th century, was to prepare the future spirituality of a new age.

Richard Wagner

From such a perspective, let us take a brief look at *Richard Wagner* himself. He was deeply connected with the old European spirituality, namely with what was living in the mythical world of the ancient Germanic culture, in the world of the Nibelungs long before 1200 when that Nibelung culture was still 'right' for its time and had not yet fallen into the soul decadence of the later 'Nibelung wildness'. It points us back into ancient Atlantis (Niflheim) with which, as we have seen, the 'stray Atlantean' was also decisively connected. Hence, Richard Wagner's deep connection with the stream of esoteric Christianity and its forces of the future, the Holy Grail, with that which is called to transform all human life and raise it to a higher level. 'Someone who is able to interpret the signs of the times even only a little,' said Rudolf Steiner in an Easter lecture,[469] 'will see in Richard Wagner's art the first rising star, how Christianity in its deepest idea arose from the narrow bounds of religious life into the wider circle of modern spiritual culture', and he speaks of Richard Wagner's Good Friday experience in 1857 and of his 'Parsifal'. In such perspectives of the future, does a Christianity not sound forth clearly that grows beyond all mere 'religion', as we wrote above (pp. 37-40) about Kaspar Hauser's relation to religion, and indeed, precisely in an intimate relation to the living presence of the gods in ancient Atlantis, in the 'pre-religious' stage of human development? In the above-mentioned Easter lecture, Rudolf Steiner speaks again of these Atlantean conditions. Is the figure who, with an innermost right, was called to bring forth a renewed priest-kingship not to be seen together with the being of the Grail kingship, which Richard Wagner, out of deep experience, presented to our eyes and ears in his 'Parsifal'? Did we not already find the figure of the unfortunate one in intimate proximity to that other 'pure portal'? Did he not know his origins or even his name? Indeed, we dare even to see the course of Richard Wagner's own life, even if only from a distance, yet in relation to everything of which we spoke earlier (p. 161, footnote): how in 1849—gripped by the impulse of the German national movement and taking part in it—during the revolution in Dresden he called on the king himself to declare his country a free state and to stand at its head. As external as that may seem, it stemmed from what Wagner longed for in those same depths of his soul from which so many powerful urges originated.

Everything, *everything* sounds together in harmony if we are only able to place it all before our souls, synthesising it from sufficient heights and rooting it in sufficient depths of spiritual becoming....

Malwida von Meysenbug, Édouard Schuré

Still other personalities, born at the right time, stood ready around the middle of the 19th century to participate actively in the great cause that sought to be inaugurated. The Crown Prince of Baden was born in 1812. Richard Wagner was born in 1813. In 1816 (in Kassel) a significant personality was born, in her soul and spirit one of the most enlightened figures of Middle Europe at that time: the unforgettable *Malwida von Meysenbug*; she too became one of the 'homeless souls'. She too had a deeply personal share in the '48 movement. Destiny led her to meetings with many important people at that time. Later, in her own full spiritual autonomy, she was part of the circle of souls gathered around Richard Wagner and his work. She shared intensely in what he sought and undertook.

'Only someone who experienced it,' she wrote[470]—about the first performances at Bayreuth in the summer of 1876, 'this first wondrous impression' (when for the first time, with the lights extinguished, the invisible orchestra sent forth its wonderful sounds 'as though from a world of spirits' and finally the curtain opened),

> this realisation of a creative ideal hardly thought possible—can grasp with what ardour the heart gave itself to this hope that a new cultural epoch, of which our greatest spirits had dreamed, would arise from this seed, that material power won through weapons could be transfigured in the best of the German spirit's heritage. No later success of the undertakings at Bayreuth could ever again equal the happiness of *this* hope, for whatever the heights that have been achieved and are still being achieved, this hope failed; the German people fell short of their mission.

It is also from Malwida von Meysenbug that we learn of Richard Wagner's own concerns about the German people, for example from a letter written at the beginning of September 1873 in Bayreuth.[471]

She tells how, together with Édouard Schuré, she spent an evening with the Wagners and how, provoked by something Schuré said, the disconcerting question of the opposition between France and Germany burst forth. 'Wagner expressed himself,' writes Malwida:

> fierily, energetically but very finely and fairly; he said, 'The point now is to see whether the actual German character still has another core and characteristic and can produce something sacred and new for the future rather than mere skill in war through the breeding of men, obedience, loyalty and doing one's duty; this will now be tested.... Germany would have to free itself from the foolish copying of what is French.' ... And again: 'Now the important thing is to see whether the German character is capable of this and capable of creating something new, beautiful and sacred out of itself; if not, then we are lost'.... It was splendid and uplifting and I hope that Édouard felt so too.

So here in the circle around Richard Wagner we see *Édouard* Schuré,[472] another great homeless soul, in whom much ancient spirituality lived and who had an intense longing for a new spirituality. He was born in 1841 and was therefore 32 years old in 1873. In 1889 his important book *Les grands Initiés* [The Great Initiates] has opened up for many people access to the spiritual movement. Later, he found his way, as is well-known, to Rudolf Steiner, who was 20 years younger, and in whom he recognised the great initiate. Schuré was the real bridge between Wagner and his circle and Rudolf Steiner....It is striking how the Franco-German motif played into his life too. He could not always cope with it.

A few years later, Richard Wagner felt himself very disappointed in his hopes. On 10 February 1878 he wrote, for example, that 'the German décadence' could 'no longer be stopped; few people imagined that the barrenness of the Prussian idea of the state should be so rapidly imposed on us as German imperial wisdom!' On 15 July 1878, he spoke of 'the ruination of the German character, which is beyond saving' and of 'the slow but also inevitable gestation of barbarism'.[473]

Ludwig II of Bavaria

For the Richard Wagner who wrote in this way about Germany, Ludwig II, King of Bavaria (1864-1886), with whom Wagner shared such a memorable destiny-laden friendship, was perhaps the *most* tragic among the tragic homeless souls of the 19th century, a personality to whom one can only do justice when one can let the unique phenomenon that was Ludwig speak to one, from whatever spiritual circles he may have come and whatever—unrealised—longings and intentions he bore in his soul, which was oriented towards what Richard Wagner was serving and for which Ludwig could not find a ground in the materialistic 19th century, which had to remain deeply alien to him because the great spiritual impetus with which a soul such as his could have united had failed to occur. It was due to this that Ludwig fell into his eccentricities and ultimately into his tragic illness.

He was born on 25 August 1845, almost exactly 33 years after the Crown Prince of Baden. At the time, Richard Wagner was writing the first draft of his 'Lohengrin', and he himself later saw Ludwig's birth at that time as having been as a meaningful gesture of destiny.[474]

From his childhood, we find the motif of the swan, which was taken up so powerfully by Richard Wagner, woven into Ludwig's life.

> Destiny arranged it that he spent a large part of his childhood at Hohenschwangau Castle, very close to where he later built Neuschwanstein Castle. ... This southwestern region of Bavaria, which would be so significant in Ludwig's destiny, had long been linked to the swan motif. The district

> known as Schwangau is there and also the Schwan-See [Lake Swan]. The nobles of Schwanstein built their castle there in the 12th century. In those times, the saga of the Swan Knights was still alive. Lohengrin was a son of Parsifal....[474]

How we can recall here what we were able to write earlier (p. 39) about the Order of the Swan in relation to Kaspar Hauser's confirmation in the 'Chapel of the Swan Knights' in the Church of St Gumbertus in Ansbach!

When in 1861 Ludwig, who was not yet 16 years old, was finally able to see a performance of Lohengrin he was deeply moved and wept copious tears.[474] Soon after acceding to the throne in 1864, in the sign of the Swan Knight, he met Richard Wagner for the first time.[474] He died in a state of tragic mental derangement at Whitsun in 1886, just as once Kaspar Hauser had appeared at Whitsun (1828) in Nuremberg for his brief, painful life 'in the world'.

Richard Wagner had himself called Ludwig the 'incorporated and potentised German Folk Spirit' and after a first meeting with Ludwig, 'Cornelius "quietly referred to him as the Emperor of Germany."'[475] It was all as if Ludwig's incarnation had been set according to very different preconditions.

His cultus, which he pursued at his palace at Linderhof and his castle Neuschwanstein in relation to his namesakes, the French 'Sun King' Louis XIV and even Louis XV, can still be perceived as a significant gesture despite all its aberrations. Ludwig XIV's Sun Kingship, itself an absolute distortion, points to the ancient theocracies of the sun kings[476] with whom the Bavarian king felt a deep kinship.

He had a great trust in Bismarck. In the founding of the Reich and the new German imperial institution he provided Bismarck with essential assistance; that is a chapter in itself. His antipathy against the new Prussian German Empire steadily stiffened, however. He wrote to Wagner: 'The consequences of '70 and '71 embitter my existence; truly, they should have turned out differently.'[477] Indeed, they should certainly have turned out very differently. In how deep a sense, he himself could not know.

Finally, his antipathy intensified until it became outbursts of hatred, even against Bismarck himself. The German Reich now 'disgusted' him—'how, unfortunately, it had shaped itself to an extreme degree, thanks to the dry Prussianism devoid of ideals under that provincial Junker' (9 August 1878).[477]

★

Constantin Frantz, a very important political thinker and an outstanding opponent of Bismarck (b. 1815), was born in 1817, and in 1819 was born the much more universal German philosopher, *Karl Christian Planck*, who also, in negative terms, became an opponent of Bismarck and of the Bismarck Reich, but more positively, fought for a social form for the Germans that would correspond to their true spirit. Constantin Frantz's opposition to Bismarck also came from a similar direction. One finds in the works of these men real treasures of profound ideas about politics and the state.

We mentioned both of them above on p. 175 and discussed them also in our book on National Socialism in the chapter 'Those Who Warned...'.[478]

Once again, without falling into any fantasies, one can well imagine how differently the destinies of the two men could have been, how their more spiritual ideas and approaches could have become really positively constructive and effective in Middle Europe if that spiritual social impulse that had actually been extirpated had become centrally important there.

Rudolf Steiner frequently referred to Karl Christian Planck who was passed over during his own lifetime and forgotten after his death (1880). In a lecture on 30 January 1917, Steiner said of him:

> ...this man had ideas and thoughts in connection with industrial and social life which ought to have been put into practice. If only there had been someone at that time capable of employing in social life the great ideas this man had, ideas truly compatible with reality, then—and I am not exaggerating—mankind would probably not now be suffering all that is going on today which, for the most part, is a consequence of the completely wrong social structure in which we are living.
>
> If people had turned to a healthy way of life such as that advocated by Planck in the 19th century, then the bloody conduct of the first third of the 20th century would at least have been ameliorated. One cannot ameliorate things with idealisms but only through realistic thinking; and realistic thinking also always means spiritual thinking.

Rudolf Steiner spoke in general terms in a lecture of 29 September that same year 1917, about the intimate connection between the failure to take up spiritual impulses and consequent physical catastrophes: how the chaos of the present has arisen 'from an unspiritual grasp of reality': one cannot ignore the spiritual world with impunity, the spirits 'take their revenge' when they are ignored here on earth. A mysterious connection exists, he says in this lecture, between human consciousness and the destructive forces in the universe. If there had been an era in the last 20 or 30 years of the 19th century in which human beings had striven for the spirit (like they had striven only for material aims), if people had striven for spiritual knowledge, spiritual impulses for social action, that would have 'paid off the destructive forces. If people had been more awake and had not slept through the last decades of the 19th century ..., the first decades of the 20th century would not have needed to bring destruction if consciousness had been stronger.'

This was said on Michaelmas Day 1917. At that time, the new spiritual impulse had been given out for many years, out of the fundamental forces of the new Michael Age that had begun in 1879 and those of the dawning Age of Light following the end of the dark age (of 'Kali Yuga') in 1899, and this new impulse expressed itself precisely in 1917 in the great ideas for human social life on earth that were in tune with reality [i.e., the ideas of social threefolding—*Ed.*]. That this new impulse found such an astonishingly poor reception is surely related in essence with the fact that in the 19th century in Middle Europe the preparation did not take place that could and should have served the impulse. But the consequences of this renewed 'falling aleep' were again the same. Destructive processes continued, powerfully intensified.

They took on a very strong accent in Middle Europe when the spiritual 'vacuum' that had developed over decades was suddenly filled, as it were, by demonic powers of destruction, first under the deceptive guise of a new development [the Reich] and a new catastrophe of the most dreadful kind was set in train.

1833-1933

When Henriette Feuerbach wrote in her letter of 2 January 1884 to her nephew in connection with the case of Kaspar Hauser about that hypothetical 'casket' (see above, p. 94) which she said she would lock and seal with the inscription 'To Be Opened on 17 December 1933' (i.e., on the 100th anniversary of the death of Kaspar Hauser), she could not have realised the profoundly shattering sense which these words of foreboding would make to us who would come after her.

A hundred years after the death of Kaspar Hauser in Ansbach, National Socialism had taken power in Germany and ruled the 'Third Reich', as the Counter-Reich. The counter-image of the new 'priest-kingship' had appeared in the form of the *Führerprinzip*: the absolute dominance of one possessed by the demonic powers of the abyss. The *Führerprinzip* was in its spiritual reality the principle of possession, the grotesque face of a new principle of initiation.

What the 'Third Reich' enabled people to experience was a very particular form of the 'encounter with evil' which makes up a really intrinsic part of our entire epoch.

Not a few people came to grasp once again through the 'Third Reich' that evil is a real spiritual power which strikes into historical and social life.

One such was the important German historian *Friedrich Meinecke.* In his book *Die deutsche Katastrophe*[479] [The German Catastrophe], written in his old age, he came to the insight that 'the work of Hitler must be reckoned among the irruptions of a satanic principle into world history'. That is a new category in conventional academic thought.

With the recognition of the objective and real satanic powers also begins for many people a recognition of the reality of the spiritual world as a whole.

The destiny of Kaspar Hauser can become for us today an image—and more than just this—of the destiny of the German people. The stabbing of Kaspar Hauser at Advent in 1833 seems like a prefiguring—and a 'preconditioning' of what Hitler did to the German people a hundred years later.

The greater a spiritual individuality is, the more powerful is the historical dimension of his or her destiny for humanity. The ongoing consequences of the exclusion of the one who was called the Child of Europe cannot easily be conceived of in sufficiently universal terms. For the failed development of *Middle* Europe robbed Europe of the right middle, without which Europe cannot flourish between its East and West, and in the larger sense, neither can the whole world in its balance between its larger East and its larger West.

In what dimensions Rudolf Steiner regarded the figure of 'Kaspar Hauser', was shown by his (well-attested) words that: if Kaspar Hauser had not lived and died as he did, contact between the Earth and the spiritual world would have been completely disrupted,—words which open still further enormous perspectives pointing to a positive reverse side to what happened with Kaspar Hauser and what was done to him. They enable us to compare that smaller event with the greatest event in Earth evolution, and even to think of it in terms of this central greatest event.

But what was intended by this 'unrealised history' remains, as we have already said, in a certain sense, and demands to be realised, in however modified a form—a demand that stands there before humanity, just as the individualities also remain. The 'unrealised history' thus transforms itself, when it is recognised, into a seed. That is its future promise, and what we must focus on.

'The essential thing,' said Rudolf Steiner in 1919,[480] 'is that from this present time onwards, into the near future, people must not be deprived of [knowledge of] what the actual driving forces of human evolution are.'

Notes

Abbreviations:

Vol. I, II, III, IV,V,VI,VII,VIII refer to: Karl Heyer, *Beiträge zur Geschichte des Abendlandes* [Contributions to the History of the West] ,Vols. I-VIII.

I. *Von der Atlantis bis Rom* [From Atlantis to Rome], Stuttgart, 3rd ed. 1964.

II. *Mittelalter* [The Middle Ages], Kressbronn 1956.

III. The Modern Age, Kressbronn 1957.

IV. *Wege der neuern Staats- und Sozialentwickelung* [Paths of New Development in State and Society]

Part 1: *Machiavelli und Ludwig XIV* [Machiavelli and Louis XIV], Stuttgart, 1964.

V. *Wege der neuern Staats- und Sozialentwickelung* [Paths of New Development in State and Society]

Part 2: *Friedrich der Grosse und das Preussentum* [Frederick the Great and Prussia], Stuttgart 1964.

VI. *Wege der neuern Staats- und Sozialentwickelung* [Paths of New Development in State and Society]

Part 3: *Gestalten und Ereignisse vor der Französischen Revolution* [Figures and Events before the French Revolution], Stuttgart 1964.

VII. *Wege der neuern Staats- und Sozialentwickelung* [Paths of New Development in State and Society]

Part 4: *Die Französische Revolution und Napoleon* [The French Revolution und Napoleon], Stuttgart 1964.

VIII. *Wege der neuern Staats- und Sozialentwickelung* [Paths of New Development in State and Society], Kressbronn 1964

Part 5: *Sozialimpulse des deutschen Geistes im Goethe-Zeitalter* [Social Impulses of the German Spirit in the Age of Goethe], Kressbronn 1964.

A new edition of these volumes under the series title

Studien-materialen zur Geschichte des Abendlandes

[Study Materials on the History of the West] is planned.

1. E.g. in the lecture of 11 April 1916 in Berlin, Rudolf Steiner *Gesamtausgabe* [Collected Works] GA 167.
2. See especially Rudolf Steiner's lectures of 14, 20, 21, 26, 27, 28 October 1917 in Dornach in GA 177. In the last of these lectures the significance of these events for a real understanding of the history of the 19th century is emphasised. (See our Vol. III, p. 69f.). See also Rudolf Steiner's lecture of 23 September 1916 in Dornach in GA 171.
3. Op. cit.—See also the lecture of 2 April 1921 in Dornach, in GA 204.
4. This was 14 years before the year 1842, often referred to by Rudolf Steiner e.g. in the lecture of 20 March 1917 in Berlin, in GA 175.
5. 23 March 1923 in Dornach, in GA 222.
6. The public lecture of 17 June 1908 was accordingly printed in the lecture cycle on the Apocalypse, GA 104.
7. G. Fr. Daumer, *Enthüllungen über Kaspar Hauser* [Revelations about Kaspar Hauser], Frankfurt-am-Main, 1859, p. 326.

7a Daumer 1859, printed in Hermann Pies, *Kaspar Hauser. Augenzeugenberichte und Selbstzeugnis* [Eye-witness Reports and Personal Testimony] Vol. I, 1st ed., Stuttgart (1925), p. 180.

8. Feuerbach, in Pies, *Augenberichte...* [Eye-Witness Reports], op. cit., I, 129.
9. See especially Rudolf Steiner's lectures of 24 December 1923–1 January 1924 in Dornach 'World History in the Light of Anthroposophy and as a Foundation for Knowledge of the Human Spirit', GA 233 and together with those lectures, also Hans Erhard Lauer, *Geschichte als Stufengang der Menschwerdung* Vol. I [History and the Process of Becoming Human], Freiburg-im-Breisgau 1956, pp. 105-136, especially p. 124.
10. Personal communication of the son of the above-mentioned personality to the author. See also the essay '*Erinnerungen an Rudolf Steiner*' [Memories of Rudolf Steiner] by Rudolf Rissmann in *Erinnerungen an Rudolf Steiner* [Memories of Rudolf Steiner] ed. E. Beltle, Stuttgart 1979.
11. See Pies, *Augenberichte...* [Eye-Witness Reports] I, 15/16.
12. Wilhelm Kunze, *Georg Friedrich Daumer und die Fortführung der Reformation. Mit einem Anhang: Eine Schülerin Daumers* [Georg Friedrich Daumer and the Continuation of the Reformation—With an Appendix: A Female Pupil of Daumer's], Nuremberg 1933. Another book that should be mentioned for the many insights it provides is the small book by Hans Kern, *Georg Friedrich Daumer. Der Kämpfer für seine deutsche Lebensreligion* [Georg Friedrich Daumer. The Fighter for his German Religion of Life], Berlin 1936, written from National Socialist perspectives, which Daumer, through his comprehensive criticism of Christianity, seemed to endorse.
13. Hans Wohlbold in the Stuttgart weekly *Anthroposophie*, 16 March 1930.

14. Hans Wohlbold in *Blätter für Anthroposophie* [Gazette for Anthroposophy] VI, 2 (Feb. 1954), pp. 56-64.
15. This, together with details, was reported to me by the person who heard it from Rudolf Steiner.
16. In *Süddeutsche Monatshefte* [South German Monthly] Vol. 11, vol. 2, April—September 1914, p. 143.
17. See *Kaspar Hauser. Über tausend bibliographische Nachweise.* [Over One Thousand Bibliographic Items of Proof] by Dr Hans Peitler and Prof. Dr Hans Ley, Ansbach 1927, Nos. 541,542, 548f. After this, the novel first appeared in the journal *Über Land und Meer* [On Land and Sea], Stuttgart and Leipzig, Nos. 1-31.
18. I am quoting here from '*30 bis 34 Auflage aller Ausgaben*' [30-34 edition of all issues], published 1925 (in Peitler-Ley No. 728 a), p. 460.
19. In Hermann Pies, *Die amtlichen Aktenstücke über Kaspar Hausers Verwundung und Tod* [Official Records of Kaspar Hauser's Wounding and Death], Bonn 1928, p. 180.
20. Hermann Pies: 1. *Kaspar Hauser. Augenzeugenberichte und Selbstzeugnis* [Eye-witness Reports and Personal Testimony] Vols. I and II, Stuttgart 1925, 2. *Fälschungen und Tendenzberichte einer 'offiziellen' Hauserliteratur* [Falsifications and Tendentious Reports from 'official' Hauser Literature], Nuremberg 1926, 3. *Die amtlichen Aktenstücke über Kaspar Hausers Verwundung und Tod* [Official Records of Kaspar Hauser's Wounding and Death], Bonn 1928, 4. Pies' contribution to *In Memoriam Adolf Bartning. Altes und Neues zur Kaspar-Hauser-Frage* [In Memory of Adolf Bartning. Old and New Information in the Kaspar Hauser Question], ed. Frau Luise Bartning, Ansbach 1930, 4. *Die Wahrheit über Kaspar Hausers Auftauchen und erste Nürnberger Zeit. Augenzeugenberichte und Selbstzeugnisse, amtlichen Aktenstücke, Fälschungen und Tendenzberichte* (abbr.: *Wahrheit über Kaspar Hauser*) [The Truth about Kaspar Hauser's Appearance and his First Years in Nuremberg. Eye-witness Reports and Personal Testimony, official records, falsifications and tendentious reports (abbr. Truth about Kaspar Hauser)], Saarbrücken 1956.
21. Pies, *Fälschungen*, pp. 3,4; Pies, *Verwundung und Tod*, p. 7.
22. Reported by Dr Wagler, *Die Enträtselung der oberrheinischen Flaschenpost von 1816* [Solving the Riddle of the Upper Rhine Message-in-a-Bottle of 1816], Nuremberg 1926, p. 3.
23. That this appeared already in the year he was first seen in Nuremberg is evidenced, for example, in the small book produced in 1830 by the Berlin Police Commissioner (Johann Friedrich Karl) Merker: *Caspar Hauser, nicht unwahrscheinlich ein Betrüger* [Caspar Hauser, not improbably a swindler], p. 92.

24. Rudolf Steiner, 14 February 1918, Munich, GA 174a, emphasis by K. Heyer.
25. Rudolf Steiner, 9 December 1917, Dornach, GA 179.
26. In his essay '*Zum Caspar-Hauser-Problem*' [On the Problem of Caspar Hauser] in the *Vossischen Zeitung* [Vossische News], Berlin, No. 450, 21 September 1924.
27. Nuremberg (undated) (1924), p. 169. Emphasis: K. Heyer.
28. Feuerbach (Pies, *Augenzeugenberichte*... 138) thought that Hauser was 15-16 years old at the time; the official record on the case of Kaspar Hauser (Pies, *Augenzeugenberichte*...II 240) has his age as 16-18.
29. Quoted from Pies, *Augenzeugenberichte*...176. Emphasis: K. Heyer.
30. See Lauer, op. cit., p. 109f.
31. Baron Gottlieb von Tucher in his essays '*Kaspar Hauser—kein Betrüger*' [Kaspar Hauser—No Swindler] (1872), printed in *In Memoriam Adolf Bartning* op. cit., pp. 195-236. See especially p. 208.
32. Georg Friedrich Daumer, *Kaspar Hauser. Sein Wesen, seine Unschuld, seine Erduldungen und sein Ursprung* [Kaspar Hauser—His Character, His Innocence, His Sufferings and His Origin], Regensburg 1873, pp. 134/135.
33. See Dr Preu in Pies, *Augenzeugenberichte*... I 247.
34. Georg Friedrich Daumer, *Enthüllungen über Kaspar Hauser* [Revelations about Kaspar Hauser], Frankfurt-am-Main, 1859, pp. 306/307. See also p. 182.
35. H. Fuhrmann in Pies, *Augenzeugenberichte*... II 118; see also in Pies, *Verwundung und Tod*, p. 80
36. Dr Preu in Pies, *Augenzeugenberichte*... I 254.
37. Dr Preu in Pies, *Augenzeugenberichte*... I 250. Emphasis: K. Heyer.
38. Feuerbach in Pies, *Augenzeugenberichte*... I 121/122.
38a Heinrich Hubert Houben in '*Karl Gutkows Leben und Schaffen*' [Karl Gutkow's Life and Achievements] in Vol. 1 of *Karl Gutkows ausgewählte Werke in zwölf Bänden* [Karl Guthkow's Selected Works in 12 Volumes], Leipzig (1908), p. 122.
39. Johannes E. Hohlenberg, *En Sjaels Tragedie*, Copenhagen 1923.
40. In *Die Menschenschule* [The School of Men], ed. C. Engler-Faye, Basel, February-May 1929.
41. Op. cit., p. 137f.
42. Karl König, '*Mignon. Versuch einer Geschichte der Heilpädagogik*' [Mignon. Attempt at a History of Curative Pedagogy]. In *Der Beitrag der Geisteswissenschaft zur Erweiterung der Heilkunst. Ein anthroposophisch-medizinisches Jahrbuch.* [The Contribution of Spiritual Science to the Furtherance of the Art of Healing], Dornach-Basel 1950, pp. 219-243, here pp. 234/235.
43. Feuerbach in Pies, *Augenzeugenberichte*... I 42.
44. Daumer 1873, pp. 136/137.
45. Daumer 1859, in Pies, *Augenzeugenberichte*... I 192/193.
46. Daumer 1873, pp. 212, 139.

47. Feuerbach in Pies, *Augenzeugenberichte*… I 126.
48. Feuerbach in Pies, *Augenzeugenberichte*… I 94.
49. Feuerbach in Pies, *Augenzeugenberichte*… I 68.
50. Ivo Striedinger, '*Neues Schrifttum über Kaspar Hauser*' [New Writings about Kaspar Hauser] in *Zeitschrift für bayerische Landesgeschichte*, [Journal for Bavarian History] Vol. 6, Munich, 1933, pp. 415-484, here p. 83.
51. In Pies, *Augenzeugenberichte*… I 147. Similarly, Feuerbach op. cit., 39.
52. Baron von Tucher 1872: *In Memoriam Adolf Bartning*, pp. 207, 216, 217.
53. Quoted from Police Commissioner Merker, *Caspar Hauser, nicht unwahrscheinlich ein Betrüger* [Caspar Hauser, not improbably a swindler], Berlin 1830, pp. 12/13.
54. Preu in Pies, *Augenzeugenberichte*… I 248/249.
55. Feuerbach in Pies, *Augenzeugenberichte*… I 94.
56. Op. cit., p. 252.
57. Daumer in Pies, *Augenzeugenberichte*… I 242.
58. Daumer in his 1873 book, p. 82, quoting his own earlier publication.
59. In his essay of 1872, op. cit., p. 219.
60. Rudolf Steiner, GA 103, Lecture 5.
61. Op. cit., pp. 57/58.
62. Op. cit., p. 413.
63. Op. cit., p. 257f.
64. Pies, *Augenzeugenberichte*… I 213f.
65. See Sigismund von Gleich, *Mysterien-Dämmerung und Christus-Erscheinung* [The Twilight of the Mysteries and the Appearance of Christ], Stuttgart (1953), p. 123.
66. For the following discussion, see Rudolf Steiner's lecture of 30 December 1913, op. cit., p. 101.
67. Feuerbach in Pies, *Augenzeugenberichte*… I 49.
68. Feuerbach loc. cit., p. 101.
69. For example, Daumer in Pies, *Augenzeugenberichte*… I 228-231, '*Träume*' [Dreams].
70. Daumer in his 1859 book, p. 92.
71. Hans Wohlbold in his essay 'Kaspar Hauser' in *Anthroposophie* XIV 4/5 (January/February 1932), p. 158.
72. Daumer in Pies, *Augenzeugenberichte*… I 224.
73. For all this, see Fuhrmann in Pies, *Augenzeugenberichte*… II 107, 120, 134, 135.
74. Op. cit., II 131/132.
75. Cf. Daumer in Pies, *Augenzeugenberichte*… I 196, 222, 224, 227; similarly, Feuerbach I 101.
76. See my essay 'Lessing' in *Das Goetheanum* V (1926) Nos. 24-29, especially No. 26.

77. Estimations of the length of his incarceration differ. The Nuremberg physician Dr Osterhausen in his expert opinion report of 1830 stated that Hauser, 'when he was incarcerated, was already 3-4 years old.' (Pies, *Wahrheit*, 154. On this question, compare the extracts that follow below from an essay by the Ansbach physician Dr Heidenreich in 1834.
78. Different from the animal: on the power of standing upright, see Rudolf Steiner's lecture of 4 October 1918 in Dornach (GA 184).
79. Report of the Nuremberg City Court Physician Dr Preu on 3 December 1830 (in G. Friedrich Kolb, *Kaspar Hauser*, Regensburg 1883, p. 82). See also Feuerbach in Pies, *Augenzeugenberichte*... I 41.
80. Daumer in Pies, *Augenzeugenberichte*... I 157.
81. Daumer op. cit., 159.
82. See Feuerbach in Pies, *Augenzeugenberichte*... I 56, Preu op. cit., 277/278, Daumer op. cit., 207.
83. Daumer in Pies, *Augenzeugenberichte*... I 161, n. 37.
84. Sophie Hoechstetter uses the motif of the 'poppy seed' in her novel on pp. 8,11.
85. Daumer in Pies, *Wahrheit* 305. (In 'Wahrheit' 236 Pies refutes Hauser's '*fabled*' skill in riding, which was a main argument of Police Commissioner Merker in Berlin for Hauser being a fraud.)
86. This expert opinion report of the Provinical Court physician Dr Albert ('Court Physicians' Reports' can be found in Pies, *Die amtlichen Aktenstücke über Kaspar Hausers Verwundung und Tod* [Official Records of Kaspar Hauser's Wounding and Death], 2nd ed., Bonn 1928, pp. 157-163.
87. Dr Heidenreich in Pies, *Augenzeugenberichte*... II 180-184 and Pies, *Wahrheit* 276-278.
88. See the lecture of 16 October 1905 in Berlin (GA 93a) and also the lectures of 31 October and 5 November 1905, op. cit.
89. Daumer in his 1859 book, pp. 327/328.
90. Daumer 1859, in Pies, *Augenzeugenberichte*... I 195/196.
91. Klara Hofer, *Das Schicksal einer Seele. Die Geschichte von Kaspar Hauser. Unter Berücksichtigung der neuesten Festellungen* [The Destiny of a Soul. The Story of Kaspar Hauser, in the Light of the Latest Research], Nuremberg 1924, p. 268.
92. Rudolf Steiner lecture of 9 April 1918, Berlin, GA 181.
93. Hermann Pies, *Fälschungen und Tendenzberichte*... op. cit. p. 40. See also p. 18. Pies discussed this comprehensively in the chapter 'Lord Stanhope and the Case of Kaspar Hauser' in the much reworked section (pp. 173-223) of his book *Wahrheit*... (see especially p. 191). Cf. pp. 245, 248, 266, 273, 297.
94. See *Fälschungen und Tendenzberichte*... pp. 38-63.
95. Feuerbach in Pies, *Augenzeugenberichte*... I 65.

96. Emil Bock (in relation to Schiller's 'Demetrius') in *Boten des Geistes* [Messengers of the Spirit], 2nd ed. Stuttgart (1937), p. 84.
97. See above, n. 39, 40. Here *Die Menschenschule* op. cit., pp. 122/123.
98. Feuerbach in Pies, *Augenzeugenberichte*... I 39.
99. Daumer in Pies, *Augenzeugenberichte*... I 156/157.
100. Feuerbach in Pies, *Augenzeugenberichte*... I 172. Similarly, Daumer op. cit., p. 159.
101. Von Tucher in *In Memoriam Adolf Bartning* op. cit., p. 227.
102. Feuerbach in Pies, *Augenzeugenberichte*... I 41/42. Cf. (on the lack of concepts) Pies, *Wahrheit*... 279 (witness: Weickmann).
103. Feuerbach in Pies, *Augenzeugenberichte*... I 69, 78/79. Emphasis in the original text.
104. Appeared posthumously in *Blätter für Anthroposophie* VI 2 (February 1954), here p. 18.
105. Von Tucher in Pies, *Augenzeugenberichte*... I 148[5].
106. Feuerbach (in Pies, *Augenzeugenberichte*... I 86) here rightly sees 'a striking witness for the state of Kaspar's soul at that time'.
107. Cf. Feuerbach in Pies, *Augenzeugenberichte*... I 54, 131; von Tucher in *Memoriam Adolf Bartning*, p. 211.
108. Feuerbach in Pies, *Augenzeugenberichte*... I 104-106.
109. Cf. Pies, *Augenzeugenberichte*... II 16-29; Daumer's 1859 book, pp. 181-188.
110. Pies, *Verwundung und Tod*, p. 144.
111. See above, n. 19.
112. Pastor Fuhrmann in Pies, *Augenzeugenberichte*... II 151.
113. Mayor Binder's 'announcement' in Pies, *Augenzeugenberichte*... II 248/249.
114. Daumer in Pies, *Augenzeugenberichte*... I 216, 218.
115. Von Tucher *In Memoriam Adolf Bartning*, p. 214.
116. Hiltel according to Feuerbach, in Pies, *Augenzeugenberichte*... I 50.
117. Feuerbach in Pies, *Augenzeugenberichte*... I 100, 120, 130, 131. Emphasis: K. Heyer.
118. Daumer in his 1859 book, pp. 297-302.
119. Daumer in Pies, *Augenzeugenberichte*... I 179.
120. Hermann Rauschning, *Gespräche mit Hitler* [Conversations with Hitler], Zurich-Vienna-New York, German ed., 4th reprint. Copyright 1940, pp. 81/82.
121. Klara Hofer op. cit., p. 129.
122. Emphasis : K. Heyer.
123. Von Tucher in Pies, *Augenzeugenberichte*... I 175, n. 59. Emphasis: K. Heyer.
124. Hans Wohlbold, '*Georg Friedrich Daumer. Ein vergessener deutscher Denker*' [Georg Friedrich Daumer—A Forgotten German Thinker] in the Stuttgart

Anthroposophie—Wochenschrift für freies Geistesleben [Anthroposophy—a Weekly for the Free Spiritual Life] XII 11, 16 March 1930, p. 85. Emphasis: K. Heyer. Cf. Wohlbold in his essay 'Kaspar Hauser' in *Anthroposophie* XIV 4/5 (January/February 1932), p. 158.

125. Rudolf Steiner speaks of this briefly in his *Occult Science—An Outline*, GA 13, in the chapter 'The Human Being and the Evolution of the World'.
126. Rudolf Steiner, lecture of 21 December 1913 in Bochum, GA 150. First emphasis: K. Heyer.
127. Rudolf Steiner, lecture of 24 December 1912 in Berlin, GA 143. It was also indicated in our book: *Aus dem Jahrhundert der französischen Revolution* [From the Century of the French Revolution], 2nd ed., Kressbronn (Lake Constance) 1956, in the description of the spiritual origins of the ideals of liberty, equality, and fraternity (here p. 69).
128. Cf. for all this, besides the lectures of Rudolf Steiner named in the text, see also those of 21 December 1911 in Berlin ('*Weihnachten ein Inspirationsfest*' [Christmas—a Festival of Inspiration], in GA 127), 23 December 1913 in Berlin, GA 150; 1 August 1915 in Dornach, GA 162; 27 and 28 December 1915 in Dornach, GA 165.
129. Helene Hirschmann, *Kaspar Hausers erstes Weihnachtsfest und andere Geschichten* [Kaspar Hauser's first Christmas and other stories], Ansbach 1929, p. 5-16.
130. Rudolf Steiner lecture 7 March 1914, Pforzheim (on the three spiritual stages prior to the Mystery of Golgotha), in GA 152.
131. Cf. the fourfold 'capacity to stand upright, capacity to speak, capacity to speak in vowels and consonants, capacity to think', also the (already mentioned on p. 49) lecture by Rudolf Steiner of 9 April 1918, Berlin, GA 181.
132. Cf. the first publication in Rudolf Steiner, 'The Spiritual Guidance of the Individual and of Humanity', GA 15.
133. Rudolf Steiner, 19 December 1910, Berlin, GA 124 ('Background to the Gospel of St Mark').
134. Sigismund von Gleich, *Mysterien-Dämmerung und Christus-Erscheinung* [The Twilight of the Mysteries and the Appearance of Christ] Stuttgart (undated) (1953), p. 25f.
135. More details on this in my Vol.I, p. 140f., Rudolf Steiner, GA 112, Lecture 2; GA 124, Lecture 5.
136. Also Daumer in his 1859 book (p. 5f.) already referred to Cyrus, Romulus and Remus and others as parallel cases to the destiny of Kaspar Hauser.
137. '*Neues über Kaspar Hauser*' [New Research on Kaspar Hauser], lecture held on 22 April 1927 by the attorney Bartning (Hamburg) in the '*Hamburgischen Forensisch-Psychologischen Gesellschaft*' ['Hamburg Forensic-Psychological Society'], Ansbach 1927, p. 51.

138. Otto Flake, *Kaspar Hauser. Vorgeschichte, Geschichte, Nachgeschichte. Der Tatsachenbericht.* [Kaspar Hauser's Story and its Antecedents and Consequences—The Factual Account], Mannheim, 1950, p. 157.
139. In my book *Aus dem Jahrhundert der französischen Revolution* [From the Century of the French Revolution], 1st ed. Breslau 1937, 2nd ed. Kressbronn (Lake Constance) 1956, Chapter 2.
140. In my book *Die Französische Revolution und Napoleon* [The French Revolution und Napoleon] Kressbronn (Lake Constance) 1953.
141. *Gestalten und Ereignisse vor der Französischen Revolution* [Figures and Events before the French Revolution], Kressbronn (Lake Constance) 1952.
142. Op. cit., pp. 191/192. Emphasis: K. Heyer.
143. Wilhelm Kunze, *Mythos, Gestalt und Schicksal von Kaspar Hauser* [The Mythos, Individuality and Destiny of Kaspar Hauser], Nuremberg-Leipzig, undated (published 1953) pp. 53/54. Wilhelm Kunze already wrote of the Rousseau motif in a similar way to ourselves.
144. Cf. my book *Gestalten und Ereignisse vor der Französischen Revolution* [Figures and Events before the French Revolution], (Kressbronn/Lake Constance 1952) in the chapter on Rousseau's experience of inspiration, pp. 98-111, especially pp. 107/108.
145. Karl Vossler, *Die romanischen Kulturen und der deutsche Geist* [The Romance Cultures and the German Spirit], Stuttgart, undated (contains lectures by Vossler given in March 1925 in Bremen).
146. Fuhrmann in Pies, *Augenzeugenberichte...* II 115.
147. Otto Flake op. cit., p. 158.
148. Dr Heidenreich in Pies, *Augenzeugenberichte...* II 178.
149. Cf. my book *Die Französische Revolution und Napoleon* [The French Revolution und Napoleon] Kressbronn (Lake Constance) 1953.
150. Cf. Merker op. cit., p. 66.
151. Vol.VII, p. 328f.
152. Cf.Vol. I 291,Vol. IV 42-45.
153. Cf. my essay '*Wer ist der deutsche Volksgeist*? [Who is the German Folk Spirit?], 1. in *Rundbriefe zur systematischen Erarbeitung des anthroposophischen Lehrgutes* [Circular for the Systematic Development of Anthroposophical Teachings], ed. Max Rebholz, No. 2 (Nov. 1946), pp.22-27; 2. reprinted in *Studienhefte für Anthroposophie* [Study Materials for Anthroposophy], ed. Max Rebholz, III 12 (March 1950), pp. 1-6. In both there are, unfortunately, a number of printing errors.
154. Rudolf Steiner lecture: 31 October 1915, Dornach, GA 254.
155. Cf. Rudolf Steiner lecture: 20 March 1917, Berlin, GA 175.
156. Edmond Bapst, French ambassador, *Une mère et son fils: La Grande-Duchesse Stéphanie et Gaspard Hauser*, Paris 1933, p. 1. Bapst specifies for the poem: '*Paul*

Verlaine (Sagesse, Chant III, no. 4)'. N.b. the other verses of the poem are of no particular relevance.

157. Cf. Frieda von Oppeln, *Das Rätsel des Kaspar Hauser* [The Riddle of Kaspar Hauser], Dresden (1922) p. 176.
158. In his essay referred to in n. 69 above.
159. Hans Kern, '*Georg Friedrich Daumer...*', Berlin 1936, p. 13.
160. Cf. my *Geschichtsimpulse des Rosenkreuzertums* [Historical Impulses of Rosicrucianism], Breslau 1938, e.g. p. 45; also, Vol. IV, pp. 154/155.
161. Wohlbold in his essay '*Georg Friedrich Daumer*' in the Stuttgart weekly magazine *Anthroposophie*, 16 March 1930.
162. Stuttgart 1952, pp. 99/100.
163. Wilhelm Kunze, *Georg Friedrich Daumer und die Fortführung der Reformation. Mit einem Anhang: Eine Schülerin Daumers* [Georg Friedrich Daumer and the Continuation of the Reformation—With an Appendix: A Female Pupil of Daumer's], Nuremberg 1933, pp. 41, 48/49.
164. Cf. my six essays titled 'Lessing' in *Das Goetheanum* V (1926) 24-29, esp. pp. 205, 211, 212.
165. Emil Bock, *Wiederholte Erdenleben. Die Wiederverkörperungsidee in der deutschen Geistesgeschichte* [Repeated Earth Lives. The Idea of Reincarnation in German Spiritual History], Stuttgart 1952, p. 148.
166. Cf. n. 17 above.
167. Rudolf Steiner, *The Guardian of the Threshold*, Scene 6, GA 14.
168. In *Lebensdienst. Gesammelte Studien, Erfahrungen und Reden aus drei Jahrzehnten* [A Life of Service. Collected Studies, Experiences and Speeches from Three Decades], Leipzig and Zurich (1928), here esp. pp. 124, 128-131, 143.
169. More correctly, it should read: 'the Luginsland at the Vestner Gate', cf. above p. 53. Feuerbach in Pies, *Augenzeugenberichte...* I 69.
170. Jakob Wassermann in his essay '*Zum Caspar-Hauser-Problem*' [On the Problem of Caspar Hauser] in the *Vossische Zeitung* No. 450, 21 September 1924.
171. Daumer in his 1873 book, pp. 1,2.
172. Antonius von der Linde, *Kaspar Hauser. Eine neugeschichtliche Legende* [Kaspar Hauser—A Legend of Modern History] Vols. I and II, Wiesbaden, 1887.
173. Pies, *Augenzeugenberichte...* II 306.
174. Daumer refers to this in his 1873 book, p. 298.
175. Ivo Striedinger, 1. '*Hauser, Kaspar, der Findling (1828-1833)*' [Kaspar Hauser—The Foundling 1828-1833] in *Lebensläufe aus Franken* [Lives from Franken], Vol. 3, Würzburg 1927, pp. 199-215 (the same essay in earlier versions elsewhere). 2. *Neues Schrifttum über Kaspar Hauser. Zur 100 Wiederkehr seines Todestages* (17 December 1833) [New Writings about Kaspar Hauser] in *Zeitschrift für bayerische Landesgeschichte*, [Journal for Bavarian History] Vol. 6, Munich, 1933, pp. 415-484.

176. *'Hauser, Kaspar'* op. cit., p. 211, '*Neues Schrifttum*' op. cit. p. 417.
177. Cf. on this and the polemical debate between Striedinger and Pies ('*Wahrheit...*,' pp. 330-347).
178. '*Neues Schrifttum*' op. cit., p. 439.
179. Dr Preu in Pies, *Fälschungen...* pp. 48-49.
180. E.g. '*Hauser, Kaspar*' op. cit., p. 203; '*Neues Schrifttum*' op. cit., pp. 430, 448, 456.
181. *'Hauser, Kaspar'* op. cit., p. 215; similarly, '*Neues Schrifttum*' p. 42.
182. '*Neues Schrifttum*', p. 421.
183. Cf. Kolb op. cit., p. 101.
184. See Pies, *Augenzeugenberichte...* II 5-104.
185. Daumer in his 1873 book, pp. 8, 82.
186. Hermann Pies, *Fälschungen und Tendenzberichte einer 'offiziellen' Hauserliteratur* [Falsifications and Tendentious Reports from 'official' Hauser Literature], Nuremberg (1926), Extract 3, pp. 38-63.
187. Pies, *Augenzeugenberichte...* II 306.
188. *In Memoriam Adolf Bartning*, pp. 180, 183. Cf. also the letter of Henriette Feuerbach (11 Jan. 1876) to Dr Julius Meyer himself in which she writes, tellingly, of 'what remains of trust in your love of truth and honour' which she had maintained, while she had 'long since lost' it in Mittelstädt (the other opponent of Kaspar Hauser). (Cf. Thomas Stettner '*Ungedruckte Briefe Henriette Feuerbachs' in Der Sonntags-Kurier, Unterhaltungsbeilage des Fränkischen Kuriers* [Unpublished Letters of Henriette Feuerbach in *The Sunday Courier*, entertainment supplement of the *Fränkisch Courier*] VII 37 Nuremberg, 11 September 1927.) A picture of Dr Julius Mayer can be found in Fritz Beyerlein, *Erinnerungen aus Ansbachs Vergangenheit* [Memories of Ansbach's Past], Ansbach 1923.
189. Eduard Engel, *Menschen und Dinge. Aus meinem Leben* [People and Things—From My Life] Leipzig (1929), p. 79f. Rather different from Eduard Engel: *Kaspar Hauser. Schwindler oder Prinz? Ein urkundlicher Roman* [Kaspar Hauser—Swindler or Prince? A Documentary Novel], 2nd ed., Braunschweig/Berlin/Hamburg, 1931, pp. 230/231.
190. '*Menschen und Dinge*', p. 79.
191. The Kaspar Hauser book mentioned in n. 189.
192. Op. cit., pp. 123, 160, 11.
193. Op. cit., p. 108.
194. In the *Nürnberger Zeitung* newspaper of 2 December 1931. The passage referred to is in Daumer's 1859 book, p. 236.
195. Hermann Pies in the *Kölnischen Zeitung* newspaper of 30 October 1931, No. 593.
196. On Engel's book, see also Ludwig Wagler: *ein Danaergeschenk Eduard Engels an die Kaspar-Hauser-Literatur* [A Greek gift from Eduard Engel to the Kaspar-Hauser literature], Ansbach 1931.

197. Cf. here also Hans Wohlbold in his often cited essay: in the weekly magazine *Anthroposophie* 16 March 1930 about Daumer, who had known these forces very well.
198. Cf. Pies, *Verwundung und Tod*, pp. 83, 101.
199. Lecture of 24 September 1909, Basel, GA 114.
200. Stuttgart 23 March 1921 during the Anthroposophical High School Course, GA 324.
201. Lecture of 23 October 1915, Dornach, GA 254.
202. For more on this, see my Vol. IV, pp. 32-34, and also the important essay by Paolo Gentilli '*Dantes Verbannung*' [Dante's Banishment] in the monthly magazine *Gegenwart* [The Present] (Bern) XVII (Feb. 1956) pp. 432-444. There, it is briefly shown which forces hindered Dante's mission and, conversely, which would have been blocked if he had remained in power. See also the essay by Roberto Passaglia, '*Die Erkenntnis des Übersinnlichen in Dantes Göttlicher Komödie*' [The Knowledge of the Supersensory in Dante's *Divine Comedy*] in *Blätter für Anthroposophie*, esp. IX 2 (Feb. 1957), p. 67.
203. Lecture of 15 January 1917, Dornach, GA 174. Rudolf Steiner here shows how the course of history would have been very different if Napoleon had had a strong navy and so would not have been defeated at sea by England.
204. Rudolf Steiner lecture of 12 October 1918, Dornach, GA 184.
205. Rudolf Steiner lecture of 8 September 1918, Dornach, GA 184.
206. Rudolf Steiner lecture of 24 September 1916, Dornach, GA 171. See also my Vol. II, p. 221.
207. August Strindberg, *Der bewusste Wille in der Weltgeschichte. Skizze zu einem Buch* [Conscious Will in World History. Sketches for a Book] German translation, Munich and Leipzig (1903?), e.g. pp. 15, 22, 24, 81, 82.
208. Leopold von Ranke in the Prologue to his *Geschichten der romanischen und germanischen Völker* [Histories of the Romance and Germanic Peoples], Vol. I, Berlin, 1824.
209. Cf. for this 'unrealised history', see my little book *Aus dem Jahrhundert der französischen Revolution* [From the Century of the French Revolution], Breslau, 1937 (Foreword and Introduction), also, Vol. II, pp. 152/153 and Vol. III p. 226.
210. Frieda von Opeln, *Das Rätsel Kaspar Hauser* [The Riddle of Kaspar Hauser], Dresden 1922, p. 8.
211. Sophie Hoechstetter, *Das Erlebnis* [Experience], Leipzig 1931, p. 71.
212. P. 58 in the text named.
213. In his essay 'Kaspar Hauser' in the monthly magazine *Anthroposophie* of January/February 1932, p. 157.
214. Cf. Meyer's *Grosses Konversations-Lexikon* [Meyer's Great Conversation Lexikon] Vol. 18, 6th ed. Leipzig and Vienna 1907, p. 107; Baedecker's *Süddeutschland* [Southern Germany], 30th ed. Leipzig 1909, p. 341; Fritz Beyerlein,

Erinnerungen aus Ansbachs Vergangenheit [Memories of Ansbach's Past], Ansbach 1923, pp. 2,3.

215. E.g. in the lecture of 23 July 1922, Dornach, GA 214.
216. About the swan, the sacred hyperborean bird of Apollo, and about swan sagas, swan knights etc., one can find much that is spiritually revealing in, for example: a) E.Ch. Wolfram, *Fixsternhimmel und Menschheit* [The Fixed Stars and Humanity], Breslau 1940, p. 151, b) Sigismund von Gleich, *Hellas und Kleinasien* [Greece and Asia Minor] (no publication details), p. 89, c) Friedrich Doldinger, *Der Schwanenritter. Dramatische Legende* [The Swan Knights—Dramatic Legends], Bremen 1949, d) Sigismund von Gleich, *Mysterien-Dämmerung und Christus-Erscheinung* [The Twilight of the Mysteries and the Appearance of Christ], Stuttgart (1953), p. 51, e) Eduard Lenz, essay '*Gottesboten*' [God's Messengers] in *Die Christengemeinschaft* [The Christian Community], June 1954, pp. 167, 169, f) Wilhelm Schneider op. cit., p. 175, g) Rudolf Meyer, essay '*Keltische Sagenschätze*' [Treasures from the Celtic Myths] in *Die Christengemeinschaft*, July 1956, p. 222, h) *Nachrichten-Blatt Dornach* [Newsletter Dornach], 29.7.1956, pp. 140/141.
217. E.g. in the lecture of 10 June 1910, Kristiania, GA 121.
218. Lecture of 28 August 1909, Munich, GA 113.
219. Lecture of 23 April 1912, Berlin, GA 133. See also above, n.4.
220. In *Memoriam Adolf Bartning*, pp. 181/182.
221. Op. cit., p. 261.
222. Such as the Head Librarian Dr Hermann Haering in his critique of Hermann Pies' *Augenzeugenberichte*... in *Deutsche Literaturzeitung* [the Journal of German Literature], January/June 1927, Berlin 1927, p. 769.
223. Archive Director Dr Ivo Striedinger in *Lebensläufe aus Franken* [Lives from Franken], Würzburg 1927, p. 199.
224. Heidenreich in Pies, *Augenzeugenberichte*... II 155.
225. Feuerbach in Pies, *Augenzeugenberichte*... I 119.
226. See Vol. III, pp. 52-60, esp. 58.
227. See above, p. 90, footnote.
228. Printed in: 1. *Anselm Ritter von Feuerbachs Leben und Wirken*... [Anselm Ritter von Feuerbach's Life and Works], published by his son Ludwig Feuerbach (the well-known philosopher), Vol. II Leipzig 1852, pp.319-333, here p. 92, footnote 2. Klara Hofer, *Das Schicksal einer Seele*... [The Fate of a Soul...], Nuremberg 1924, Appendix pp. 280-297, here p. 70.
229. Peitler-Ley, op. cit., Nos. 106, 109.
230. Peitler-Ley, op. cit., Nos. 192, 200.
231. Eduard Vehse, *Geschichte der Häuser Baiern, Württemberg, Baden und Hessen* [History of the Houses of Bavaria, Württemberg, Baden and Hesse] Part 4, Hamburg 1853, p. 292.

232. Daumer in his 1873 book, pp. 362, 414.
233. Georg Friedrich Kolb, '*Kaspar Hauser*', Regensburg 1883, p. 68.
234. Pp. 6, 190.
235. Daumer in his 1873 book, pp. 362, 414.
236. A great deal can be found concisely summarised in the often-cited book by Otto Flake (but mostly without sources).
237. See, for example, Fritz Klee, *Neue Beiträge zur Kaspar Hauser-Forschung* (Nuremberg, 1929) [New Contributions to Kaspar Hauser Research], p. 102.
238. In Pies, *Die amtlichen Aktenstücke über Kaspar Hausers Verwundung und Tod* [Official Records of Kaspar Hauser's Wounding and Death], Bonn 1928, p. 186.
239. Nuremberg 1928, p. 15.
240. Part 4, Lepizig 1889, pp. 361/364.
241. *Gedanken und Erinnerungen von Otto Fürst von Bismarck* [Thoughts and Memoirs of Prince Otto von Bismarck] New ed., Vol. 1, Stuttgart and Berlin 1923, p. 334.
242. Peitler-Ley, op. cit., pp. 1-76, Nos. 1-503.
243. Jakob Wassermann, *Mein Weg als Deutscher und Jude* [My Path as a German and a Jew], Berlin 1921, pp. 79. See also above p. 80, footnote.
244. In *Velhagen und Klasings Monatshefte* [Velhagen and Klasing's Monthly Bulletins], September issue 1908, pp. 156-158.
245. For a deeper discussion of the Demetrius problem, those interested are referred to: 1. Emil Bock, *Boten des Geistes. Schwäbische Geistesgeschichte und Christliche Zukunft* [Messengers of the Spirit—Swabian Spiritual History and the Christian Future], 2nd ed. (1937), p. 83f., 2. Herbert Hahn, *Gewaltiger als das Schicksal* [More Powerful than Destiny], Stuttgart, 1939, pp. 87-91, 130, 3. Paul Michaelis' literary portrayal, *Demetrius. Tragödie*, [Demetrius—A Tragedy] Karlsruhe 1956. See also, for example, René Fülop-Miller, *Macht und Geheimnis der Jesuiten* [The Power and the Secret of the Jesuits], Berlin 1929, pp. 411-417, 5. Johannes Scherr, '*Der falsche Dmitry*' [The false Dmitry] in *Menschliche Tragikomödie* [Human Tragi-comedy] Vol. 3, Leipzig 1884, pp. 136-166, 6. Theodor Hermann Pantenius, *Der falsche Demetrius* [The False Dmitry], Bielefeld and Leipzig 1904.
246. In *Aus der Mansarde Streitschriften, Kritiken, Studien und Gedichte. Eine Zeitschrift, in zwangslosen Heften herausgegeben von G. F. Daumer* [From the Garret: Polemics, Critiques, Studies and Poems. An Informal Journal published by G. F. Daumer] No. 4, Mainz 1861, pp. 107/108.
247. Cf. Daumer's 1873 book, pp. 381, 409.
248. Cf. Gustav Berthold Volz, *Der Graf von Saint-Germain* [The Comte de St Germain], Dresden 1923, pp. 28/29, 290f.
249. Pies, *Wahrheit...*, p. 330.

250. Cf. also Klara Hofer op. cit., p. 226f and Fritz Klee op. cit., p. 53.
251. Cf. above, p. 68.
252. Cf. Wilhelm Mommsen, *Die politisch Anschauungen Goethes* [Goethe's Political Views], Stuttgart 1948, p. 60.
253. Emil Bock, essay '*Zur Ketzergeschichte*' [The History of Heretics] in *Die Christengemeinschaft* [The Christian Community], February 1953, pp. 52/53.
254. Cf. Eduard Heyck, *Geschichte der Herzoge von Zähringen* [History of the Dukes of Zähringen], Freiburg-im-Breisgau 1891, p. 3, where it is even stated that the House of Zähringen was justified 'by its age—by which is meant its ancient importance and power—in placing itself before all other reigning dynasties'.
255. Cf. our Vol. II, p. 66/67.
256. Cf. our Vols. IV, V.
257. Part 4, Book 16. Similarly in Part 4, Book 18. Cf. also Part 3, Book 12 (in relation to Klopstock's invitation to the Karlsruhe court.)
258. Cf. Arthur Kleinschmidt, *Karl Friedrich von Baden*, Heidelberg 1878, p. 99.
259. Cf. Gustav Berthold Volz, *Der Graf von Saint-Germain* [The Comte de St Germain], Dresden 1923, p. 314. On St Germain, see also my book *Aus dem Jahrhundert der französischen Revolution* [From the Century of the French Revolution], 2nd ed., Kressbronn (Lake Constance) 1956.
260. With regard to this section about Baden and Karl Friedrich, see the following: 1. The above-mentioned works by Heyck and Kleinschmidt, 2. Friedrich von Weech, *Badische Geschichte* [Baden's History], Karlsruhe 1890, 3. The essay by David Friedrich Strauss, '*Klopstock und der Markgraf Karl Friedrich von Baden*' [Klopstock and Margrave Karl Friedrich von Baden] in *Historische Zeitschrift* [The Historical Journal] 1859, Vol. I, pp. 424-448, 4. Karl Brunner, *Badische Geschichte*, [A History of Baden] Leipzig 1904, 5. Rolf Gustav Haebler, *Ein Staat wird aufgebaut. Badische Geschichte 1789-1818* [A State is Built. The History of Baden 1789-1818], Baden-Baden 1947.
261. J.W. Goethe, *Dichtung und Wahrheit* [Poetry and Truth], Part II, Book 9; Part IV, Book 16.
262. Cf. Alfons Rosenberg, *Der Christ und die Erde. Oberlin und der Aufbruch zur Gemeinschaft der Liebe* [Christ and the Earth: Oberlin and the Coming of the Community of Love], Olten and Freiburg-im-Breisgau 1953, p. 271.
263. *Johann Heinrich Jung's (genannt Stillings) Lebensgeschichte* [Johann Heinrich Jung's (Stilling's) Life Story], 3rd. ed. Stuttgart 1857, p. 611.
264. See Emil Bock, *Wiederholte Erdenleben* [Repeated Earth Lives], Stuttgart 1952, p. 53.
265. Rudolf Steiner, *Briefe I 1881-1891* [Letters I 1881-1891], Dornach 1948, p. 136/137.
266. Published as a book in Basel 1941.
267. Lecture of 4 November 1916 in Dornach, GA 172.

268. On St Martin, see my Vol. VI, pp. 215-239.
269. Lecture of 20 March 1917, Berlin, GA 175.
270. Op. cit., p. 760.
271. Op. cit., p. 811.
272. *Lebensgeschichte* [Life Story] op. cit., p. 730.
273. Eduard Vehse, *Geschichte der deutschen Höfe seit der Reformation* [History of the German Courts since the Reformation], Vol. 27, Hamburg, 1853, p. 188.
274. Cf. above, p. 99.
275. For the facts in relation to Jung-Stilling here, see Alfons Rosenberg op. cit., pp. 111-123, 301 and Haebler op. cit., pp. 216/217.
276. On the 'Holy Alliance' see my Vol. VIII, pp. 261, 263, 265, 267f.
277. Cf. my Vol. VII, especially p. 328f.
278. Cf. above, p. 97.
279. Cf. above, p. 97.
280. Cf. my book *Geschichtsimpulse des Rosenkreuzertums* [Historical Impulses of Rosicrucianism], Breslau 1938, esp. the chapter '*Ein Ereignis am Anfang des 17. Jahrhunderts*' [An Event at the Beginning of the 17th Century] (pp. 20-25) [New ed. Perseus Basel 1992].
281. Cf. Pies, *Wahrheit...*, p. 333. Such an example—*Mittelstädt* op. cit., p. 126.
282. Lecture of 15 May 1915, Prague, GA 159/160.
283. Cf. my essay '*Arabertum und Islam als weltgeschichtlicher Kulturimpuls*' [Arab culture and Islam as a World-historical Impulse] in *Die Drei* [The Three] II 10/11 (1923); also, numerous references in *Beiträgen...* [Contributions] especially Vols. II and III (see the Index in Vol. III)
284. Lecture of 13 March 1911, Berlin (in '*Exkurse in das Gebiet des Markus-Evangeliums*'), GA 124.
285. Lecture of 15 September 1912, Basel, in the lecture cycle '*Das Markus-Evangelium*', [The Gospel of St Mark], GA 139.
286. '*Schopenhauer Gespräche*' [Conversations with Schopnhauer], ed. Arthur Hübscher, in *Zwanzigstes Jahrbuch der Schopenhauer-Gesellschaft. Für das Jahr 1933* [20th Yearbook of the Schopenhauer Society. For the Year 1933], Heidelberg 1933, p. 63.
287. '*Über die vielfache Wurzel des Satzes vom zureichenden Grunde*' [On the Multiple Root of the Theorem of Sufficient Reason] in Arthur Schopenhauer, *Sämtliche Werke* [Complete Works], Brockhaus ed., Vol. 1, Leipzig 1937, p. 73f.
288. In '*Parerga und Paralipomena*', Complete Works op. cit., Vol. 5, Leipzig 1938, p. 123.
289. Complete Works Vol. 5, p. 145. Vol. 4, Leipzig 1938 in the Preface to *Über den Willen in der Natur* [On the Will in Nature], pp. XII, XXIX (1854).
290. In relation to Rudolf Steiner's statements discussed on p. 93 above.
291. Lecture of 19 January, Berlin, GA 157.

292. Cf.Vol.VIII p. 121.
293. Cf. p. 96 above in this book.
294. E.g. lecture of 1 November 1918, Dornach, GA 185.
295. In his essay '*Schiller und Goethe*' ('Fifteen Essays') 1st set, 3rd ed., Berlin 1884, pp.173/174.
296. Cf.Vol.VIII p. 121 and Rudolf Steiner's important comparison with the effect that the *Buddha* had once had on the general life of the people.
297. Cf. all this with the chapter '*Unpolitisch*' [Unpolitical] in my Vol.VIII (p. 181f.).
298. Cf.Vol.VIII, p. 145.
299. Lecture of 2 April 1921, Dornach, GA 204.
300. Eugen Diesel, *Diesel, der Mensch, das Werk, das Schicksal* [Diesel, the Man, the Work, the Destiny] Hamburg (1937), p. 23.
301. In *Die Neue Propyläen-Weltgeschichte* [The New Propylaean World History] ed. Willy Andreas, Vol. 5, Berlin 1943, p. 412.
302. Rudolf Steiner lecture of 24 January 1919, Dornach, GA 188.
303. Rudolf Steiner lecture of 15 September 1920, Stuttgart, GA 302a.
304. Cf. Rudolf Steiner lecture of 23 May 1923, Berlin, GA 224.
305. Rudolf Steiner lecture of 6 July 1919, Stuttgart, GA 192.
306. Rudolf Steiner lecture of 11 March 1923, Dornach, GA 222.
307. Cf. Rudolf Steiner lecture of 2 April 1921, Dornach, GA 204.
308. '*Die geistige Signatur der Gegenwart*' [The Spiritual Signature of the Present], GA 30.
309. Cf.Vol.VIII, pp. 8, 9.
310. Cf. Vol. V (*Friedrich der Grosse und das Preussentum* [Frederick the Great and Prussia]).
311. E.g. in the lectures of 22 January 1917, GA 174 and 21 December 1918, Dornach, GA 186.
312. Lecture of 13 April, Dornach, GA 190. Cf. my Vol.VIII, pp. 159/160.
313. Cf. my Vol. VII, esp. the chapter '*Freiheit, Gleichheit, Brüderlichkeit*' [Liberty, Equality, Fraternity].
314. In the year of the great crisis, 1842 ('Fall of the Spirits of Darkness', see p. 74), Hauser would have been 30 years old and 35 when the Revolution of 1848 broke out.
315. See my Vol.VIII p. 169/170.
316. Rudolf Steiner lecture of 17 February 1918, Munich, GA 174a. Emphasis: K. Heyer.
317. Rudolf Steiner lecture of 25 October 1918, Dornach, GA 185.
318. Rudolf Steiner lecture of 25 October 1918, Dornach. See also the lecture of 30 May, Dornach, GA 198, and on the subject of Liberalism also Count Ludwig Polzer-Hoditz, *Erinnerungen an den grossen Lehrer Rudolf Steiner. Rückschau eines Österreichers* [Memories of the Great Teacher Rudolf Steiner. An Austrian Remembers] Prague 1937, pp. 99/100. [New ed., Dornach 1985].

319. Haebler op. cit., pp. 74/75.
320. For the genealogical connections, see the family tree of the Beauharnais family in Friedrich Walter, *Stéphanie Napoleon*, Baden-Baden (undated—1946 or thereafter); see also family tree of Prince Adalbert of Bavaria, *Eugen Beauharnais*, Berlin 1940, after p. 496.
321. The complex diplomatic story prior to this marriage can be found in Friedrich Walter, op. cit., p. 57f.
322. See Friedrich Walter, op. cit., p. 105f., Haebler op. cit. pp. 119f., 150f., 222f. Also worth mentioning is the book by Jos(eph) Turquan, *Eine Adoptivtochter Napoleons I. Stéphanie, Grand Duchess of Baden, übertragen und bearbeitet von Oscar Marschall von Bieberstein* [An Adopted Daughter of Napoleon I—Stéphanie, Grand Duchess of Baden, adapted and revised by Marshal Oscar von Bieberstein] Leipzig 1902, but it was also warned against by von Bieberstein as a superficial and irresponsible book which, amongst other things, tends to include criticism of Stéphanie which does not appear to be objectively justified.
323. For the dangerous consequences for the state of Baden of the non-consummation of the marriage, see Haebler op. cit., pp. 120, 151.
324. E.g. Kolb op. cit., pp. 31, 49, 113, 119.
325. Flake op. cit., p. 23, see also Haebler op. cit., p. 218.
326. Haebler op. cit., pp. 153, 218-221.
327. K.A. Varnhagen von Ense, '*Denkwürdigkeiten und vermischte Schriften*' [Memorabilia and Miscellaneous Writings] Vol. 9, Leipzig 1859, p. 406.
328. Haebler op. cit., pp. 204/205, Friedrich Walter op. cit., pp. 274, 277, 280.
329. Friedrich Walter op. cit., p. 200.
330. Pies, *Wahrheit...*, p. 305.
331. Julius Trumpp, *Kaspar Hauser. Napoleon und Stéphanie*, Gerabronn (Württemberg) 1953.
332. On such connections between Napoleon and Stéphanie, see also a comment by Stéphanie in Friedrich Walter, op. cit., pp. 100/101.
333. See Haebler op. cit., p. 223.
334. Op. cit., p. 436.
335. Quoted from Daumer's 1873 book, p. 415.
336. Friedrich Walter, op. cit., pp. 8, 100.
337. Friedrich Walter, op. cit., p. 9.
338. See lectures by Rudolf Steiner of 18 December 1912 in Neuchâtel, GA 130, and of 22 December 1912 in Berlin, GA 141. See also my book '*Geschichtsimpulse des Rosenkreutzertums*' [Historical Impulses of Rosicrucianism] Breslau 1938, p. 20f. [New ed., Perseus, Basel 1992].
339. Hauser came from the Rosicrucian stream. On the connection between Christian Rosenkreuz and the transformative mission of the Buddha on Mars., see n. 338 above.

340. See both in general and in detail: Vol.VII, pp. 309f., 313, 335.
341. Aubry, op. cit., Vol. II, p. 38, 46f.
342. For part of the other side of this story (the nationality principle), see Vol.VII, p. 310.
343. *Oeuvres de Napoleon III, Tome premier*, Paris 1854, p. 15-233; '*Des Idées Napoléoniennes*', here p. 144.
344. Vol.VII, p. 330.
345. Octave Aubry, *Der König von Rom* [The King of Rome], German translation, Erlenbach, Zurich, undated.
346. Aubry op. cit., pp. 141, 148, 190, 218, 233, 252/253, 262, 267, 269, 301, 380, 400, 421, 422, 439.
347. What Wilhelm Kunze writes in his book op. cit., p. 42 shows that he has been on the trail of the whole complex even if he has not yet been able to identify the actual starting point of it. It is also not without interest that Franz Otto in *Das Buch merkwürdiger Kinder* [The Book of Remarkable Children] (5th ed., Leipzig and Berlin 1884) in two successive chapters (15 and 16) deals first with the King of Rome and then after it, with the foundling Kaspar Hauser.
348. Aubry op. cit., pp. 251, 203.
349. Aubry op. cit., pp. 207, 255.
350. Von Prokesch-Osten in Aubry op. cit., p. 272.
351. Aubry op. cit., pp. 153, 197, 206.
352. Rudolf Steiner lecture of 15 February 1920, Dornach, GA 196.
353. See for example the lectures of 22 and 23 October 1920, Dornach, GA 200.
354. Cf. Friedrich Walter, op cit., before p. 497 the 'Family Tree of the House of Baden'.
355. Haebler, op. cit., pp. 59, 213.
356. Cf. my Vol.VII pp. 192/193.
357. Op. cit., pp. 211,237, 239.
358. In his lecture of 12 April 1919, Dornach (the 'Nibelungs lecture') in GA 190.
359. See my Vol.V, pp. 255-257, 259, see also Vol.VIII, pp. 227-229.
360. Vol. III, pp. 167-169, Vol.Vii, pp. 126, 135, 164, 183, Vol.VIII p. 33.
361. See Vol. III, pp. 122-133, 166-169.
362. In that lecture of 12 April 1919, Dornach, GA 190.
363. On this, see the chapter 'Saint-Martin' in my Vol.VI.
364. Rudolf Steiner lecture of 30 January 1917, Dornach, GA 174. Emphasis: K. Heyer. See also Rudolf Steiner's lecture of 8 October 1917 in Dornach, GA 177.
365. For ancient times, see my Vol. I '*Von der Atlantis bis Rom*' [From Atlantis to Rome], also in Vol. II '*Mittelalter*' [The Middle Ages], for the modern period, Vol. III the extract on p. 203ff.: '*Entstehung und Werdegang des neueren Staates in grossen Zügen*' [The Development and Growth of the Modern State in Broad

Outline], Vol. IV '*Maschiavelli und Ludwig XIV*' [Machiavelli and Louis XIV], Vol. V '*Friedrich der Grosse und das Preussentum*', then the chapter 'Joseph II' in the book *Aus dem Jahrhundert der französischen Revolution* [From the Century of the French Revolution]. The phrase '*Die Wandlungen des Fürstenbegriffs*' [The Transformation of the Concept of the Monarch] stems from Rudolf Steiner himself. With it, he set the author a historical and social science task, which ultimately became the basis of the majority of his historical writings. This happened on 29 September 1912 (see Vol. IV, n. 2), a date which, if this half-personal remark may be permitted, subsequently had a strong impact on the author, after he had begun (from late autumn 1952) to occupy himself intensively with the figure of Kaspar Hauser.

366. E.g. see the Collected edition '*1848—The Preliminary Struggle for German Unity and Freedom*' by Tim Klein, Munich and Leipzig 1914; Friedrich Payer, '*Anno 48*', Frankfurt 1923; Wilhelm Mommsen, '*Grösse und Versagen des deutschen Bürgertums, Ein Beitrag zur Geschichte der Jahre 1848-1849*' [The Greatness and the Failure of the German Bourgeoisie—A Contribution to the History of the Years 1848-1849]; Theodor Heuss, '*Ein Vermächtnis. Wer und Erbe von 1848*' [Legacy—The Deeds and the Inheritance of 1848], Stuttgart (1955).
367. Wilhelm Mommsen op. cit., p. 218.
368. Heuss op. cit., p. 108.
369. Malwida von Meysenbug, '*Memoiren einer Idealistin*' [Memoirs of an Idealist] Vol. I, 10th ed., Berlin and Leipzig 1906, p. 252.
370. On 2 January 1921, Stuttgart in the second lecture of the Course for Upper Silesians. Emphasis: K. Heyer. GA 338.
371. Op. cit., p. 169.
372. See Rudolf Steiner's lecture of 28 July 1920, Stuttgart.
373. Quoted from Jacques Bainville, *Frankreichs Kriegsziel* [France's War Aim] (German translation of Bainville's book *Les conséquences politiques de la paix*, [The Political Consequences of the Peace] 1920) Hamburg 1939/40, pp. 90/91.
374. See Heuss op. cit., p. 182.
375. E.g., see B.W. Mommsen, op. cit., pp. 134/135.
376. Op. cit., 135/136.
377. W. Mommsen op. cit., p. 211.
378. W. Mommsen op. cit., p. 125.
379. Lecture of 12 December 1918, Bern, GA 186.
380. See my essays : 1. '*Vom Reiche des 'silbernen Königs' in der Geschichte*' [From the Realm of the 'Silver King' in History] in the weekly, *Das Goetheanum* VII 26, 24 June 1928f., 2. '*Staats-Kunst*' [Statecraft] op. cit., VIII 23, 2 June 1929, p. 180f.
381. Op. cit.

382. Reprinted in '*Das Goetheanum*' VII 12, 18 March 1928, p. 91f. Also, what follows the passage we have quoted, when properly understood in a sufficiently broad context, fits in with our view.
383. For more detail, see, for example, Friedrich von Weech, '*Badische Geschichte*' [A History of Baden], Karlsruhe 1890, p. 574f.
384. Wencker-Wildberg, op. cit., p. 118f.
385. Otto Flake op. cit., p. 146.
386. Wencker-Wildberg, op. cit., p. 118f.
387. Cf. here p. 105 the indication that Mittelstädt's publication of the documents followed instigation by Kaiser Wilhelm I.
388. See, for example, also the very striking account in Klee op. cit., p. 49; also Bapst, *Une mère et son fils* [A Mother and Her Son] op. cit., pp. 165-167, 227; Flake op. cit., p. 146f.; Pies, *Wahrheit...* pp. 302, 365; a contrary view in Striedinger, *Neues Schrifttum über Kaspar Hauser*, op. cit., p. 456.
389. In his essay '*Henriette Feuerbachs und Dr Julius Meyers Stellung zur Kaspar Hauser*' [The Positions of Henriette Feuerbach and Dr Julius Meyer with Regard to the Kaspar Hauser Question] in *Der Fränkische Bund* [The Frankish League], April/May 1926, p. 99.
390. See also a letter from Henriette Feuerbach (8 February 1876) to Dr Julius Meyer, printed in an essay by Thomas Stettner in *Der Sonntags-Kurier, Unterhaltungsbeilage des Fränkischen Kuriers* [The Sunday Courier, entertainment supplement of the Fränkisch Courier] Vol. 8, No. 37, 11 September 1927, p. 144.
391. A. Krieger, *Badische Geschichte* [A History of Baden], Berlin and Leipzig 1921, p. 115.
392. *Süddeutsche Monatshefte* [South German Monthly] Year 11, Vol. 2, April 1914 to September 1914, Munich, p. 141.
393. Herman Grimm in his essay '*Fürst Bismarcks Briefe an seine Frau und Gattin*' [Prince Bismarck's Letters to his Wife] (this book was published in 1900) in *Aufsätze zur Literatur* Gütersloh 1915, p. 271.
394. Vol. 67, 1898, No. 32 (13 August).
395. Lecture of 14 November 1919, Dornach, GA 191.
396. In No. 15 of the magazine (of 12 October 1921) in the interview of Rudolf Steiner by the correspondent of *Le Matin*, Jules Sauerwein, about the unpublished memoirs of the late Chief of the German General Staff von Moltke, in GA 24. Rudolf Steiner's Bismarck essay was printed in GA 31.
397. *Reden Bismarcks nach seinem Ausscheiden aus dem Amte* [Bismarck's Speeches after Leaving Office], Leipzig undated p. 51/52.
398. Leonhard von Muralt, *Bismarcks Verantwortlichkeit* [Bismarck's Responsibility], Göttingen 1955, pp. 63/64.
399. In the fortnightly magazine *Die Gegenwart* [The Present] III 62, 10 July 1948, p. 15.

400. Quoted from Otto Westphal, '*Bismarcks Feinde*' [Bismarck's Enemies], Munich and Berlin 1930, p. 205.
401. *Reden Bismarcks nach seinem Ausscheiden aus dem Amte* op. cit., p. 48.
402. More precisely: *Ein treuer deutscher Diener Kaiser Wilhelms I* [A Loyal German Servant of Kaiser Wilhelm I].
403. Lassalle died on 31 August 1864 from a fatal wound he had suffered in a pistol duel with a Mr J. von Racowitza [Prince Iancu Racoviţă (1843–1865)—*Ed.*] near Geneva.
404. Quoted from Arnold Oskar Meyer, *Bismarck. Der Mensch under der Staatsmann* [Bismarck—the Man and the Statesman] Stuttgart (1949) p. 456. (In context, the word refers to the *Pope* as a man who has the consciences of 200 million human beings at his disposal.)
405. W. Mommsen op. cit., p. 8.
406. For example, the—in this sense—excellent, objective work by the Swiss historian, Leonhard von Muralt, '*Bismarcks Verantwortlichkeit*' [Bismarck's Responsibility] should be noted.
407. *Bismarck. Die gesammelten Werke* [Bismarck—Collected Works], Vol. 10, 1028, p. 140. See also Georg Büchmann, *Geflügelte Worte* [Winged Words], 9th ed. Berlin 1876, p. 304; op. cit., 1915, p. 313; Eduard Heyck, '*Bismarck*', Bielefeld and Leipzig 1904, pp. 84, 94; Karl Mielcke, *Bismarck in der neuen Forschung* [New Research on Bismarck] Braunschweig 1954, pp. 31, 34f. The brilliant comments by Roman Boos with regard to 'Blood and Iron' should be noted, which can be found in his *Reichsgeist und Schweizergeist* [Imperial Spirit and Swiss Spirit], Elgg/Canton of Zurich 1945, pp. 35-40; see also his n. 116 in Rudolf Steiner, *Geschichte und Überwindung des Imperialismus*, Zurich/New York 1946, pp. 192/193. GA 196.
408. In Mielcke op. cit., p. 16.
409. Op. cit., pp. 99/100.
410. A.O. Meyer op. cit., p. 161.
411. E.g. Robert Saitschick, *Bismarck und das Schicksal des deutschen Volkes* [Bismarck and the Destiny of the German People], Munich 1949—in its whole conception a very ignorant and fallacious book—includes the chapter (pp. 16-33) '*Bismarcks Machiavellismus*' [Bismarck's Machiavellianism].
412. Saitschick op. cit., p. 23.
413. Karl Heyer, *Der Machiavellismus* [Machiavellianism], Berlin 1918, p. 49.
414. Lecture of 14 November 1919, Dornach, GA 191.
415. See Vol. V pp. 250-254, Vol. VIII pp. 215-219.
416. Op. cit., p. 36f.
417. Emanuel Geibel, *Ausgewählte Gedichte* [Selected Poems], Stuttgart und Berlin 1904, p. 170. (See also Eduard Heyck, '*Bismarck*' op. cit., p. 92.) For another

comment by Geibel which one can find paradoxical in view of what is quoted here, the reader is referred to my Vol. VIII, pp. 174/175.

418. For an illustration of the coat of arms from the year 1365, see Heyck, op. cit., p. 2.
419. Erich Eyck, 'Bismarck', Vol. 3, Zurich (1944), p. 637.
420. E.G. Eyck, op. cit., p. 497, Hermann Oncken, *Lassalle. Eine politische Biographie* [Lassalle—A Political Biography], 4th ed. Stuttgart and Berlin 1923, pp. 256, 269/270.
421. Op. cit., p. 169.
422. Quoted from Oncken, op. cit., p. 177.
423. In the weekly *Das Goetheanum* VIII 50, 8 December 1929.
424. In important connections Lassalle can, of course, also be included *together with* Marx, even if in another and indeed, a decisive respect, he is a kind of counter-pole to Marx. For interested readers, the dates of a few lectures by Rudolf Steiner should be referred to in which Lassalle is mentioned or briefly discussed: 28 October 1917 GA 177; 19 October 1918 GA 185; 16 November 1918 GA 185a; 13 December 1918 GA 186; 21 February 1919 GA 189; 20 July 1919 GA 192.
425. Erick Marcks in a university lecture of 16 December 1913 in Munich.
426. Quoted from Oncken op. cit., p. 445. See also Oncken p. 504.
     With regard to the subject of Bismarck and Lassalle, the book by Gustav Mayer, *Bismarck und Lassalle. Ihr Briefwechsel und ihre Gespräche* [Bismarck and Lassalle—Correspondence and Conversations] place of publication unknown, 1928.
427. Erich Marcks op. cit.
428. H. Oncken op. cit., p. 392.
429. A.O. Mayer op. cit., p. 203.
430. See Eyck op. cit., p. 500.
431. New edition as special publications, Bern 1946 p. 24.
432. Princip—the man who shot Austrian Heir Apparent Archduke Franz Ferdinand and his wife in the assassination in Sarajevo on 28 June 1914.
433. E.g., cf. Oncken op. cit., p. 482f.; see also Helene von Racowitza (b. von Dönniges, *Meine Beziehungen zu Ferdinand Lassalle* [My Relations with Ferdinand Lassalle], e.g. 7th ed., Breslau 1879.
434. GA 28, Dornach 1962, pp. 462, 463.
435. Jacob Burckhardt, *Briefe* [Letters] ed. Fritz Kaphahn, 4th ed., Leipzig (1940), p. 338.
436. *Reden an die deutsche Nation von Johann Gottlieb Fichte* [Addresses to the German Nation, by von Johann Gottlieb Fichte] with an Introduction, ed. Imanuel Hermann Fichte, Leipzig 1871, p. XXXII.
437. *Kaiser Friedrich III. Das Kriegstagebuch von 1870/71*, ed. H.O. Meisner, Berlin and Leipzig 1926.

438. Lecture by Rudolf Steiner, 23 October 1920, Dornach, GA 200.
439. E.g. cf. Erich Marcks, *Der Aufstieg des Reiches* [The Rise of the Reich], Vol. 1, Stuttgart, Berlin 1936, pp. 207, 209.
440. Lecture of 15 November 1918, Dornach, GA 185.
441. On the positive attitude of the young Rudolf Steiner to this legislation (1884), see Roman Boos, *Die Dreigliderungs-Idee, das Goetheanum und das Driegliederungs-Ideal* [The Idea of Threefolding, the Goetheanum and the Ideal of Threefolding], Münchenstein and Lörrach (1930?), pp. 19/20.
442. E.g., see B.A.P. Meyer, op. cit., p. 467.
443. Wilhelm Mommsen in his essay '*Der Kampf um das Bismarck-Bild*' [The Struggle for the Image of Bismarck] in the journal *Universitas* V 3 (March 1950), p. 279.
444. Stuttgart 1919, p. 107f. Immediately prior to this, the subject is the Austro-Hungarian state structure and *its* failure.
445. Rudolf Steiner, lecture of 20 February 1920, Dornach, GA 196.
446. In GA 23, Dornach 1961, p. 157f.
447. E.g. in the lectures of 17 November 1918 in Dornach, GA 185; of 15 December 1918 in Dornach, GA 186; and of 28 July 1920 in Stuttgart, GA 335.
448. Friedrich Nietzsche, *Unzeitgemässe Betrachtungen* [Untimely Meditations] (Kröner's paperback edition, Vol. 71, Stuttgart 1955, p. 3). See Otto Westphal, '*Feinde Bismarcks*' [Enemies of Bismarck], Munich and Berlin 1930, p. 124f.
449. Lecture of 16 November 1918, Dornach, GA 185a.
450. Lecture of 15 December 1919, Dornach, GA 194.
451. See Rudolf Steiner, lecture of 6 April 1919, Dornach, GA 190, for more detail.
452. Maria von Rumänien, '*Traum und Leben einer Königin*' [The Dream and the Life of a Queen], Leipzig 1935, p. 185.
453. [Endnote missing in the original text—Ed.]
454. Stuttgart 1919, p. 112.
455. Confirmed by a well-informed source.
456. This Preface is in the Folk Souls' lecture cycle ('*Die Mission einzelner Volksseelen im Zusammenhang mit der nordisch-germanischen Mythologie*') [The Mission of the Folk Souls], GA 121.
457. Rudolf Steiner lecture of 24 November 1921 in Kristiania, GA 209. For the whole complex, see also 1. Guenther Wachsmuth, *Rudolf Steiners Erdenleben und Wirken* [Rudolf Steiner's Life and Work], 2nd ed. Dornach 1951, pp. 155, and 379/380, 2. Herbert Hahn, '*Die Geburt der Waldorfschule aus den Impulsen der Dreigliederung des Sozialen Organismus*' [The Birth of the Waldorf School from the Impulses of the Threefolding of the Social Organism] in M.J.Krück von Poturzyn, '*Wir erlebten Rudolf Steiner. Erinnerungen seiner Schüler*' [We Experienced Rudolf Steiner. Memories of his Pupils], Stuttgart 1956, pp. 90/91.

458. See W. Quenzer, '*Ein liberaler Prinz*' [A Liberal Prince] in '*Stuttgarter Zeitung*' No. 260, 6 November 1954.
459. Quenzer op. cit., also Wilhelm Keil, '*Prinz Max von Baden*' in '*Der Bürger im Staat*' [The Citizen in the State] Stuttgart IV 11 (November 1954), p. 187f.
460. Rudolf Steiner, '*Die Kernpunkte der sozialen Frage*' [The Core Points of the Social Question a.k.a. Towards Social Renewal] GA 23, Dornach, Dornach 1961, p. 155. Similarly, in the lecture of 21 April 1919 in Stuttgart, GA 192.
461. Roman Boos, '*Rudolf Steiner während des Weltkrieges*' [Rudolf Steiner During the World War] Dornach, (1933) Introduction p. XXVII.
462. See, for example, Rudolf Steiner's notably reluctant words in his lecture of 21 August 1920 in Dornach, in GA 199, which reflect his objective, great disappointment in the Prince.
463. Paris 1930, p. 315, n. 1. We reproduce the passage here in our own translation. Emphasis: K. Heyer.
464. My emphasis.
465. Op. cit., pp. 35-41. Cf. also pp. 7/8.
466. Flake op. cit., pp. 145/146. See also 148/149.
467. Maurice Paléologue, *Alexandre I. Der rätselhafte Zar* [Alexander I—The Mystery Czar] German translation, Berlin undated (1937), p. 408. Paléologue was the French ambassador in St Petersburg, 1914-1917.
468. Lecture of 10 June 1923, Dornach, GA 259.
469. Lecture of 13 April 1908, GA 102. See also the essay '*Gestalten und Motive der Ostervorträge Rudolf Steiners*' [Figures and Motifs in Rudolf Steiner's Easter Lectures] by Hermann Reuter in *Blätter für Anthroposophie* [Gazette for Anthroposophy] V 4 (April 1953) p. 130f.
470. Malwida von Meysenbug, *Im Anfang war die Liebe. Briefe an ihre Pflegetochter* [In the Beginning was Love—Letters to her foster-daughter], ed. Berta Schleicher, Munich 1926, pp. 15/16.
471. Op. cit., p. 313.
472. On Schuré, see, for example, B. K. H. Reuter, '*Édouard Schuré, 1841-1929*', essay in *Die Kommenden* X 17, 10 April 1957, p. 8.
473. Werner Richter, *Ludwig II. König von Bayern* [Ludwig II—King of Bavaria], Erlenbach, Zurich und Leipzig (1939), p. 333.
474. Rudolf Frieling in his important and illuminating essay '*König Ludwig II von Bayern Zur 70. Wiederkehr seines Todes*' [King Ludwig II of Bavaria—On the 70th Anniversary of his Death] in the monthly magazine *Die Christengemeinschaft* [The Christian Community] XXVIII 6 (June 1956), p. 174f.
475. Werner Richter, op. cit., p. 218.
476. [Endnote missing in the original text—Ed.]

477. Quoted from Werner Richter op. cit., p. 310.

478. *Wenn die Götter den Tempel verlassen ... Wesen und Wollen des Nationalsozialismus und das Schicksal des deutschen Volkes* [When the Gods Leave the Temple ... the Being and Will of National Socialism and the Destiny of the German People], Freiburg-im-Breisgau 1947, pp. 98-101. [New ed. Perseus Basel, 1991]. For Constantin Frantz, see also Sigismund von Gleich's essay on Constantin Frantz in *Die Kommenden* VII 4, 25 February 1953, p. 3. For Karl Christian Planck, see also my essay '*Die Geschichte Europas in den letzten 200 Jahren*' [The History of Europe in the Last 200 Years] Part IX, in *Die Kommenden* VII 14, 25 July 1953, p. 4.

479. 2nd ed. Wiesbaden 1947, p. 26. With regard to Meinecke, see also our Vol. VIII, pp. 220-225, 258/259.

480. Lecture by Rudolf Steiner, 15 November 1919, Dornach, GA 191.

Index of Names